ERP
WITH
CONFIDENCE

Disclosure

The goal of this book is to share my first-hand sales experience in the enterprise resource planning (ERP) industry. It is important to note that this book has not been endorsed and is not associated with Microsoft, Oracle, Sage, SAP, Workday, Salesforce, or any other leading software developers. When I sell ERP software as part of my everyday profession, I receive a commission through my employer, and over the years, I have acquired shares in Microsoft. Notwithstanding these relationships, I refer to several leading software developers and consultants in the marketplace throughout this book to highlight products and services designed for the middle market without making any direct recommendations. References to specific companies are designed to assist the reader in navigating the ERP journey.

ERP
WITH
CONFIDENCE

THE ULTIMATE GUIDE FOR MIDDLE MARKET PROFESSIONALS NAVIGATING THE ERP JOURNEY

C H R I S   K U T T

ERP with Confidence:
The Ultimate Guide for Middle Market Professionals
Navigating the ERP Journey

Editing Services by Tom's Touch
Book Design by YellowStudios

Published by

Yard-Hard Multimedia Company LLC
Denver, Colorado

Paperback ISBN: 979-8-218-26025-5
Library of Congress Control Number: 2023914954

CONTENTS

You look at where you're going and where you are and it never makes sense, but then you look back at where you've been and a pattern seems to emerge.

—*Robert M. Pirsig*

INTRODUCTION

I have been tremendously fortunate to work in the enterprise resource planning (ERP) community for over twenty years. It wasn't the most auspicious of beginnings as I replied to a "help wanted" advertisement in the Sunday edition of the *Denver Post*. But at that time in my life, I was ready for a new challenge and was fortunate to land a good job.

In January of 1999, I began working for an award-winning Great Plains value-added reseller by the name of Frederic Wells Inc. Just one year earlier, Frederic Wells had been recognized as the "Outstanding Partner in the US" by Great Plains Software, and it planned on continuing the positive momentum by growing the practice.

I joined as a marketing assistant, and over time that grew into a marketing manager position, which eventually led to a sales position. By this time, Frederic Wells had been acquired by a leading consulting firm that strategically acquired several resellers across the country to become one of the first national Great Plains partners. The consulting firm eventually grew into one of the most prolific ERP practices for middle market companies in the United States.

Once in a sales position, I found that the world got a whole lot bigger. For the first time, I was in meetings and software demonstrations with prospects and clients based on their business requirements. The decision makers in most of these meetings were comprised of chief executive officers (CEOs), chief financial officers (CFOs), chief information officers (CIOs), financial controllers, and accounting managers.

During this time, I was surrounded by some of the best mentors to come out of the ERP community, including Jon Pratt, Matt Kenney, Jim Auer, Paul Maynell, and the late Paula Hendley. Having worked directly with these fantastic mentors, I was able to learn a lot about ERP software, technology, accounting, and people.

These mentors provided significant guidance, helping me to grow both personally and professionally. I learned from each meeting and conversation, each software demonstration, and each proposal, and in the meantime, I grew my communications skills. Ultimately, what was once a good job eventually became a great career.

Over the passage of time, I have been privileged to have worked with hundreds of clients and prospects as they navigated the ERP journey. When it comes to selecting and implementing the right ERP software system, I have learned there are some companies that are simply more successful than others.

When you meet with business decision makers, you can often tell who is prepared for the journey while others seem to be all over the place. Why is one company successful at the ERP journey while another company is not? Why are there so many stories of failure, discontent, or buyer's remorse?

There are several reasons why some companies are more successful than others at evaluating, selecting, implementing, and maintaining ERP software systems. The companies that flourish in navigating the ERP journey are willing to learn, embrace, and execute what it takes to succeed.

The ERP journey is neither an art nor a science. It is a process of open-mindedness, continuous alignment, and timely problem-solving, all of which is supported by leadership, corporate culture, technology, reasonable expectations, budget, and execution. Although this may seem to be an overwhelming list, the reality is that this is how successful businesses operate each and every day.

ERP with Confidence is intended to offer insights into an approach to assist business professionals to be more informed in the preparation and the execution of the ERP journey. Not surprisingly, readers of this book will discover that the journey requires leadership, vision, investment, and effectiveness in execution. There also has to be a level of enthusiasm throughout the entire organization to learn and grow through the ERP journey.

The information contained in this book offers insights into technology and innovation without being overly technical, and it covers financial management topics at a high level without being a textbook for practical accounting principles. However, the concepts listed throughout the book highlight the ways to prepare for the ERP journey.

There is an emphasis on how to evaluate ERP software, select a consultant for the software implementation, and prepare the team for the deployment of the new system. The execution of this sequence of events will assist your company in realizing an ERP software solution that can take your company to the next level.

While there is never a right time for beginning this journey, many businesses eventually reach a period in their growth and evolution that clearly indicates the need to implement enterprise resource planning (ERP) software. It's not surprising that all companies evaluate ERP software differently.

When the time arrives, members of the finance team—such as the CFO, financial controller, and accounting managers—often lead the ERP evaluation process. After all, the ERP software represents the core of the business and all financial operations. Although the evaluation might be in good hands, that doesn't mean there won't be many mistakes.

There are cognitive biases and subjective reasoning that occur throughout the ERP evaluation process. Therefore, variables such as price, corporate pressures, previous professional experiences, existing relationships, preprogrammed knowledge (sometimes misguided), and hubris all seem to join the evaluation process. When this happens, business requirements can inadvertently become secondary.

Rather than dwelling on these variables, this book takes a look at some of the good news, which is that there are several great products and consultants in the marketplace. So unless a company goes down a severe rabbit hole, there is a really good chance of achieving a successful implementation. That is why there is no reason to say one ERP software is the best, to rank providers in any type of order, or to even discuss product features and functionality. CFOs and financial controllers already use the internet for that type of *"research,"* so there's no use in wasting time on it here.

Today, technology and innovation are moving faster than ever, so businesses need to rely on an ERP package to track, manage, and report all financial transactions and activities. It enables executive management in making critical business decisions in a timely fashion and communicate results to investors, business partners, and team members.

However, in order to get into this position, there first needs to be a way to gain insight into the right information to shape the vision and successfully navigate this journey. There has to be a foundation, which includes several main themes: appreciate time, invest in technology, demonstrate leadership, and align people, technology, and other aspects of the organization.

Having this foundation will assist in formulating the vision and also provide a necessary means to reaching the desired future state of increased efficiency, more productivity, and better results. As the great basketball coach John Wooden once said, "Success is not a destination, it is a journey" (Wooden & Jamison, 2005).

Appreciate Time

Time is the most precious resource in life and in business, and once it has been consumed, it cannot ever be replaced. In life as well as the workplace, it is important to properly allocate time and focus its use on productive tasks and activities in order to achieve goals.

When unproductive actions take place, time is wasted, and that negatively impacts the bottom line of a business. When time is used properly in the workplace, it can become one of the most powerful resources for the business. By appreciating time and using it wisely, you can unlock its true potential.

Time can be utilized within your organization to assist in the planning, preparation, and execution to achieve goals, reach quotas, and generate profits. The most successful people in the world understand that time is of the essence and "the essence of success is time" (Wooden & Jamison, 2005).

The purpose of implementing a new ERP software system is to transition from several time-consuming manual tasks to a more proactive approach, which leads to increased productivity, greater output, and better results. Ultimately, the ERP journey will assist in better utilizing precious time in the future for the purpose of increasing productivity and generating greater results in the workplace.

Invest in Technology

Business is all about money. A company executing upon its growth strategy is not only focused on making money but also investing these dollars back into the business for future gains. These businesses invest in their assets, such as product research and development, intellectual property, employee acquisition and talent development, acquiring machines and vehicles, and implementing information technology.

It is absolutely necessary to invest in information technology for your business. The willingness to pay for the right tools, technology, and consulting resources goes a long way toward increasing the probability of being successful. The same is true when it comes to ERP software systems. Properly budgeting for the acquisition of a new ERP software system assists in not only paying for the software but also funding the professional consulting services to implement it and being able to receive the necessary support.

Now, it's easy to be cheap. After all, financial controllers and accountants alike tend to have a reputation for being cheap. However, skimping is not the same as saving. Being cheap often leads to taking shortcuts, which can dramatically impact having the right software and/or proper consulting resources available. These constraints greatly reduce the possibility for a successful ERP implementation.

However, investments made in technology and infrastructure should be viewed as the application of resources toward business improvement (Hayden, 2014). The investment in an ERP software system and implementation can directly lead to improved controls, processes, production, and financial reporting.

As with any special project in life, there will be times when something will happen unexpectedly. With a proper budget in place, your team will be prepared during these special circumstances. Instead of having a crisis on your hands, there will be a cool sense of confidence that the situation is workable and can be resolved, which in many cases requires the need for additional software, professional services, or training.

The willingness to budget and tactically invest in information technology is an absolutely critical component of a successful ERP journey.

Demonstrate Leadership

There are several reasons for making the change to a new ERP software system, which may or may not be obvious to the people in charge of the organization. If you are tasked with leading team members in overcoming challenging goals in the marketplace, especially in an extremely competitive environment, it only makes sense to continuously strive to discover a means for achieving success.

A strong leader is purposeful, resourceful, and determined to discover the best way for increasing the probability of success. A strong leader also understands the direct connection of business goals, processes, departments, people, and data. With a focused approach on meticulous execution, a leader recognizes that the best way to tie everything together is with an ERP software system.

Unfortunately, not all people in executive management are blessed with strong leadership skills. There are many executives filling C-level positions—such as CEO, CFO, and CIO—who simply do not have *the juice*. They may not have a clear vision of the future, understand the changing marketplace, or feel the need to make strategic improvements. Whatever the case may be, these people believe *business as usual* works just fine.

Then somewhere in the middle, there are the leaders who simply *cannot pull the trigger* and make the decision on moving forward with a new ERP software system. These are members of executive management who have the power, vision, and understanding of the impact of their business, but they *lack the gumption* to make decisions out of the fear of making the wrong decision.

These people take several months or even sometimes years to evaluate software. These people waste time trying to spread the responsibility through steering committees and executive team members. Even worse, they become overly consumed with having to understand how each particular ERP software package handles every possible situation or transaction, anomaly, or business exception. With this type of *analysis paralysis*, many ERP software search initiatives lead to *no decision*, which is truly unfortunate.

Ultimately, it takes a leader to "make a call" to decide to move forward with a new system, motivate the team, and execute on the strategic vision (Willink & Babin, 2015). A leader expects all team members to produce at a high level, which often consists of *raising their game* in how they produce in the workplace. It takes strong leadership, courage, and conviction to move to a new ERP software system.

Alignment

Lastly, and probably most importantly, there is alignment. The first model of alignment in business dates back to the 1960s. Dr. Harold J. Leavitt, a psychologist of management and a pioneer in the academic study of organizational behavior, developed the Leavitt's Diamond Model (Umar, 2020).

Leavitt's Diamond Model first illustrated a balance of four equal components of organizational change: structure, tasks, people, and technology. Over the following decades, the components of structure and tasks naturally merged together into a more modern component, known as process.

By the late 1990s, the concept of people, process, and technology (PPT) was popularized by a security technologist named Bruce Schneier. Today, commonly referred to as the "three-legged stool," the PPT concept is used for leading organizational change and modern digital transformation (Khanduri, 2022).

While understanding the importance of balance within the PPT framework, what often gets lost is the level of connection and interdependence these elements have in everyday business. As people work each day, they play a critical role within several key processes that are supported by technology. While processes make people more efficient, technology can automate and dramatically increase productivity. The planned connection and interdependence among each of these elements are known as "alignment."

Alignment can take many forms and is critical for the advancement of strategies, working together, communication, collaboration, and execution. In any business or organization, ownership, executive management, and team members have to be aligned. When there is alignment, it enhances the ability to communicate together, develop a plan, solve complex problems, and achieve success.

When teams and strategies are not aligned, they perform poorly. Where there is no alignment, initiatives from management go nowhere, complex problems never get resolved, special projects are not completed, and people just simply go through the motions each and every day. But it doesn't have to be this way.

When there is alignment, everyone understands the common goals, the shared values, and the strategic vision. In situations where there is alignment, strategies are implemented, team members work together, communications are clear, and special projects are completed. When everyone works together toward a common goal, good things happen.

The ERP journey is all about alignment. The entire process of developing a shared vision, producing a list of requirements, evaluating ERP software packages, formulating a decision, and working on the implementation is fundamental alignment.

Summary

A chief financial officer once posed this question: "Why is this information such a secret?"

While there is a very intentional information gap in the ERP marketplace, there is an enormous amount of accessible information to those properly searching for it. Unfortunately, it's not as simple as checking the answers published in the back of the book.

The information is readily available for those wanting to learn more and are willing to take the necessary steps forward into unfamiliar territory. One at a time, these steps will assist in eventually reaching objectives.

Let these pages serve as a guide for developing a framework from which to create an objective approach and go-forward plan for gathering information, evaluating systems, selecting an implementation partner, and ultimately going live on a new ERP software system. With the right plan in place, you will utilize your new ERP software with confidence and successfully navigate the ERP journey.

SECTION I

ERP FOR THE MIDDLE MARKET

How you gather, manage, and use information will determine whether you win or lose.

—Bill Gates

1

WHY ERP IS ESSENTIAL

Your company was established and founded with the intent of selling a product and/or service in the open marketplace. Now, assuming there is competition in the marketplace, your business has to strive to differentiate itself to stand out to potential customers by means of providing a better product, superior service offering, or enhanced value.

A company strives to become successful by generating revenue, growing its profit margin, and rewarding investors. From the very beginning, a company has to develop its team, its hierarchy, procedures, communications, and the right tools for executing upon its mission. Depending on your industry, these tools can be a geographic location, forklifts, trucks, ovens, or software.

Software? Yes, software. To be more specific, an enterprise resource planning (ERP) software package. ERP is a software system of fully integrated applications or modules that standardizes and integrates critical business processes across a business. Those processes include finance, operations, and sales (Perkins, 2020). A successful company has a growth roadmap that requires the right

ERP software package to automate business processes for the purpose of collecting, storing, and managing the business transactions, which are functions needed to execute on the vision.

The importance of ERP software to your business is to increase both productivity and profits through a structured and collaborative technology environment that provides the ability to track activities, tasks, transactions, and revenue. This may include accounting, inventory, assets, and even payroll.

Specifically, an ERP software package plans and tracks all the necessary activities for revenue-generating transactions, profits, and reports to investors. The software will automate business processes, allow multiple departments to share data for collaboration, and provide strong reporting of financial results with analytics.

Without the right ERP software to execute upon the mission, management is demonstrating a lack of leadership by not providing the software tools to succeed. They waste the time of their employees by forcing them to play catch-up with redundant efforts, thus sacrificing the ability for them to be proactive in key situations. With inefficient tools, outdated technology, and redundant processes, this represents the devaluation of technology and software as tools for driving business success.

Deprived of the right tools and technology for the company, the corporate strategy becomes reliant on team members performing time-consuming activities, manual processes, and repetitive tasks each day. These are all examples of internal threats to the success of the business. Those threats are rooted in complacency, daily crisis management, and recurring distractions. The consequences of this strategy are countless meetings, emails, and spreadsheets to ensure everyone is on the same page. The additional workload can tear down the morale of your team.

Many of these time-consuming tasks are necessary due partly to team members being stuck using old legacy business software systems that are either antiquated or lacking in the capabilities of a modern ERP system. Most legacy systems are a byproduct of initial shortsighted decision-making by management letting individual departments acquire their own stand-alone software packages and treating each department as if it were its own island.

Perhaps over twenty years ago, the stand-alone legacy software packages made sense by meeting the needs of a single departmental function, such as general ledger, asset tracking, quoting, shipping, billing, etc. However, the result is typically a software landscape comprised of disparate legacy systems with no two systems talking to one another.

With disparate systems, business data and information have to be manually patched together with the use of spreadsheets to combine information in the hopes of getting the pulse of the business. Business data essentially *duct-taped* together with spreadsheets often becomes latent, stale, and static. And it may even include outdated, inaccurate, or missing data by the reporting deadline. A Gartner study says poor data quality is the reason "40% of all business initiatives fail" to reach their intended targets (Friedman & Smith, 2011). There should not be any doubt in anyone's mind that manual processes and the reliance on static spreadsheets are more susceptible to human errors.

However, business professionals often justify the continued embrace of these legacy systems by saying, "We invested a lot of money in this system several years ago." Therefore, there are no plans to change at this time. Well, the only way to achieve a better result is by making a change to a better system, which may save time (and money) by automating tasks and having real-time insight into data.

With manual tasks, legacy systems, and stale data, how can anyone expect management to make good business decisions or grow the business? How can a company be an innovative or competitive business or possibly land future investors based on bad data? Once a strategic course of action is determined with bad data used as a base of a key decision, it may take days, weeks, or even years to potentially reverse course and right the ship. Is this the right approach to achieving a meaningful growth strategy?

The only way to change this process is by taking a different approach and embracing modern technology platforms. To be a fast-moving company, businesses embrace modern tools, software applications, and unified communications. With the right tools and technology, a business will attract the best talent, be more productive, with management having more insight into the business, and possibly grow and expand to multiple locations, possibly even becoming a global company.

With too many time-consuming activities and ad hoc processes and not enough automation or collaboration, the business naturally creates a slippery slope of constantly needing more meetings, conference calls, and discussions to execute on the mission of the business. It is going to be hard to continue to differentiate your business if you are not leveraging the right tools, technology, or automating processes.

An excellent term coined by Ward Cunningham, one of the most well-known computer programmers of all time, is "technical debt" (Fowler, 2019). Technical debt will naturally happen when a business embraces less expensive, short, quick, or dirty solutions in the near term rather than choosing the best approach, consisting of a well-designed, long-term solution.

The technical debt has monetary consequences, such as monetary debt. If the technical debt is not paid off, then this will naturally cause the accumulation of interest. The interest is comparable to making it harder and more expensive to implement the right solution at a future date.

By devaluing the role of technology in an organization, an executive is sending a clear message to the team that its members will never get the tools needed for success. Furthermore, a business operating at a high level of technical debt may never be able to achieve its overall mission because it's impossible for team members to have a reasonable amount of time to perform proactive tasks.

These businesses are functioning in a state of chaos, trying to limp along in a reactive state instead of having the right tools for being proactive. These businesses will let all or parts of their systems fall far behind in technological capabilities, reporting tools, and automation. There may be several components—such as hardware or software, including security provisions—that need to be brought forward for a significant cost that executives are simply unwilling to spend (despite the fact that this is also known as the cost of doing business).

There are several ERP systems in the marketplace that offer a scalable platform with modern technical capabilities that can assist in eliminating technical debt. Now, especially with cloud-based technology (the ability to access software, databases, and hardware over the internet from anywhere in the world), there has never been a better time to modernize systems and bring technology forward (Cloudflare Inc, 2021).

In many ways, a cloud-based technology approach provides a vehicle and opportunity for eliminating technical debt nearly immediately. Instead of having to replace and modernize hardware and various types of, software, including databases, operating systems, firewalls, switches, and other technical components, all these tools may be a part of a single cloud-based offering, thus eliminating the technical debt with a robust and modern ERP system and strategy.

By embracing a modern ERP software platform, a company can automate processes, increase productivity through collaboration, eliminate separate departmental silos of information, and make insightful business decisions in real time. It can do that by having the ability to analyze information, including data mining, performance management, and reporting. The use of a modern ERP system platform assists in reducing human errors and emphasizes improved controls that will allow for effectiveness and consistency. Moreover, once employees spend their time wisely, they will be happier in the workplace and perform at a higher level, which will increase productivity and overall efficiency.

A new ERP software system is essential to any organization because of the following:

- It easily automates time-consuming tasks for the entire organization.
- It increases efficiency and precision and minimizes mistakes.
- It securely maintains critical business data.
- It provides security and control.
- It allows data to be shared among multiple teams and departments for collaboration.
- It keeps track of key business processes and increases productivity.
- It provides insight into the business to executives, investors, and business partners.
- It captures the data, which may be analyzed to find trends, anomalies, and growth opportunities.

Summary

Companies embracing the right tools and technology are naturally in a better position to accomplish more in less time, enabling them to focus on strategy, innovation, execution, and growth. Being proactive through tools, technology, collaboration, and execution naturally leads to increasing business success with faster and better decisions. The first step is to acknowledge and accept the importance of an ERP software system. Once executives understand the positive impact of a modern ERP system, they will be in the position to take the next step by leading a change for the overall business.

Everything's intentional. It's just filling in the dots.

—David Byrne

2
EVERYTHING ROLLS UP TO THE OFFICE OF THE CFO

In any business, all the financial activities ultimately rollup to the office of the CFO. In taking this a step further, all the financial activities of each individual department—such as sales, marketing, production, and human resources—culminate in cash flow management, budgeting, and financial analysis. And so, everything does eventually "roll up" to the office of the CFO.

In the middle market, the office of the CFO has varying positions, roles, and responsibilities. There may be a CFO, financial controller, accounting manager, staff accountants, and clerks all playing an important part in the activities of the finance team each and every day.

Traditionally, the CFO has been focused only on the numbers, spending time on tactical analytics, monetary tasks, budgets, and daily financial decisions. Today, a chief financial officer may be focused on more external responsibilities. These external responsibilities may vary and could include investor-based relations, fundraising, corporate governance, and communicating the financial viability of the company to internal and external stakeholders.

19

In addition, over the last several years, there has been a natural unification of the CFO position with the traditional chief operating officer (COO) position. The traditional COO handled day-to-day administrative and operational functions of a company (Freedman, 2020). However, today there are more operationally focused CFOs taking on more day-to-day responsibilities. The operational responsibilities of the CFO have grown to include traditional departments such as administration, information technology, and human resources.

With a broader set of responsibilities, the CFO naturally relies heavily on the financial controller. The position of a financial controller has also expanded to include several areas, including all accounting oversight, financial planning and analysis (FP and A), establishing and executing internal controls, tax governance, and due diligence on potential acquisitions. The financial controller is responsible for tracking and reporting (keeping score) with regard to the financial health of the business and understanding all company facets from which the information has been derived, such as sales, costs, labor, etc. (Ernst & Young LLP, 2008).

The financial controller meticulously tracks and analyzes all the financial aspects of the business, including the general ledger, payables, receivables, budgets, financial statements, and sales analysis. Furthermore, the financial controller, along with the accounting team, has to perform transactional daily tasks, such as accounts payable, invoicing, accruals, adjustments, and bank reconciliations.

In tracking all the financial aspects of the business, the financial controller and the accounting team provide communications to executives, upper management, investors, bankers, and the board of directors of the organization, offering financial insight into the business (Whatman, 2022). These communications include key metrics, financial statements, and financial ratios—such as cash flow to debt and net profit margin—to convey the financial health and long-term sustainability of the company.

The communications and financial reporting require accuracy and detail because the information is vital to all the primary stakeholders. If the numbers are incorrect, then the accounting team has an immediate credibility problem, which can directly affect the growth strategy (Lampton, 2019). There is a never-ending demand for this information, so it has to be generated as fast as possible and in multiple easy-to-read formats so there are no surprises. As everyone knows, nobody likes surprises (Treece, 2021).

It is very possible for the financial controller and the accounting team to pull together the financial information and data from disparate business systems. The financial information is obtained through various exports, so it may be brought together with the assistance of multiple spreadsheets. These spreadsheets are configured with pivot tables, financial models, and macros to gain financial insight into the business.

The numerous hours invested in compiling information will ultimately lead to important month-end financial reporting. Once again, the distribution of financial communications and reports to management has to happen as fast as possible in multiple formats and be correct.

The reality is that the financial controllers, accounting managers, and accounting team members have to consistently work late—often over the weekend and even well into the evening—trying to compile and report the information for decision makers to rely upon. The process can be tremendously overwhelming and time-consuming because there are so many ad hoc tasks being managed behind the scenes. This creates a heavy workload for the accounting team, which often leads to unhappiness and potentially team members exploring new career opportunities.

When this situation becomes too burdensome, the accounting team has clearly reached a crossroads. There are only a couple of simple ways to alleviate the pain: (1) hire more people to help perform a bad, manual, time-consuming processes or (2) invest in technology, systems, process improvement, and automation.

If the first option is considered to be the best approach, then there may be simply an element of complacency fueling a lack of desire to improve processes or increase business success. Or perhaps the answer may be a bit more straightforward: Management simply does not understand how to solve problems with technology. Whichever the situation, adding more people to the mix to solve the larger problem only serves as a temporary bandage, and the wound will continue to be expensive and time-consuming.

If there is a desire to alleviate painful, time-consuming processes by investing in technology, process improvement, and automation to save time, increase efficiency, and be in a better position to make business decisions, then this book is the right place to start. Investing in a new ERP software system will assist in creating a platform for utilizing more features and functionality, automating processes, and generating accurate financial information in a sensible fashion to ultimately save time and money.

With the pressures associated with a changing business environment, added emphasis on growth, and limited resources, there is an increasing need to gain a strategic advantage through technology. With all the growing responsibilities within an organization, the CFO now typically oversees the business systems of the organization, including the ERP.

The office of the CFO needs to embrace these challenges by seeing this as an opportunity to become more effective in several areas. A new ERP system assists in saving time and money both now and in the future, so there is no reason not to take advantage of the opportunity to optimize daily operations. It is here that you begin to see the office of the CFO develop the alignment of people, processes, and business systems.

The financial controller is the most likely candidate for *gathering information* on ERP systems available in the marketplace, such as understanding the capabilities, reviewing the pricing on licensing, and learning about what the implementation services entail. The financial controller may not be the final decision maker, but he or she often plays a significant role in the ERP software evaluation process, thus leading to the final overall recommendation and implementation of a new system solution.

A joint study from the Institute of Management Accountants (IMA) and Deloitte highlights the challenging roles of the financial controller. "The roles are (1) *steward*, managing risks and preserving assets, (2) an *operator*, running an efficient and affective finance operation, (3) a *strategist*, influencing the future direction of the company, and (4) a *catalyst*, helping to drive execution" (Waelter, et al., 2018). These roles provide a regular framework for the financial controller and uniquely positions him or her for evaluating ERP software.

Obviously, there are instances in which an ERP software evaluation may begin with the president, CFO, or CIO, but this process usually begins with the financial controller because everything rolls up to the office of the CFO. Whomever it may be, the individual tasked with leading the ERP software evaluation for your company will find it important to gather the right information.

In leading this process for a company, there is an opportunity to avoid the typical turn to the internet to perform research. This type of rudimentary research consists of downloading and reviewing marketing materials such as brochures, filling out online questionnaires, skimming blog posts and articles, and more or less wasting time trying to learn anything about ERP systems. Although this is how the majority of people begin an ERP purchasing process, substantial information is limited through such a search.

Spending time on the internet conducting research only leads to becoming fresh bait for software salespeople to try to "hook you" as fast as possible in the form of a new *hot lead*. All you have to do is Google the words Microsoft, Oracle, SAP, Workday, and Sage to begin an uncharted path of evaluating ERP systems and being contacted by direct sales representatives with hard and fast software quotas.

Instead of online window shopping under the false pretense of research, the process of moving to the next level from tedious, time-consuming manual processes to a more robust future state actually begins with your own chart of accounts (COA). The chart of accounts is financial instrument that provides a detailed list of every account in the general ledger itemized into subcategories for purpose of tracking financial transactions during specific accounting periods, such as month, quarter, or year-to-date (Liberto, 2022). Knowing and understanding the chart of accounts of the business is the first step in the path toward successfully navigating toward a new ERP system.

Although each company is unique, each has a chart-of-accounts structure designed to track the financial aspects of the business, including assets, liabilities, equity, revenue, and expenses. When it comes to researching a new system, all information for a company rolls up to the chart of accounts, which means so do the business requirements for a new ERP. It's similar to how everything rolls up to the office of the CFO.

The chart-of-accounts structure serves as the backbone of the system (Knab, 2019). All the payables and receivables transactions will post to the chart of accounts. More commonly known as the core financial layer, this includes the general ledger, payables, receivables, bank reconciliation, fixed assets, and financial reporting.

The additional features and functionality available in the system—such as sales, procurement, and fulfillment—are considered the transactions layer, which naturally builds off the financial layer. While each department will have its own set of business requirements, all of them eventually connect to the financial layer because everything ties back to the office of the CFO.

The CFO has one of the most influential positions for not only developing a strategic vision for a more desirable future state but also for inspiring others to accomplish it. Ryan Davies and Douglas Huey of McKinsey point out, "It's important that CFOs step up to play a broader role, one that includes modeling of desired mind-sets and behaviors in transforming the finance function itself" (Davies & Huey, 2017). Therefore, it is vital to communicate the strategic vision to the entire team.

Although this can take significant time and can be repetitive, communicating the strategic vision with the team is critical. All team members, including executives, managers, and employees, need to be prepared because lots of hard work and several challenges are ahead (Mead, 2022). With the strategic vision properly communicated to the team, a strategy becomes actionable.

With the power allocated within a typical corporate structure, with the technology decision-making authority, and with standard business processes, the office of the CFO has the greatest leverage and the most influence in developing a strategic vision for a more desirable future state. The strategic vision needs to be based on bringing the current team, existing processes, and technology all forward on to a new platform.

Summary

The office of the CFO has become the central nervous system for a business. The official role of the CFO has grown significantly over the last several years. The responsibilities of the financial controller have increased as well. The reason is simple. All the departments of an organization either report to the office of the CFO or have financial ties with the office of the CFO through sales, budgets, reports, and controls. With this being the case, all the financial aspects of the company roll up to the chart of accounts. It only makes sense to develop processes that encompass the financial aspects of a company and also form a strategic vision for taking it to the next level.

Should you find yourself in a chronically leaking boat, energy
devoted to changing vessels is likely to be more productive than
energy devoted to patching leaks.

—Warren Buffett

3
WHEN IS THE RIGHT TIME TO ACQUIRE NEW ERP SOFTWARE?

There are several identifiable characteristics indicating a company
is going through an evolutionary period, which is usually associated with growth or factors potentially prohibiting growth. These
characteristics compel leadership to acknowledge the reality of the
situation and demonstrate the courage to take the next step by changing these circumstances.

These characteristics may be affecting planned strategic initiatives, team member performance, and overall execution, but they
also serve as the primary drivers for deciding when it is the right
time to move to a new ERP package. These characteristics can be
grouped into categories such as corporate strategy, current system
limitations, environmental factors, or immediate triggers.

The practice of keeping costs down is innate to any business, and trying to find workarounds and inexpensive options is commendable. However, ignoring change-demanding characteristics and trying to justify not investing in a new ERP system can lead to missed opportunities or even detrimental results.

Any one of the characteristics listed below (or perhaps any combination) is a clear indication of experiencing limitations in the current environment that require a resolution. Ultimately, the correct resolution is the deployment of a new ERP solution.

Below are the primary categories and the corresponding characteristics for justifying a move to a new ERP platform.

Corporate Strategy

A corporate strategy is designed to include a long-term strategic vision for the purpose of creating value for owners and customers. It is a continuous process, which requires constant effort to manage by making decisions for the purpose of growth and strategic direction (MyAccountingCourse.com, 2022).

Maintain Competitiveness

If two separate companies are selling similar products and services within the same market, they are competing against one another. If one of these companies leverages technology to execute on their growth strategies, they may be able to gain a competitive advantage.

Technology can assist in increasing operational efficiency for delivering goods and services to a company's existing customers and future prospects. In addition, technology can also enhance customer intimacy and increase satisfaction. In business, there has to be a willingness to embrace technical tools, innovative technology, and strategies to maintain competitiveness.

In the digital age, several companies have been labeled "disruptors" by the financial news media (CNBC Staff, 2021). However, not all companies have to be disruptors. They may simply have better systems for execution, and that's how they win. If the competition is using technology to increase customer satisfaction, by fulfilling orders on a timely basis, and by delivering quality products and services, then this can have a dramatic effect in the marketplace.

In order to maintain competitiveness, investing in technology is an absolute must. These systems are designed to enable collaboration, streamline processes, and increase throughput. By leveraging technology and modern systems, businesses can become more productive and achieve better results in a highly competitive marketplace.

Increase Automation

One of the best ways to use technology for the purpose of gaining a competitive advantage is through automation. Automation reduces manual human intervention, which helps eliminate costly errors, lessen operation costs, and increase productivity (Cameron, 2022).

Automation can immediately replace repetitive, time-consuming, ad hoc tasks and paper-driven processes to increase speed, efficiency, and throughput. For instance, financial processes—such as order to cash (O2C), procure-to-pay, and record-to-report are a few of the most automated business processes (workato, 2022).

ERP software contains a natural path for automating backend processes because they are built on top of a relational database. Without being too technical, a relational database stores information, but it also provides access to data points that have a relationship to one another (Pattinson, 2020). Therefore, the attributes in an ERP package can have a one-to-many relationship for the purpose of managing sales, inventory, and financial transactions.

In addition to the natural flow of information, several ERP systems provide easy-to-use workflow automation tools. Workflow automation offers the ability to enhance business processes based on actions, conditions, and triggers to streamline approvals, payments, service requests, and several other activities. These workflow tools require some training, but they do not require a software programmer or software developer.

Beyond workflow, several ERP systems offer enhanced automation, such as artificial intelligence (AI), robotic process automation (RPA), and machine learning (ML). These tools recognize repetitive tasks, trends, and tone and then automate, accelerate, and escalate activities without human intervention. When these tools are used together, it is considered "intelligent automation" (IBM Cloud Education, 2021). Although this functionality is more prevalent in the enterprise space (companies with over $1 billion in annual revenue), these tools are becoming more accessible to companies located within the middle market.

The latest in ERP technology offers several tools available for the purpose of increasing automation. Automation tools assist companies in moving away from busy repetitive tasks and activities that squander time and opportunity. With automation, team members can become more strategic by spending more time on higher-value tasks and increased productivity.

Gain Control

As a small business evolves into a medium-sized business, the roles within an organization begin to change. At the beginning, it may have been necessary for team members to *wear many hats*, but with growth there eventually becomes a need to hire more people and institute formal policies and procedures (Kokemuller, 2022).

Instituting formal policies and procedures means establishing a hierarchy within an organization, including the creation of job roles with corresponding responsibilities, and ensuring there is separation of duties (Greer, 2020). It is not enough to have a diagram on paper. A software system has to be able to enforce internal controls.

A software system can be used to establish a framework of internal controls that provides an environment with tighter financial reporting, the reduction of costly errors, and minimization of exposure to fraud. Without system controls in place, data is susceptible to manipulation, alteration, or worst of all, possible deletion.

An entry-level system is priced to be inexpensive, so although one may be economical for starting a business, it will not provide the necessary controls to get to the next level. An entry-level system is created to be easy to use, so it does not have tight controls or audit trails, and data can be deleted at any time.

Once there are multiple accounting team members accessing an entry-level system, it is time to move to an environment with better controls and security. An ERP system provides internal controls with a security layer to protect the business from potential fraud, to assist with compliance, and to provide an auditable trail

The Sarbanes-Oxley Act of 2002 (SOX) requires financial controls to be in place for publicly traded companies. This legislation was born out of several high-profile accounting scandals, most notably the Enron scandal of December 2001 (Constable, 2021). A company running on an entry-level system wanting to *go public* will never pass a SOX readiness assessment performed by a reputable consulting firm, so this is a logical entry point for an ERP procurement.

Private companies also need to avoid high-risk accounting practices, so if there is a desire to seek new investment in the form of private equity or venture capital, or to potentially go public in the future, then those investment efforts are reasonable entry points for a new ERP package.

Although an entry-level system works well in getting a company started and serves a great purpose, it cannot provide sustainable controls for growing businesses. Growing businesses have a responsibility to institute formal polies and procedures, and the only way that can happen is by gaining control.

Current System Limitations

The purpose of entry-level accounting software is to assist entrepreneurs in launching their small businesses. These entry-level accounting software systems contain basic financial management capabilities but are not designed to scale to meet the long-term needs of businesses experiencing growth.

A growing business relies on accounting team members to process transactions, compile information to create personalized reports, and communicate the financial health of the company to owners and executive management. Although these outputs are normal, behind the scenes they may be comprised of manual, time-consuming, and highly repetitive activities caused by the limitations of the current accounting software. These activities lead to mistake-prone situations that can be frustrating and burdensome.

Although an entry-level accounting software package serves its intended purpose very well, it has several limitations that are easily identifiable. These are the limitations accounting professionals experience first-hand, which can eventually lead to accepting the idea that it may be time to move to a robust ERP solution.

Duplicate Data Entry

As businesses grow, software decisions might be made on the basis of specific needs or by decision makers within individual departments. The department-based software implementation approach eventually leads to team members having to enter information into several different packages within the software landscape.

The process of entering the same information into multiple places is called duplicate data entry. Duplicate data entry happens when vital information—such as sales, fulfillment, time entry, project tracking, payroll, and financial information—has to be entered into multiple systems.

Worst of all, duplicate data entry taking place each day over a significant period of time has a way of masquerading as a legitimate process. In fact, the process of duplicate data entry slows down sales order processing, inventory fulfillment, bank reconciliation, and financial reporting.

It probably goes without saying that, in addition to slowing down critical processes with time-consuming data entry, the process of entering the same information into multiple systems increases the likelihood of making mistakes. These data duplication errors can dramatically affect any reporting or data output.

The best way to reverse course is by moving from department-based software decision-making and by eliminating systems that only handle a single function within the organization. ERP software brings departments together so that several functions are taking place within a single platform. There is a single point of entry for business data, which saves time, reduces errors, and increases reporting integrity.

The Need for System Integration

Outside of department-based software decisions, companies often deploy standalone software packages to serve unique business needs. These unique needs may be related to industry, regulation, compliance, or multiple sales channels. Many of these software packages are standalone, so they immediately become disparate systems.

Make no mistake, the outcomes of having disparate systems are similar to deploying department-based systems. With disparate systems, there's a need for time-consuming duplicate entry, which increases the chance of creating errors and creating unreliable data. However, these systems cannot be easily replaced since they are necessary for achieving business success.

These disparate systems may be based on a particular industry, business model, or potentially proprietary (secret sauce) software, so there's significant justification for their deployment. For instance, health care companies use medical billing systems to track patient information, verify insurance, process payments, and submit claims for reimbursement (Byrd, 2022). In the health-care industry, having a medical billing system is an absolute necessity.

While health care serves as a good example for the pluses of having disparate systems, there are many other examples: a hospitality company needs a reservation system; an event venue needs a ticketing system; a retail store needs a point-of-sale system; and an e-commerce company needs an online storefront. In addition, there are several smaller systems utilized by thousands of companies across the country that provide distinct functionality, such as expense management, sales tax automation, and shipping software.

The bottom line is that disparate systems are often an integral part of the business, and they're not going anywhere. In these circumstances, the back-office accounting system needs to "talk" with these systems through system integration. There are several integration tools available that perform this task, but we will get to that later. Most entry-level software packages lack the ability to integrate with other systems.

The need for system integration quickly arises in these circumstances due to the high volumes of data, which cannot be simply "rekeyed" into the system by a staff member. The data needs to be uploaded on a scheduled basis based on a business process or a specific event trigger. With system integration, data from disparate systems may be imported into an ERP system on a regular basis, thus eliminating separate silos of information, duplicate entry, and time-consuming tasks.

Limited Reporting Capability

The purpose of reporting is to assist owners, executives, managers, or any decision-maker in the ongoing guidance and tracking of corporate progress and strategic growth. In business, there are several reports needed for tracking financials, sales, revenue, budgets, and inventory levels.

Robust reporting tools publish data at a macro level with the ability to drill down to a micro level to gain multiple perspectives on historical information. With these detailed reports, management can review data and gain insight into trends or unforeseen irregularities to assist in navigating the business.

However, with an entry-level accounting software package, the reporting available is simply too basic and lacks visibility. There are limitations to the reporting tools and amount of data that may be presented. In addition, the charts, graphs, and metrics tend to be inflexible for viewing in multiple formats.

When users are unable to get the reports they need from an entry-level system, they are forced to create standalone reports outside of the system. The result is a manual compilation of spreadsheets with static information, which makes gauging the financial health of the business difficult.

Owners and executives need to assess the performance of the business by having real-time insight into revenue, sales, debt, labor, etc. The only way to understand the financial health and viability of the business is by understanding where the numbers are coming from and how they tie together.

Executive management needs access to accurate, up-to-date information so that decisions can be made based on real-time factors. Often these decisions affect the scale of the business and investment, and they can sometimes impact several full-time employees or team members.

If too much time is being spent building and maintaining spreadsheets for reporting purposes outside of the current accounting software, then it is evident the current system is out of date. The lack of reporting will eventually hinder the ability to make reliable decisions.

Multicompany/Multicurrency

There are two basic ways to grow a business. The first is by expanding your product or service offering into new markets (domestically or globally), and the second is selling additional new products and services in existing markets. In both instances, this expansion may necessitate having multiple companies.

In the middle market, it's normal for a business to have multiple companies. There may be a holding company with subsidiaries, various business units, or divisions. These entities may represent different ownership scenarios, properties, or brands, and they may be based in the United States or internationally.

The process of tracking multiple companies with entry-level software is difficult. It requires establishing multiple licensed or subscription accounts so that users can switch from one company to another for processing transactions. Using multiple accounts is annoyingly repetitive, time-consuming, and limited.

The primary limitation is the ability to perform intercompany transactions (due to and due from). For many businesses, the process of transacting between these entities may be essential (Parcells, 2015). In these situations, the transaction needs to flow through multiple subledgers or over multiple corporations.

Another limitation is inadequate financial reporting. Entry-level software is unable to run consolidated financial statements or generate individual profit and loss statements. The accounting team is forced to export data from each entity into a spreadsheet and manually consolidate financial information.

Furthermore, most entry-level software has basic multicurrency functionality and is unable to handle complex foreign currency exchange situations or localization. There are more middle market companies conducting business on a global scale than ever before. In these situations, there has to be a way for tracking multiple entities based on foreign currencies.

A business has to execute on its growth strategy in order to be successful. It only makes sense to expand into new regions across the globe, which ultimately requires multicompany and multicurrency transactions and financial reporting.

Using an entry-level system for multicompany and multicurrency transactions is analogous to "playing musical chairs." It cuts into productivity as everyone is trying to compensate for software limitations with workarounds and spreadsheets.

No Control

It's no secret that entry-level accounting software is designed for small businesses. It simply cannot handle the added complexities associated with growth, especially when it comes to controls.

With very basic architecture, transactions can be deleted or undone by basically anyone with access to the software. In addition, the concept of maintaining an audit trail is nonexistent. Without an audit trail, it's easy to question the legitimacy of financial transactions and reporting.

Furthermore, as the company grows, so does the chance of real money actually walking out the door. Without controls, there are numerous ways for a perpetrator to commit white-collar crimes such as fraud (wire fraud, payroll fraud, double paying a vendor), embezzlement, skimming, or money laundering (Hayes, 2022).

With any small or midsize company, there is a strong chance that thousands of dollars—if not hundreds of thousands of dollars—per year may be lost due to hemorrhaging caused by fraud. While this may be due to lack of controls in entry-level accounting software, part of the blame might also be allocated to putting too must trust in employees.

For a growing business to minimize exposure and a potential single point of failure, accounting controls need to be established. These accounting controls need to be based on real processes, discipline, and rigor, and they need to be enforced by technology (Thakur, 2022).

Establishing security around individuals (user identification and passwords) based on their role within an organization goes a long way. With a software-enforced security layer, organizations can establish separation of duties (approvals), with an audit trail to provide control and enforce compliance (industry or regulatory).

Too Many Time-Consuming Tasks

Due to the limitations of entry-level software, there are too many time-consuming tasks. With all the tasks, activities, and work-arounds, one eventually reaches the point of asking, "Is the juice worth the squeeze?"

There are numerous examples of time-consuming tasks, such as keying data, manually compiling information for reports, and trying to find a formula error in a spreadsheet. With several spreadsheets, each with its own purpose, this happens over and over each week or month like clockwork.

These time-consuming tasks evolve into manual monthly processes to ensure timelines are being met. For instance, a manual process may require team members to pull data from multiple sources (disparate systems), compile this information into a spreadsheet, massage the data to ensure it is cohesive, and then apply formulas and pivot tables to summarize large amounts of data.

Although this particular process may take several hours, days, or perhaps even a week, the hope is to reach a point of confidence in the information being presented before an eventual deadline. Upon reaching the deadline, it is time to forward this information for review. Ultimately, owners, investors, or executive team members consume this information. God forbid one of the formulas in the report is wrong or any of the information is incorrect.

However, the real issue is that as a company grows, the manual processes become lengthy, and the workarounds become harder to accomplish. There is only so much time in the day, and working in a current state of having to "play catch-up" all the time can be extremely aggravating.

The sheer volume of time-consuming tasks leads most rational individuals to question whether there is an easier way. It only makes sense to explore systems to assist in being more productive so that necessary tasks are being performed proactively and efficiently.

Environmental Factors

In addition to the system limitations listed above, there may be environmental factors influencing the decision to explore a move to an ERP package. These environmental factors are conditions that surround the current software and that, if left unattended, might lead to a critical situation.

Provider Instability

There are several examples of provider instability presenting a number of challenges. The current provider may have financial issues or limited resources for development or support, or the provider might bring other unforeseen real-world challenges you never anticipated.

All software developers and implementation providers are in business, which means they go through the traditional pains associated with growth, such as generating sales, managing employees, servicing customers, and trying to increase profit. It is not easy, and unfortunately, not all providers are successful.

Both the mainstream horizontal players and vertical niche providers face challenges, but some are unable to "right the ship" and may perhaps land in financial trouble. While some providers are able to raise capital or be acquired to get through tough situations, many niche players may experience more enduring struggles.

Although a provider may be facing challenges, that may not be immediately noticeable. However, eventually the instability of the provider will either affect the software you are running or the support you are receiving. Over time, you may notice that the software is slow to be updated or that the support has become sluggish in response to requests for assistance.

If the customer base of the provider is not growing, there will be implications, such as a natural reduction in the number of developers and/or consultants available to support the application. Having a software package with several limitations or having to wait hours, days, or weeks to resolve a system issue can each be problematic.

There are several industry-specific software platforms that address specialized niches for customers, but these offerings present a slew of other issues. Perhaps the developer is located on another continent, or perhaps there are only a handful of consultants supporting this platform all over the world. Although you have an industry-specific software package, perhaps there is only one person in the country supporting it.

There are other circumstances in which a software developer or partner may bring in consultants with offshore resources to assist with the implementation. Although the hourly rates are cheap, the challenges of working through multiple time zones and communication barriers may eventually sour the experience for the purchaser.

Whether the provider is having issues financially, has limited staff resources for development and support, or brings other unforeseen challenges to the game, these should all be considered examples of provider instability. It does not take a SWOT (strengths, weaknesses, opportunities, and threats) analysis to determine that this is a threat in relation to achieving everyday success (Kenton, 2022).

Preparing for an IPO

When a company desires to make an initial public offering (IPO), it has to comply with Section 404 of the Sarbanes-Oxley Act of 2002 (Cohn, 2022). SOX requires internal controls and procedures to be applied to the existing environment, and those controls and procedures must be comprehensive and sustainable (Shives, 2022).

To be more specific, SOX requires members of the executive management team to create and maintain controls for two significant purposes. The first purpose is to establish a level of corporate responsibility for all financial reports while the second is to be able to provide disclosure in "real time" of both financial and operational conditions (Pathlock, 2022). The failure to comply can directly lead to financial penalties to corporate officers.

Without going into too much detail, entry-level accounting software does not offer the features and functionality needed to comply with SOX. The limitations of system security (lack of control) and the simplistic financial reporting are too basic.

In moving toward an IPO, there are several steps required that can take anywhere from a few months to a couple of years to complete (Fernando, 2021). One of the first steps is to move from an entry-level software package to a more complete ERP system, which offers the robust security features and reporting capabilities needed.

The base platform of an ERP system includes controls, security, the ability to segregate duties, and the ability to generate reliable financial reporting with audit trails. If there is any desire to ever launch an IPO, then one of the first steps in the strategy has to be moving away from entry-level accounting software.

Compliance Needs

Whether your company is private, public, local, regional, or international, the regulatory landscape continues to become more complex.

The best way to stay on top of the rules and regulations is by having ERP software that can handle these challenges.

For instance, there are specific regulatory requirements for companies in the life sciences, food and beverage manufacturing, and energy industries. In the life sciences and food and beverage sectors, compliance includes the ability to track the origin of every piece of inventory in case of a product recall (Bolton, 2019). In order to be compliant, ERP capabilities such as lot control, serialization, and audit trails are absolutely necessary to fulfill this obligation.

In addition to regulatory compliance, there may be accounting compliance requirements and standards that need to be maintained, depending on the industry. In these situations, a software system has to track, report, and comply with the Accounting Standards Codification (ASC) of the Financial Accounting Standards Board (FASB) (Financial Accounting Foundation, 2014).

For example, revenue recognition (ASC 606) is based on recognizing revenue on contracts with customers and representing new revenue reporting standards for both public and private companies for each of their entities (Intrasinghathong, 2019). ASC 606 is significant for technology companies using software as a service (SaaS) and other high-tech offerings. The adoption of the standard has an impact on multiyear contracts with customers that may include software licenses, software subscriptions, hardware, professional services, and an on-going support contract.

Another current example highlighting the need for compliance is ASC 842. ASC 842 is now the lease accounting standard, which means the majority of operating leases have to be reported on a company's balance sheet (Leese, 2020). Once the standards are assessed and the impact is determined, the lease data needs to be migrated into the ERP for long-term management rather than continue to live in a spreadsheet.

ASC 842 impacts any industry with leases, including energy companies, hospitality providers, restaurants, supermarkets, and fitness companies (gyms, studios, and equipment sellers) (Goldstein, 2021).

Companies in these industries may have anywhere from dozens to hundreds of leases (if not thousands). More often than not, when you see commercial trucks, vans, buses, and industrial equipment, there is a strong chance these items are leased rather than owned by the company.

As a company grows over time, the regulatory landscape continues to become more and more complex. Entry-level accounting software packages were not designed to handle these circumstances. A more robust ERP software system provides the ability to track this level of complexity, automate repetitive tasks, and create an auditable trail.

Modernize the Software Landscape

In situations where there is significant technical debt, there is a need to modernize the software landscape and move away from legacy systems. In many cases, legacy systems can become obstacles to new business initiatives because automated processes are needed to support them (Gartner, 2022).

There are several ways for modernizing the software landscape. Most notably, a business may update the on-premises hardware infrastructure, move business applications to a data center (private cloud), adopt cloud-based business applications (public cloud), or a combination of each of these options together (hybrid cloud) to form a full solution (Cloudflare Inc, 2021).

The first step is overcoming a culture in which people have become comfortable with technical debt and falling behind on technology. Whether the "debt happens inevitably with time", or "accrues both inadvertently and deliberately", there has to be a decision point for moving away from these antiquated systems (Pluralsight LLC, 2022).

The modernization of the software landscape at a company requires leadership, executive sponsorship, and investment in technology. The investment in technology packages in areas such as ERP,

CRM (customer relationship management), productivity, and collaboration helps to change a corporate culture. As former football coach Tony Dungy once wrote, "Small changes lead to big shifts" (Dungy, 2022). The process of modernizing the software landscape by replacing legacy systems and overcoming technology impediments certainly represents a big shift.

With cloud-based technology, companies are able to modernize software landscapes faster than ever before and no longer have to rely on antiquated legacy software. It is here where a company can begin to advance into the future with systems that support key initiatives and the processes behind them.

Immediate Triggers

Beyond system limitations and environmental factors, there are some immediate triggers that may spark the need for a new ERP package faster than anticipated. In these situations, a high amount of urgency is placed on making a change. Any number of events may spark an immediate trigger for new ERP software, but the examples below are common.

New Sheriff in Town

Ever heard the term "There's a new sheriff in town"? It is an idiom used when a new person has come into power at a company and is going to be making changes (Wiktionary, 2022). In the world of ERP, the classic instance of the "new sheriff" is likely to be a CFO, but it can also be a financial controller, CIO, or even the CEO.

In this scenario, the new sheriff inherits an entry-level system or an antiquated legacy ERP system or simply just wants to get his or her fingerprints on the business system to take ownership. In these circumstances, a new sheriff may understand the magnitude of switching to a new ERP system but might be clearly focused on replacing the old way of doing things regardless of the impact.

Here the new sheriff essentially becomes a disruptor by taking team members, departments, and perhaps paid consultants outside of their comfort zone. There is really no telling how people respond to this disruption, but one thing is clear: changes are coming very fast.

Hopefully the new sheriff is sponsoring this change to strengthen processes, tighten controls, and enhance financial reporting with the goal of taking the team and the entire company to the next level. However, there are instances in which the new sheriff exerts executive bias only to acquire a specific software package or chooses to work with consultants already known through past experiences.

Whatever the situation, the new sheriff brings power, budgetary say-so, and authority, plus the ability to formulate the vision and make this type of decision. The combination of these forces can create an immediate level of urgency to acquire a new ERP package.

Private Equity Acquisition

When a private equity firm acquires a company, it immediately becomes a part of its investment portfolio. Since the company becomes part of the portfolio, the private equity group will make several calculated investments into the company to increase efficiency and sales.

The goal of the private equity group is to rapidly increase the value of the portfolio company so that it may eventually exit with the highest profit possible for its investors. In many instances, the company that has been acquired has problematic issues such as poor financial performance, operational inefficiency, or slow growth.

Once a private equity group is involved, it will take bold steps to steer the company through "rapid performance improvement" (Barber & Goold, 2007). These actions may include a greater emphasis on management, increasing operational efficiency, improving financial reporting, and enhancing the overall execution of business operations.

While each situation is unique, there may be an emphasis on replacing the entry-level or legacy system or just moving away from daily management by spreadsheet. Any one of these situations can lead to an ERP evaluation for the purpose of increasing efficiency and growing the business.

Corporate Carve-Outs and Spin-Offs

In a global market where mergers and acquisitions are commonplace, corporate carve-outs and spin-offs happen all the time. In these situations, a company may partially divest an asset, portfolio of assets, or business unit by selling a minority interest to outside investors or by spinning off a business unit to create a new independent company (Luu & Thomson, 2019).

Upon the close of the deal, in either case, there will be a transitional service agreement (TSA) between the buyer and the seller. The TSA provides for specific services to be performed by the seller for the buyer at a predetermined price for an agreed upon length of time, such as six months (Deloitte, 2021).

The TSA is designed to provide the new company essential services such as administration, accounting, human resources, and information technology (VelocityGlobal, 2022). With these services temporarily in place, the new company can focus on assembling the rest of the organization, including appointing members to the management team, hiring staff, planning IT strategy, and acquiring business software.

When it comes to a new carve-out or spin-off, time is of the essence. The TSA will provide "air cover" only for a limited period of time. However, the new company has to move swiftly. In terms of a new ERP package, there is an accelerated level of urgency to acquire, implement, and completely stand up a new system before the expiration of the agreement.

Mission-Critical Situation

When an essential software package, piece of hardware, component, or device fails, there is a disruption to business operations. When the accounting and business software package fails, it can be catastrophic to any organization, and that quickly turns into a mission-critical situation.

There are several scenarios that can lead to a mission-critical situation. The most common scenarios are system incompatibility, infrastructure failure, cyberattacks, or acts of God. A mission-critical situation affects the entire business and disrupts nearly all financial and operational processes.

When the accounting system is down, everyday processes come to a full stop: Transactions cannot be processed, vendors cannot be paid, orders cannot be fulfilled, and historical data may be lost. In this situation, the company is on life support as it's no longer capturing transactions and tracking revenue.

Worst of all, the mission-critical situation may have been self-inflicted through a lack of preparation due to IT complacency, cheapness, passive resistance, or laziness. What led to the single point of failure will eventually be scrutinized, and the outcomes may not be pretty.

In times of chaos, problem-solvers strive to find a solution. When it comes to an ERP package, in many instances a short-term solution is to find a new location for the legacy on-premises ERP software to reside. However, the most realistic and best long-term solution to this situation is to stand up a new ERP system in the cloud. In any case, the goal will be to try and get back to everyday business (transacting, reporting, etc.) as soon as humanly possible.

Summary

There are several identifiable characteristics to help decision makers recognize it's time to move to a new ERP. The ability to identify these characteristics as early as possible assists in setting the stage for future success. Ignoring them could lead to an unfortunate set of circumstances.

Whichever of these easily identifiable characteristics drive the process, the goal is to utilize the tools and technology to get to the next level. A new ERP system brings automation, control, better reporting, system integration, and new insights into the business that will assist in propelling the business forward.

The good news is that each of these easily identifiable characteristics really indicates an evolutionary period in the growth and success of the business. It is truly time for an ERP system to do the bulk of the heavy lifting and become a valuable tool for a business to rely upon for many years to come.

Knowing is half the battle.

—G.I. Joe

4
ERP SYSTEMS FOR THE MIDDLE MARKET, SMBs, AND PRIVATE EQUITY

According to Fortune Business Insights, "The global enterprise resource planning (ERP) software market size was valued at USD 45.82 billion in 2021" (Fortune Business Insights, 2022). The ERP software market is comprised of several leading mainstream ERP software developers and numerous vertically-focused ERP vendors, so the industry is a fiercely competitive battlefield.

The leading mainstream ERP software developers have solutions designed for prospective customers located throughout the middle market on a global scale. These developers play an active role in the middle market, SMB market (small- and mid-sized businesses) and strive to forge relationships with private equity groups. All of this is done to gain as many new customers as possible to increase overall market share.

Furthermore, the leading mainstream developers have highly developed and experienced partner channels. Also fiercely competitive, these partner channels are comprised of trained and certified consultants coming from accounting firms, value-added resellers, and independent consultants.

These channel partners have the ability to assist customers in the middle market and SMB market, and also forge relationships with private equity groups. Rather than being driven by market share, these consultants are focused more on growth with the initial sale, one-time implementation, and generating recurring revenue through ongoing support. Once the ERP package has been deployed, these consultants will be able to provide service and support for many years to come.

Also in the marketplace, vertical ERP applications are industry-based systems (as opposed to the mainstream players offering horizontal applications). A vertical ERP application intentionally brings more industry-specific functionality, operational processes, formulas, and leading practices into the ERP application. While vertical ERP applications may not be as commonly known, they are developed to address unique business challenges.

Since there may only be one or two possible entry points for a new ERP software package during the entire life of a business, the stakes are incredibly high for leading mainstream ERP software developers and many vertically focused ERP vendors to add new customers. Once a new ERP system is deployed, it may be ten or more years before it is replaced.

The process of small- and medium-sized businesses transitioning to a new ERP platform can be a big leap technologically, culturally, and financially. However, these ERP software systems have been specifically designed, packaged, and able to be supported for companies making this transition.

The ERP industry understands the characteristics of small- and medium-sized companies, the capabilities needed by these potential customers, and how to package the software to fit businesses of all sizes. The capabilities available in these ERP software platforms (or in some cases multiple platforms) offer robust features and functionality designed to appeal to as many small- and medium-sized businesses as possible.

One thing most middle market and SMBs have in common is the eventual need for an ERP system. In fact, these companies spend a significant amount of money on information technology, which creates momentum and growth for well-known software developers such as Oracle, Microsoft, SAP, Epicor, and Sage.

The leading ERP software developers have a firm grasp on the unique characteristics of the middle market and SMBs. The software products, licensing, and pricing are all geared toward assisting companies within this marketplace. This makes the ERP marketplace a battlefield in which software developers try to *land and expand* by starting small and eventually growing their footprint with each customer (Alexandra, 2021).

Middle Market

It's apparent the middle market is not going to win any popularity contests. While politicians love to talk about small businesses, and consumers love name brands of some of the largest companies in the world, the middle market is the segment with the least amount of attention, and it seemingly glides under the radar (Maney, 2011).

Yes, the easiest way to describe the middle market is the space between small business and big business, but that's not good enough. Most middle market businesses are privately owned and have established processes, multiple entities, a diverse range of complexities, and operations as part of both the US and global economies. However, they are unique in many ways. They represent different types of investors, varying degrees of purchasing power, a mixture of technical capabilities, and wide-ranging possibilities for growth.

At the turn of the millennium, the middle market was characterized as businesses larger than a mom-and-pop shop but smaller than a global Fortune 500 Company. In terms of annual revenue, a business had to have greater than $2 million and less than $500 million.

Today, whether based on annual revenue or even employee size, there are several different definitions of what constitutes the middle market. A good barometer for measuring the middle market would be companies with annual revenue between $10 million and $1 billion (The National Center for The Middle Market, 2022).

In this range, there are approximately 350,000 middle market businesses within the United States. Those businesses account for a third of the US private sector gross domestic product (The National Center for The Middle Market, 2022). While a great many of these businesses are not household names, they are tremendously important players in the marketplace.

These middle market businesses have a huge impact on our growing economy by filling different types of office parks (research, industrial, and business) all over the country and creating important jobs that communities need for expansion (Cantelme, 2016). They span across multiple industries and access capital from banks and investors to achieve significant growth.

In addition, there are all types of ownership scenarios in the middle market. These companies are more mature and may be entrepreneur-driven, owned through partnerships, established as family businesses, impacted by multiple generations, or backed entirely by private equity investors.

However, there is one major issue: Many prospective ERP buyers do not see themselves as middle market customers. Often the leaders of middle market companies believe their companies are too small for a robust and scalable ERP (Maslen, 2021). Those companies are used to being nimble and believe they cannot afford a better solution.

While this disconnect may create a feeling of being misunderstood by vendors, the real issue for many of these companies is a failure to embrace their own market identity (Carucci, 2016). As a company reaches a middle market size, its leaders need to embrace the fact that it has needs that are similar to those of large corporations (Maslen, 2022).

Companies in the middle market need robust solutions, the assistance of experienced consultants, and on-going support. Business leaders simply need to become more comfortable with the characteristics of the middle market so that they know they exist within this space.

SMB Market

According to the US Small Business Administration, there are over 30 million small businesses across the United States today (U.S. Small Business Administration—Office of Advocacy, 2019). The software industry uses the term SMBs to highlight a portion of the marketplace filled by fast growing small businesses and the lower end subset of the middle market. One method used to classify the SMB market are companies and organizations with less than $50 million in annual revenue (Gartner, 2022).

The reason for this designation is that SMBs operate on the scale of middle market and enterprise-sized companies. There are three types of small businesses that distinguish themselves in the SMB market: (1) traditional small businesses experiencing organic success and growth, (2) entrepreneurs leveraging technology and digital tools to compete with much bigger players, and (3) fast-moving, tech-enabled start-ups trying to disrupt a particular market through innovation.

The most fundamental way for these companies to play and compete with middle market and enterprise-sized companies is through the adoption of technology (Cloudwell, 2022). One of the primary areas of technology adoption is an ERP package that synchronizes business functions and processes with the ability to scale for growth.

The first example is of a small business experiencing organic growth over an extended period. That company will eventually need more sophisticated systems. These companies grew their businesses by being standardized on entry-level software products—such as QuickBooks, Xero, or FreshBooks—because those products were affordable and easy to use.

As small businesses achieving exceptional growth, these companies will eventually experience first-hand the limitations of entry-level software. It will eventually become apparent that a more scalable ERP software will provide a better solution for addressing the needs of a growing business.

In addition to small businesses achieving organic growth, there are even smaller companies created by entrepreneurs and even solopreneurs (a person that runs an entire business on their own) that are leveraging technology as much as possible (Saar, 2022). By embracing the latest in technology, they are able to grow their businesses faster than ever.

These small enterprises are taking advantage of several digital tools, such as social media (Twitter, LinkedIn, and Facebook), API-based applications (Zoom, Slack, Mailchimp, HubSpot, etc.), analytics (Google Analytics and Amazon Web Services) and e-commerce capabilities (Shopify, Wix, and WooCommerce) (Deloitte, 2018). These are small companies doing more with less right out of the gate, but ultimately the success they experience will require an ERP system, which can be inserted into this environment.

Lastly, there are startup communities all over the country in places such as Silicon Valley, Boulder, and Boston. Here, newly established businesses begin with an entrepreneur, and a brand-new idea receives funding from incubators, angel investors, venture capital firms, and private equity groups to accelerate growth.

In order to move this fast, these startups assemble strong team members, utilize scalable technologies, and pursue new markets. There's a high amount of risk and a lot of uncertainty but also the chance for reaping great rewards. It's a "go-big-or-go-home" mentality, with the intention of achieving a successful exit by reaching an IPO or a sale to a much larger company within three to five years (Ledgard, 2022).

On paper, many of these companies are small businesses with less than $2 million in annual revenue (and they may even be preprofit) and fewer than thirty employees. In these situations, the team and technology are being put into place for immediately scaling up with growth, and that often means a new ERP package and a willingness to accept "affordable losses" over the short term (Jongen, 2019).

While these businesses can temporarily run on an entry-level accounting software, the fast-growing businesses in the SMB market cannot succeed using software with limited functionality and scalability. These businesses need to graduate to the next level and adopt an ERP system.

Private Equity—Enter the Dealmaker

As the economy has continued to expand, there has been a rapid increase of investment into the middle market and SMBs by private equity groups (Langer & Heaton, 2022). These dealmakers focus on growing an investment portfolio comprised of companies based on a specialty that fits a certain size, industry, sector, geography, or ownership structure.

The way it works is private equity groups establish investment funds to give private investors the ability to make direct capital investments into private companies (Baldwin, 2021). Once a company has been acquired by the fund, it becomes part of the private equity group's investment portfolio.

The primary objective of the portfolio company is to increase earnings, drive growth, and unlock hidden value to provide investors with better returns than they would receive in the public market. Therefore, with every acquisition there's an exit strategy, which leads to an eventual sale of the company to either a corporate buyer, a larger private equity group, or an initial public offering by taking a company public (McKinsey & Company, 2019).

In addition, private equity firms perform several types of deals in the form of mergers and acquisitions (M&A), corporate carve-outs of underperforming divisions of larger companies, the purchase of distressed assets, and investment in preprofit startups (Chen, 2022). These deals are attractive to investors as long as there is a realistic strategy to increase margins and return profits to investors upon exit (buy low and sell high).

With any transaction, dealmakers perform due diligence on potential acquisition targets. The operational due diligence process includes evaluating the technology operations, including full-time IT employees, infrastructure (hardware and software), business applications, and cybersecurity (Patel, 2022). They search for potential gaps, holes, and vulnerabilities so that there are no surprises after closing on the acquisition.

Assuming the deal eventually closes, dealmakers exhibit "relentless focus" on the execution of their strategy (Barber & Goold, 2007). Although each situation is unique, the basic formula remains the same: keep costs down, drive up sales, and increase operational efficiency.

The only way to fill in the technology gaps of a portfolio company is by putting the right solutions in place. Dealmakers understand the importance of an ERP system since it controls financial operations and provides visibility into the portfolio company (Agrawal & Selimkhanov, 2020). Dealmakers have to assess whether the current ERP software is worth keeping or if it needs to be replaced. Quite often this means acquiring new ERP software because dealmakers know growing companies need robust ERP systems (D., et al., 2017).

When it comes to a new portfolio company and assessing the current state of the ERP software, there are several real-world scenarios worth mentioning. For instance, the new acquisition may have a large, enterprise-sized ERP system that is expensive and difficult to maintain; antiquated software unsuitable for upgrading or optimizing; entry-level software lacking scalability; or maybe no ERP software at all. These situations all point to making a change.

With a lot at risk, dealmakers hire people with unique skills and strong fundamentals to lead departments of their portfolio companies (Harvard Business Review, 2016). In many instances this process will undoubtedly include a new CEO, chief financial officer, and potentially a financial controller with a proven track record and previous experience in replacing ERP systems.

Dealmakers bring a lot of common sense to an ERP evaluation process. The primary goal is to modernize the ERP software in a relatively short time frame without making things complicated or affecting EBITDA (earnings before interest, taxes, depreciation, and amortization).

In many instances this means increasing reliance on technology by exploring mainstream ERP software options with a strong belief in not wasting time or money or taking on additional costs associated with overly complex business systems (Kimberling, 2018). Here there is a narrow focus on *have-to-have* capabilities rather than *nice-to-have* capabilities to achieve a rapid time to value.

Dealmakers embrace ERP systems offering out-of-the-box functionality instead of the larger, more complicated systems requiring significant design and build-out and greater financial investment (Kimberling, 2018). Furthermore, dealmakers bring an increased level of determination and urgency throughout this process because they can "size-up a situation and make quick and smart decisions" (Anderson, 2019).

Summary

The ERP marketplace actively targets companies within the middle market and the SMB market because they compete with large enterprise-sized corporations head-to-head each and every day.

The ERP industry understands middle market businesses and SMBs have similar ERP needs as large corporations. However, business leaders must embrace their true market identity and stop hiding behind the "we're a small company" catchphrase.

For many of these companies, a lot can be learned from the no-nonsense approach exhibited by dealmakers dialed in to focus on exactly what's needed in ERP software. They have an uncompromising desire to deploy mainstream ERP systems in a sensible time frame and at a reasonable price point to achieve a rapid time to value.

There are many ways for growing businesses to reach their potential, but they're simply not going to get there without an ERP package. It is the one software package that allows for the synchronization of business functions into a modernized business process that can scale for growth for many years to come.

You are what your record says you are.

—Bill Parcells

5
GOING FROM LAGGARD TO DIGITAL TRANSFORMATION

The first edition of *Diffusion of Innovations*, published in 1962 by Dr. Everett M. Rogers, first reasoned that consumers of innovation may be characterized as innovators, early adopters, early majority, late majority, and laggards (Rogers, 1962). Over the years, the work and research by Rogers has become repeatedly referenced by social scientists, technology studies, and online bloggers.

The Rogers innovation adoption curve highlighted these five categories. Together, these categories represent a traditional bell curve since some companies are on the bleeding edge of technology and innovation while the rest eventually catch up over an extended period of time (Management.Net, 2022). Each one of these characterizations is represented in the middle market. It's the businesses residing in the latter categories (late majority and laggards) that need to "see the light." In these situations, business leaders have to accept the reality of the current software landscape and choose to do something about it.

If the current software landscape is old, antiquated, and complex, that situation increases the level of exposure and vulnerability to several unfortunate circumstances. Choosing to rely on antiquated and complex legacy systems leads to functionality gaps, compatibility issues, error messages, a lack of productivity, or even, worst of all, unfortunate mission-critical situations (breakdowns, ransomware, etc.).

Under another scenario, instead of the current software landscape being dominated by old legacy systems, it might be characterized by several entry-level packages with limited capabilities. In these situations, separate siloes of information develop, and that situation leads to manual processes, duplicate entry, and numerous spreadsheets. While these systems are inexpensive and serve a good purpose, there is only so much they can do for a growing business before ultimately reaching their limitations.

At the other end of the spectrum, fast-growing startups may begin on entry-level software packages that do not have the baggage of legacy systems. They have a corporate culture that looks for ways to solve problems with a combination of technology and creativity (Hisrich & Soltanifar, 2020). While there is more enthusiasm toward embracing the latest in technology, those companies can become attracted to bleeding-edge software products.

Whatever the status of the current software landscape, it is all based on decisions from the past. Accepting the state of the current technology environment means letting go of the past, including the time and effort and previous financial investments in hardware and software.

These past decisions were merely stepping stones to help pave the way to achieve more progress in the future. Ultimately, what matters is whether the current software can perform today and produce positive results in the future. If it cannot, then it is time to proactively deal with it.

With today's acceleration of technology, the current software can be modernized faster than ever before. If the system is outdated, limited, or inadequate, software can be implemented in a reasonable amount of time to create a platform for modernizing the current system.

It is through this acceleration of technology that businesses began referring to this experience as digital transformation (Farris, 2020). As luck would have it, companies moving from an old legacy system to a modern system will experience digital transformation because technology naturally improves performance (Westerman, et al., 2014).

In the TechTarget article "How to choose the right ERP for digital transformation," Linda Rosencrance precisely notes, "ERP forms the core of digital transformation" (Rosencrans, 2020). Therefore, the shortest path from laggard to digital transformation is by replacing the ERP system.

Summary

Regardless of the current situation, it takes leadership to not only identify the limitations being experienced in the present but to also become the agent of change for the future. Business leaders have to accept reality, understand the strengths and weaknesses of the current software, let go of the past, and choose to make a change.

There are modern tools and technology available that can be used to improve performance, scale for growth, and consistently achieve positive results. In order to get there, use the current environment as a launchpad for beginning the ERP journey, which means adopting a technical basis for addressing business requirements and developing a strategic vision for a better future.

THE ERP JOURNEY BEGINS IN THE BUILDING

Failure to prepare is preparing to fail.

—*John Wooden*

6
BEGINNING THE ERP JOURNEY: FORMULATE A STRATEGIC VISION AND DEVELOP A LIST OF REQUIREMENTS

Unfortunately, when it comes to evaluating a new ERP system, many experienced business professionals go straight to the internet to "conduct research" and seek inspiration. Although well-intentioned, trying to gather detailed information on the internet for new ERP software is a time-wasting exercise.

There is very little substance or relevant guidance beyond vaguely written product information sheets, shiny literature, and web landing pages designed to influence visitors towards a *call to action*. These materials are graphically appealing and eye-catching because they were created by the best and brightest marketing professionals in the world.

These marketing materials intentionally contain written copy with ambiguous generalizations and promises of enhancing collaboration, increasing productivity, and accelerating sales, but they don't contain specific details on how this might be achieved. The only goal here is to generate ERP software leads.

There is an entire community of business professionals who base their research and software evaluation on novice opinions and commercial literature such as product sheets, white papers, and blog posts. Teaser information offers very little insight, so perhaps it's time to step away from the internet.

In order to embark on a successful ERP journey, it is important to start at the very beginning. Executives and business professionals have to be intentional and truly look inside the business.

By looking inside, business leaders can see the limitations of the current software, recognize manual processes, and identify all the static spreadsheets being utilized. They can also define a greater vision for the business based on a desire to be in a better place in the near future.

Start at the beginning by formulating a strategic vision statement for the future system. This is the opportunity to brainstorm ideas and identify all the immediate goals and needs as well as create a wish list of cool features and functionality available in a modern business system.

A strategic vision is a guide for influencing the path of the evaluation process. It can be referred to at any point of the evaluation process to assist in keeping the team aligned and everyone on track. Whatever is chosen for the strategic vision, it should represent the business, the goals, and the desire for a better future.

While everyone's perspective is unique, one example of a strategic vision statement is as follows:

Deploy a proven ERP system that provides accessibility, control, mobility, and reporting and that can be enhanced, scaled, and supported as our company grows into the future.

Once a strategic vision for the new ERP system has been developed, the next step is to formulate a list of requirements based on the business. The list of requirements needs to be developed with the assistance of key team members and departments leaders, and it needs to include the primary processes performed every day.

The exercise of creating a list of requirements will generate internal discussions (perhaps several) and help to create organizational alignment. The unification of vision, team, and requirements becomes a productive force in the evaluation because knowing what you want and need in a new ERP package is the key to success.

Now, it is extremely important to avoid making short-sighted decisions or, worse, fail in learning from the mistakes made in the past. (Unfortunately, history often repeats itself, even in business.) Having a detailed list of requirements based on existing challenges, limitations, problems, and pain points will help the businesses transform its technology and operations.

Creating a list of requirements can be very easy, but there needs to be caution associated with this exercise. Avoid getting *into the weeds* by focusing on specific features, functions, or reports that exist in the legacy system and need to be re-created in the new ERP system.

The objective is to not re-create the current software. Requirements based on how the legacy system is used today can become obstacles in evaluating a new ERP system and getting to the next level.

Here is a short list of examples of requirements that are disconcertingly based on re-creating a legacy software package. These requirements are examples of essentially highlighting *what not to do*.

An Example of an Inappropriate List of Requirements (What Not to Do!)

1. The system needs to be able to export data into a spreadsheet to update information and formulas.
2. The system has to be able to generate an aging report.
3. Payables has to be able to print checks twice per month.

4. The system needs to be able to add our logo to an invoice.

5. The system needs to be able to print.

In addition to trying to re-create the legacy software to perform daily activities, this list specifies some of the most fundamental capabilities available in modern ERP software. Imagine going to a car dealership and telling the salesperson, "I only want to look at cars with motors." It's just an approach that is too limited.

In formulating a list of requirements, assume a new ERP package offers thousands upon thousands of capabilities. Leading developers such as Microsoft, Oracle, and SAP have been building these systems and enhancing them for several years. It is safe to assume the application has a general ledger as well as the ability to run reports, print checks, add a logo to an invoice, or print when needed.

Use the strategic vision as a statement of purpose for formulating a list of business requirements for new ERP software. This way, specific needs can be identified while the big picture remains in focus. Here is a short list of example requirements highlighting *what to do*.

Example of an Appropriate List of Requirements (What to Do!)

1. The system has to be accessible through the web so that users may work remotely or be mobile.
2. Reports need to be refreshable so that management can make timely business decisions.
3. The system needs to automatically reconcile our bank accounts with our financial institutions.
4. The system needs to integrate data from our other software applications on a daily basis.
5. The system needs to have controls in place so that our organization can have a separation of duties.

Let the strategic vision drive the business requirements and assist team members in visualizing a business system for the future that will save time and money and increase productivity. Armed with a strategic vision and a list of business requirements, business professionals can know what they are looking for in a new ERP package.

The strategic vision and the list of requirements can be sent to consultants, partners, and developers in advance of any discovery conversations, software demonstrations, or presentations. In addition, this information may be referred to at any point to ensure the evaluation process is staying on track.

Summary

In order to evaluate a new ERP system, the first step is to understand the current situation. Understanding the current situation includes gaining insight into the challenges, pain points, limitations, and manual processes existing today.

These obstacles can form the basis for developing a future vision statement and creating a focused list of requirements. Having these tools in place assists in creating a guide for evaluating new ERP software packages and building a path toward a more desirable future.

It is no different than going to a grocery store with a shopping list. Without a shopping list, one can become lost by picking up random items and spending money on the wrong things. Having a shopping list is intentional and focused, which helps to save time, energy, and money.

We live in a society exquisitely dependent on science and technology, in which hardly anyone knows anything about science and technology.

—Carl Sagan

7
EMBRACE THE DISCOVERY PROCESS

Once a strategic vision and a list of business requirements have been developed, they are ready to be sent to consultants and partners representing the ERP software products you wish to evaluate. The strategic vision and list of requirements provide insight into the critical aspects of the ERP evaluation and assist potential consultants in determining whether an ERP product is potentially a good fit or not.

Assuming there is a good fit, the consultant will request one or perhaps multiple meetings to discuss the requirements in more detail. Obviously, consultants can learn about the business by reviewing this information, visiting your website, reading news releases, and making general assumptions based on employee size, annual revenue, or the industry as a whole. However, the best way for the consultant to gain insight into the business requirements is through a discovery process, which consists of meetings and conversations using all of this valuable information as a launchpad.

It is important to embrace the discovery process. Discovery meetings provide an open dialogue for discussing the business requirements in more detail. Through these conversations, ERP consultants gain insight into the current challenges of the software landscape, technical constraints, team resources, and any other variables impacting the transition to a new ERP package.

Furthermore, the right people need to be available to participate in the discovery meetings based on their roles in the organization, the business requirements, and system dependencies. Invite the primary stakeholders, including the CFO, the financial controller, subject matter experts (IT, fulfillment, etc.), and any critical, hands-on power users (people that will use the software the most often). Once the primary stakeholders have been identified, their availability to participate in the ERP discovery meetings has to be a high priority.

Although the discovery meetings may be repetitive and time-consuming, the process is beneficial for both the potential client and the consultant. While the goal is to evaluate a new ERP system, the interactions between client and the consultant may eventually lead to a long-term, strategic working relationship.

The ERP consultant gains an understanding of the business, key processes, strategic goals, and multiple perspectives within the organization. All of the information gathered during the discovery process assists the ERP consultant in preparation for a personalized software presentation, the creation of preliminary pricing on software licensing and implementation services, and familiarization with the potential client's team.

The discovery meetings and conversations also assist in keeping the team aligned and focused on the end goal of evaluating a new ERP system throughout the process. Plus, this is also the opportunity to get to know the ERP consulting teams, gain insight into their implementation methodology, and determine if they are teams you wish to work with not only on this special initiative but also potentially beyond.

Similar to dating, the discovery process is the foundation for building a long-term strategic relationship between your business and an ERP consultant. Often overlooked by people wanting a "bid," the forming of a strategic relationship with an ERP consultant should be viewed with the same importance as doing so with any other critical business partners, such as attorneys, certified public accountants, or bankers.

Based on their past experience, the ERP consultants have most likely worked with unique businesses and solved complex issues with ERP solutions. They're trying to earn your business and will be able to answer questions, provide additional insight on best practices, and offer options for implementing system solutions. The right partner may truly develop into a trusted adviser to your business for many years.

Scheduling Software Demonstrations

When it comes to scheduling the software demonstrations, all the primary stakeholders from the discovery meetings once again need to participate. If key players are unable to attend, especially from the executive team, then the demonstration should be rescheduled for another day so that they can actively participate.

Without the executive-level decision makers or significant team members being present, the demonstration rapidly becomes a time-wasting exercise, which reflects poorly on your organization. Furthermore, if the primary stakeholders are not in the demonstrations, this can also lead to gaps in the overall solution.

In order to get the right people to participate, plan to align schedules for demonstrations perhaps weeks or months in advance. Send meeting invitation placeholders on the calendar for two hours to each of the participants. With the daily responsibilities and inevitable distractions of a normal business day, a meeting with multiple team members trying to proactively absorb new information can only realistically be two hours.

If for whatever reason the demonstration is scheduled for three hours or more, then extended breaks need to be built into the session, or else people will begin to lose focus, and their minds will slowly drift to other priorities. Keep in mind that there is a reason most movies are two hours in length or less. The audience can only process so much information in one sitting before having to get on with the rest of the day.

If there is a need or desire to cover more information beyond two hours in length, the best approach is to schedule a follow-up demonstration for another day in the near future (staying clear of Monday mornings and Friday afternoons because the audience will have the shortest attention span then).

Be Present at Software Demonstrations

Once the demonstration begins, be mentally present by actively listening, absorbing information, taking notes, and asking questions. These sessions are meant to be an interaction to assist in visualizing how the business may potentially use the ERP system in the near future.

Also, take the additional step of kindly putting away your cell phone. This is not the time for checking emails or text messages. Not only is it rude and disrespectful to the presenter (who has likely spent several hours preparing the demonstration), but it shows a true lack of focus. If you have to respond to an urgent call or a message, simply excuse yourself for a few minutes to address the issue and then return. If you must excuse yourself for beyond a few minutes, it looks like you're just "pulling a Houdini."

By being engaged in the meeting, you will help the demonstration remain on point, and the team will be able to better synthesize the information being presented. As you participate in the demonstration, try to visualize yourself using this ERP software package and working with this partner. If you cannot visualize it, then odds are that this may not be the right fit.

The ERP Software Demonstration

The consultants invited to participate in the evaluation process will provide the software demonstrations on a specific product (or perhaps multiple products) for your team. These demonstrations are crafted based on the vision, the list of system requirements, and information gathered during the discovery meetings.

The software demonstration will provide a high-level overview of the ERP software, which includes the system navigation, key features and functionality, and reporting tools. While it is impossible to create a full system implementation for a demonstration, the consultant can personalize the demonstration using sample customers, items, and reports to assist in providing relevant examples of how the ERP software performs.

Throughout these demonstrations, give thoughtful consideration to how the ERP software capabilities will impact the business. There may be a sense of confidence that the majority of the functionality within the software—such as performing transactions, processing orders, and generating reports—will work for the team.

Use this time wisely to compile a list of follow-up questions regarding very specific capabilities you wish to explore in more detail. These questions should be based on how the system will work for the business, with a goal of understanding the benefits of the ERP system being evaluated.

A list of questions identified may lead to follow-up conversations with the consultant or possibly a desire to schedule a second demonstration to drill down on specific functionality. The goal is to narrow the focus on the areas mattering the most, such as order entry, fulfillment, revenue reconciliation, or financial reporting.

Coming into the home stretch of the ERP software evaluation, the most critical aspects of the system need to be evaluated closely to ensure the system offers the necessary capabilities. This can be done by follow-up Q and A sessions or perhaps through a short, highly targeted demonstration.

While exploring the software, also observe whether the ERP consultant exhibits a reasonable amount of knowledge, expertise, and experience in this area. The investigation of the features and functionality also assists in evaluating the software and the implementation partner.

As mentioned earlier, the relationship with the consultant is just as important as the features and functionality within the software itself. If the consultant is able to demonstrate, articulate, and share first-hand experiences of successfully assisting other clients in these significant areas, then he or she may likely be in the best position to assist your team to successfully lead the implementation.

Leave No One Behind

Through the power of observation, take notice of team members resistant to this initiative. Get their thoughts and feedback early and often so that they remain engaged in the discovery meetings and demonstrations, which will hopefully overcome their concerns. If they are left alone with their thoughts and fears, you may lose them.

These feelings are mostly rooted in the fear of the unfamiliar. However these folks can quickly hijack a discovery meeting or software demonstration by going down irrelevant rabbit holes based on rare one-off situations. Usually one of them is the first person to proclaim, "This software will not work for us."

These folks want to know how they will perform their jobs with the new software. They want to see where specific reports are located or how many clicks it takes to complete a task. These folks will need to be reassured that they are being heard and that they will receive the necessary training needed to acquire the skills associated with successfully performing their jobs in the new ERP environment.

There are several ways to leave no one behind and keep the "train on the tracks." Any special concerns raised by individuals on the team need to be addressed. However, those concerns may be better addressed in offline conversations rather than including the entire team in addressing them. Work on always keeping the big picture in focus and engage in critical dialogue with team members throughout the entire ERP software evaluation.

Potential Next Steps—Going from Ballpark to Detailed Pricing

Information gathered during the discovery meetings provides consultants with an understanding of the complexity of the needs to be addressed by the new ERP system. The consultants understand which modules need to be configured, the number of users accessing the system, the corresponding software licensing, the amount of training required, and the level of comfort the team will have transitioning to a new ERP package.

With all of this information, the consultants will be in a position to provide a detailed estimate for software and implementation services. In moving away from general ballpark estimates, this information will be based on all the conversations, meetings, and presentations performed throughout the discovery phases.

In addition, the detailed pricing will be based on the necessary software licensing and the level of effort needed to deploy the features and functionality in the system. This will also include any system dependencies since many capabilities are interconnected, and it will include leading practices based on implementation methodology.

Although this may not be the final pricing based on negotiation, the detailed pricing and the level of comfort with the consultant is critical to the decision-making process. As far as the evaluation goes, this is the information that needs to be analyzed before making a final decision.

Summary

The best way to exchange the information that everyone needs is by embracing the discovery process. These meetings and conversations bring together the strategic vision, business requirements, software capabilities, and potential implementation consultants.

The participants will get an opportunity to see multiple ERP software solutions first-hand and gain insight into the features and functionality available in each one of the software packages. They will also have an opportunity to get to know the consultant and members of the consultant's team to help determine whether this is or is not a consultant they wish to partner with on this project.

The consultant will get to know the internal workings of the business, the people on the team, key processes and activities, and the current technology landscape. The consultant will use all of this information to formulate the software licensing and develop an estimate for the implementation of services.

Over the years, there has been many a business professional who has tried to keep a distance between the company's team and its consultants. They are attempting to standardize the evaluation process by formulating a matrix spreadsheet in an attempt to compare information side by side for making a final decision.

While it may be helpful to compile all this information into a single document, this should not be the standard for making a final decision on a new ERP system. Through a thoughtful discovery process, people should have an opportunity to communicate their challenges with someone who understands what they are going through on a daily basis and can communicate the options available for achieving a better tomorrow.

Let's kick the tires and light the fires, big daddy.

—*Harry Connick Jr.*

8

HOW MUCH IS THE ERP GOING TO COST? THE ANSWER IS COMPLICATED

In evaluating a new ERP system, the question of cost arises very quickly. Before a business purchases any product or service, the topic of price becomes an issue first and foremost; it needs to be addressed before proceeding forward with any potential next steps of the software evaluation.

In making any purchase in life, it is only natural to see a product and then immediately glance over at the price tag to determine if this product is something you can afford. Just like walking through a car lot to "kick some tires" and checking the sticker price in the window, a business wants to know the price before wasting any time on a pursuit it cannot afford.

In the middle market, not all businesses have a dedicated purchasing department. However, the ones that do are frequently tasked with exploring prospective purchases, whether they are technology-related or not. A purchasing department may create a request for information, or request for proposal, and send it to several vendors in the hopes of receiving the price information the department wishes to review.

For the rest of the companies in the middle market, when it comes to software acquisition, perhaps an IT person may be assigned to gather initial information and pricing. However, when it comes to an ERP software system, the financial controller usually tends to be the person on the front line exploring new potential options.

Whether the person is the financial controller or from IT, once again, he or she will typically attempt to find pricing first via the internet before speaking to another human. In some instances, searching the internet for software pricing may be fruitful. There are developers or third-party product providers in the ERP software community who may post initial pricing based on a "per user" basis, such as $99 per user per month.

However, for an ERP software application developed by one of the mainstream players in the marketplace—such as Microsoft, Oracle, or Sage—the best place to get the pricing for a system is through an implementation partner. The ERP implementation partner has the best understanding of the complexity of the base software system, the corresponding licensing, and any necessary third-party products—all of which are based on actual business requirements of the prospective customer.

Once you have found an ERP partner, the initial conversation tends to take a sharp turn early toward the topic of cost (usually within the first few minutes). It is certainly an important issue to address in order to understand the financial commitment and resources necessary to acquire and implement a new ERP system.

Most people have never been on this ERP journey and need help understanding the costs involved for the ERP software and for obtaining the necessary consulting services to implement that software. In this discussion, there is a fine line between "not wanting to waste time" and actually getting educated about the fact that business requirements actually drive the pricing.

In order to provide any realistic pricing, a dialogue has to take place to discuss the company business model, how many people need access to the system, any specialized functionality requirements or necessary compliance (for instance, revenue recognition, FDA compliance, etc.), and whether there are other unique business systems being used (proprietary, point of sale, e-commerce, etc.).

All of the information shared from the initial discussion will assist the partner *in creating a preliminary ballpark software estimate and professional services estimate.* The preliminary estimates assist in establishing a budgetary price point and expectation for the new ERP software and implementation. However, in reviewing this software estimate for the first time, there is a strong chance you may experience *sticker shock*.

Experiencing sticker shock is understandable. You may have previously purchased an entry-level system such as QuickBooks, FreshBooks, or Xero. These solutions are inexpensively priced. (Back in the day, this was commonly referred to as buying software "in shrink-wrap" from Best Buy, Office Depot, etc.) Having experience buying an entry-level system can potentially lead to an unrealistic budgetary expectation and unpreparedness for a six-figure (and in some instances seven-figure, based on size and scope) price tag for an ERP system platform.

Although the price tag for an ERP software package is going to significantly jump up from an entry-level software package, this is an opportunity to take the initial step of the journey with your eyes wide open. The good news is that a partner will assist you throughout this process to create and refine estimates throughout the software evaluation process based on information gathered during meetings, discovery conversions, and demonstrations. The discovery process will assist in ensuring the licensing and professional services are scoped out as thoroughly as possible, based on the specific needs of your business, thus limiting exposure to any future surprises.

Unfortunately, off to the side, there are always going to be the people with the "I don't want to waste any time" attitude. These are the folks who will make the minimum effort to get on the phone for a couple of minutes with a partner and say, "How much is this going to cost? I just need a ballpark!" Without having an open dialogue with a partner about the company's business requirements for thirty minutes, the consultant has no way to provide a reasonable estimate. If you're going to force somebody to just give you a number, that person is only going to cautiously provide an inflated number because there are too many unknown variables that are going unaccounted for with a real estimate. These people who complain about time expenditure only want a "number" so that they can tell their boss they have done the research and are able to prove that a new ERP system is too expensive.

Now, in understanding the pricing for any ERP software package, one must keep in mind that the leading software providers have poured millions upon millions of dollars into development, testing, enhancing, and packaging their systems over many years, and in some instances decades. With research and development, they have placed emphasis on the importance of usability and capabilities to appeal to a wide range of users and types of businesses, and they have all incorporated very specific industry attributes (inventory, projects, manufacturing, revenue recognition, etc.) in these systems. The product features and functionality are consistently enhanced based on a product roadmap strategy and time line for releasing new features into the marketplace, usually every several months.

With all that goes into the development of the software, the pricing of the ERP package correlates to the number of users and the modules included in the package. A system with five users will cost less than a system with twenty-five users, fifty users, or more. Furthermore, a system licensed to provide only financial management capabilities will cost less than a system that includes financial management, supply chain management, and manufacturing modules.

The ERP software pricing you receive for your business will incorporate users (licenses) and the level of functionality needed in the system. All of this information will culminate in the overall price point for the software.

In addition to the software pricing, there will ultimately be a price for a reasonable level of effort in the form of billable consulting hours for the professional services necessary to deploy the features and functionality of a new ERP package. These consulting hours correspond to the software estimate by incorporating the number of users, the modules to be deployed, and any personalized system design going into the new ERP configuration, such as data migration, system integration, or application development. It is very difficult to provide a professional services estimate following an initial conversation, but perhaps a rough order of magnitude may be furnished as part of an initial estimate.

There used to be a saying that the professional services for an ERP implementation were provided on a "one-to-one (1:1)" cost ratio or "one-to-two (1:2)" cost ratio compared with the amount of software dollars spent. In terms of ratios, ERP partners used to say to a prospective client, "For every dollar you spend on software, it is likely that you will spend a dollar on (professional consulting) services (1:1)." Then over the passage of time dating from the late 1990s through the early twenty-first century, this ratio evolved into 1:1.5, 1:2, and even 1:3 between software and services. These old standbys have become outdated due to ever-changing marketplaces and the increased level of complexity built into ERP software packages.

Since this information is clear as mud, it is helpful to develop situational awareness by understanding the current ERP environment in the marketplace. This will assist in getting past the grandiose marketing messages and the vague product descriptions, and it will assist in comprehending the necessary information for eventually making an informed decision as part of the ERP evaluation.

User Licenses

When a business licenses ERP software, it is paying the developer for access to the application, module capabilities, and corresponding user licenses. These users are essentially licensing to use the application for the length of the subscription or software maintenance plan.

While each ERP software system is different, there are varying types of user licenses available. The licensing is designed to provide team members with the necessary access to the system based on their roles within the organization and the tasks they have to perform on a daily basis. Once a team member has a user license, security roles and privileges may be applied to it.

The goal is for users of the system to be as productive as possible, but to only be able to see and touch the information they truly need to be successful. With the correct user roles and privileges applied, key processes can be configured, and the right people will have access to the appropriate information. As the company grows, the software licensing may be scaled to include more users at any time in the future.

Although there are several different systems in the marketplace, there are similar "user types" available for licensing. These license types will need to be factored into the software research and system evaluation as they will correspond to the number of people on your team accessing the system.

It will be necessary to understand the ERP licensing model, including what a user license entails and what its potential limitations are. These licenses will factor into the system configuration and ultimately influence the pricing for the system, regardless of whether it's perpetual or SaaS (more on that a little but further down).

Potential User Type Licenses

- **Full users**—In the system transacting each day (read, write, and append)

- **Limited users**—Partial functionality accessing information (for instance, approvals and dashboards)
- **Self-service users**—Extremely light functionality (for instance, submit time, expenses, or requisitions)

Special Notes: (1) A "read only" license in the ERP space is extremely rare and for the most part should be considered nonexistent. (2) Don't skimp on user licenses to save money.

The number of licensed users accessing the ERP system is a large factor in determining the price of the software. Furthermore, the number of users directly impacts the implementation services, such as the areas of applying role-based security and providing end-user training. It takes courage to financially commit to the proper number of user licenses.

Software Modules

In addition to the user licenses, an ERP package is comprised of several software modules. These software modules represent subsections of the ERP application that are designed to perform specialized routines.

These specialized routines assist companies in performing critical business processes. During the licensing of ERP software, the modules selected and purchased should reflect the business requirements of the company with the goal of successfully executing critical business processes.

At the base of ERP is the financial layer. The financial layer consists of the general ledger, payables, receivables, and bank reconciliation. These modules work together to create a core platform from which additional functionality can be expanded. For instance, sales orders and invoices are linked with receivables while purchase orders are linked with payables.

In each ERP software package, there are also modules designed to provide advanced capabilities in very specific areas, such as financial management, supply chain management, manufacturing, and project accounting. Therefore, a mainstream horizontal ERP software package can conceivably be a good fit for companies with critical business processes in the service, nonprofit, distribution, manufacturing, and professional service industries.

One case in point: A manufacturer may need specialized modules such as materials requirements planning, manufacturing bills of materials, sales forecasting, and demand planning. On the other hand, a company in the service industry may only need general ledger, payables management, and fixed assets. These modules are addressing completely different needs, but they may both be using the same ERP software.

ERP software is designed so that all the modules work together, which means additional modules may be added at any point in time to gain more features and functionality. For instance, a distribution company may decide to bring light assemblies and kitting (a collection of multiple products to form another product) in-house. A bill of materials module may need to be added for the purpose of defining the materials and parts needed to complete finished goods.

From an ERP evaluation perspective, it is safe to assume that the more modules needed, the more expensive the software pricing is going to be. This is also a reflection of the complexity of the business. It's easy to say, "We are a simple business." However, if a company has several critical business processes, such as manufacturing, there is a need for a more complex and more expensive ERP package.

Software Licensing Models—Perpetual and SaaS

Over the years, the marketplace has evolved from only on-premises, one-time-only software purchases into annual recurring subscriptions for cloud-based ERP systems. Today, both these options are available to customers. However, cloud-based ERP systems have gained significant popularity. In particular, the advances in cloud-based ERP systems led to user-based pricing, automatic upgrades, mobility, and special incentives for getting a subscription.

However, traditional ERP software packaging is commonly referred to as perpetual licensing. Perpetual licensing is based on a one-time purchase of the software application with an annual software maintenance plan that can be renewed every twelve months. The annual software maintenance plan is calculated as a percentage of the system list price (generally between 15 percent and 18 percent). The plan entitles the licensee to receive the latest and greatest code releases from the software developer.

The software developer uses the dollars from the software maintenance plan as a means of reinvesting into research and development for future enhancements of the ERP product. With this offering, the ERP software is licensed and then installed on a server (office, colocation data center, or public cloud) and may be upgraded every couple of years by a consultant to keep current on the latest version of the software.

In addition to traditional software licensing, today subscription pricing has become more prevalent in the marketplace with a software as a service (SaaS) model. With a SaaS (pronounced "sass") model, ERP systems are immediately provisioned (upon written acceptance of a contract) in a cloud environment with upgrades and enhancements taking place automatically two to four times per year.

The SaaS subscription model includes all the pricing for the corresponding ERP software application (users and capabilities), hardware, database, operating system, and the upgrades. The SaaS-based subscription model aligns nicely with fast-growing companies since they tend to be comfortable with the cloud and less enthusiastic about maintaining infrastructure in-house (on-premises) or having the staff to maintain it.

Whichever software application approach works best for your business, it is important to note the practice that the acquisition of licensing is founded upon. A software developer is the copyright owner of the ERP application that it develops, and it makes money by licensing the software to businesses so that those businesses can manage their accounting, supply chain, projects, manufacturing, etc.

On-Premises or Cloud

In committing to the necessary licensing, CFOs and financial controllers may be tasked with the responsibility of comparing and contrasting an on-premises system and a SaaS-based system. Understandably, there may be a little bit of discomfort approaching this topic because it seems to be more suitable for members of the information technology team than the finance team.

However, IT staff continues to be reduced in the middle market. When there is IT staff, there has traditionally been a lack of interest in supporting the ERP software because it is outside of the staff's comfort zone. Therefore, IT is not going to be the primary candidate for leading an ERP evaluation and implementation.

All is not lost for the finance team leading the ERP software initiative. Although these systems continue to evolve at an exceedingly rapid rate, a business professional whose career spans over a decade will likely have first-hand experience using both on-premises and SaaS-based systems, whether in the ERP space or through another software product.

In generally broad terms, the baby boomers (born 1946–1964) may be the least comfortable with cloud-based systems while the millennials (born 1981–1996) only know and comprehend cloud-based systems. Business professionals within the Generation X (born in the 1960s and 1970s) seem to be the most cross- generational in the workplace, with experience and comfort in both of these areas (Valentine, 2021).

Whichever generation you may be from, throughout your career, each morning business professionals "log on" to their computer, whether the software is on-premises or in the cloud, and they use these applications to perform tasks and execute on daily responsibilities. In addition to using workplace business applications, most people are already relying on the internet to shop, manage personal finances through online banking, participating in fantasy football leagues, and perhaps engaging in online dating.

In exploring options, it's wise to embrace the technology strategy of the business. In many instances, the IT department can provide insight into the current software landscape and share a preference for an ERP deployment to be on-premises, in a data center, or in the cloud. If there are no full-time employees in the IT department, then utilizing cloud-based technology may become more appealing.

On-Premises

Deploying an on-premises system typically requires a higher initial up-front cost for purchasing licenses, annual ongoing software maintenance, and the hardware and software specifications needed to support it. The software maintenance plan provides the latest code from the developer, including future releases, service packs, and hot fixes to customers. With this approach, there will be additional costs for a server hardware (dedicated to the application based on system requirements), plus a database server, an operating system, and any ancillary components to ensure the application resides in a supported environment.

If your business is currently in a position of significant technical debt, then this approach may require strategic planning, a lot of money up front, and the guts to see the process turn into reality. However, if your company is already maintaining systems in a modern server environment, then you may be in a position to scale (improve the hardware gradually) the current technical landscape to meet the system requirements to deploy a new ERP system. In many scenarios, these are larger, mid-market-sized businesses already using proprietary-based systems or maintaining compliance protocols, which makes moving to the cloud less realistic.

In many instances, the on-premises approach provides more control over your systems and data. With control comes the responsibility to maintain everything that goes along with it (IT resources, hardware, software, databases, etc.), but if there is a level of comfort with an on-premises approach, this may be the way to go.

Cloud

The prospect of moving to a cloud offers the luxury of bundling software, hardware, databases, an operating system and all the ancillary components under a single subscription at a predictable cost. The subscription also outsources the responsibility of maintaining the hardware, software licenses, software agreements, warranties, etc. to the developer.

With a cloud-based ERP, any technology debt associated with current software, databases, servers, components, and operating systems can be overcome almost instantly. Instead of having to update these areas with new hardware and software, perform upgrades, and ensure system compatibility, the move to the cloud represents the adoption of an altogether new strategy.

Cloud-based applications offer accessibility through several devices, such as workstations, laptops, and mobile phones. A user of a cloud-based ERP can essentially work anywhere internet access may be established, including a home, the airport, or a coffee shop.

Capital Expenditure Versus Operational Expenditure

A perpetual, on-premises software package may cost more initially but less over an extended period of time. In this scenario, the software developer is placing a premium on the license price entirely up front, followed by an annual software maintenance fee, which is based on a percentage of the system list price.

With this approach, the company looking to acquire perpetual ERP licenses may create a special one-time budget for this initiative, potentially line up lease financing to pay for it, or simply find the cash to make this purchase in the form of a one-time capital expenditure.

A SaaS-based subscription software package is invoiced on an annual basis with a predictable cost to the customer, which may be fewer dollars initially compared with a perpetual system. With an annual recurring software subscription, the customer is opting to take on an additional operational expense similar to paying for rent or insurance. With this approach, there is a lower cost up front but probably a higher spend over an extended period of time, such as three to five years.

The Quick Lowdown

Perpetual/On-Premises	SaaS/Cloud
Higher Initial Investment	Higher Investment over Time
Control Access with Responsibility to Maintain	Access & Maintenance Outsourced
Dedicated Environment	Shared Environment
Upgrades—Scheduled and Performed Customizations Easier to Maintain	Upgrades Are Automatic Supported Customizations Only
Capital Expenditure	Operational Expenditure

Comparing Apples-to-Apples Costs

In comparing SaaS and perpetual systems, one may become enchanted with the opportunity to compare costs from an apples-to-apples standpoint. Accountants, being accountants, want to see both sets of numbers to try to determine which is the better deal. The goal is to determine which option is less expensive, or potentially offers the best value.

As Matt Kenney wrote in the white paper "Apples to apples: Comparing ERP costs accurately," "Regardless of the deployment method, an organization will pay for everything from disk drives to databases to the application itself" (Kenney, 2013). This white paper emphasizes that there are several variables needing to be taken into consideration over an extended period of time to perform this comparison, including software applications, licensing, technical environment, consulting fees, and support for at least two years.

Going down this path can inadvertently shift the focus from the big picture ERP evaluation into analysis paralysis. In many respects, this exercise is synonymous with falling down a rabbit hole. If too much time is being spent micro analyzing the sticker price for each one of these options, then the overall ERP evaluation process is not getting the attention it truly deserves.

Developers spend a lot of time and money investing in their applications, licensing, and packaging, so they've figured how they are going to get paid for the software. From a consumer perspective, it is either going to be more up front through a one-time purchase or over an extended period of time through an annuitized subscription.

Here is a hypothetical example of common viewpoints:

> **Financial controller:** "We are interested in moving to a new ERP system. Our current software is very limited and does

not provide the reporting we need, so we spend a lot of time each day working in spreadsheets."

Software vendor: "Yes, we are able to assist. We partner with several leading ERP developers, offering cloud-based and on-premises ERP options. Have you decided which approach is best for your company?"

Financial controller: "It depends on how much the software is going to cost. Before going any further, I'm going to need to see the pricing for both options so that I can determine which one is better for us."

The prudent approach is to logically determine whether cloud or on-premises is the more desirable approach by aligning the current software landscape, business requirements and strategic vision. If the ERP evaluation process gets stuck on the apples-to-apples comparison, all that happens is that valuable time becomes wasted.

Stop Wasting Time

As previously mentioned, in comparing the two approaches from a software and hardware costs perspective, one can assume an on-premises perpetual system costs more initially than a SaaS-based system. However, over an extended period, you will likely pay more for a SaaS-based system because it is based on an annual recurring subscription.

With the information gathered on pricing through the software evaluation process, the spend comparison of the two approaches needs to be calculated over several years. In most instances, by year four, you are officially paying more for a SaaS-based system. Whichever approach is adopted, the benefit will be that everything associated with the ERP system will be modern and maintained in terms of functionality and security.

However, when it's time to initiate conversations with potential vendors regarding ERP options, topics such as software features and functionality, accessibility, security, and product roadmap tend to take a back seat to the cost of the system. Whether it's prudence, fear of the unfamiliar, or just being cheap, most people begin the ERP evaluation process with the price of the software.

You Can't Outsmart Microsoft

Instead of wasting time comparing the pricing of cloud and on-premises systems, it is important to recognize that leading software companies have a well-thought-out and ever-evolving pricing strategy. As is the case for the ERP marketplace, there is a need to maintain a delicate balance of providing value to customers, gaining market share in a competitive environment, and consistently reaching revenue targets.

There are several leading software developers in the mid-market ERP marketplace with multiple products in their product portfolio, and they are based on-premises, in the cloud, or in some cases they're available in both options. These developers provide similar pricing to the middle market for cloud-based systems on the one hand and on-premises systems on the other.

As mentioned earlier, the ERP software developers will either make their money up front through an initial purchase of perpetual software or over an extended period of time with a SaaS subscription. There is no company in the marketplace that has demonstrated this better than Microsoft.

Under the leadership of CEO Satya Nadella, Microsoft has led a remarkable transition from selling traditionally packaged software licensing products into a cloud-first, subscription-based company (Miller, 2021). Microsoft offers several ERP software options primarily focused on SaaS customers, but it still maintains a significant list of perpetual customers. With the customer buying either through an initial purchase or a subscription, the developer will ultimately get paid. It is unreasonable to believe you can outsmart the pricing strategy of Microsoft, Oracle, SAP, or Sage.

If a company wishes to compare apples-to-apples pricing between a traditional, perpetual software license and a cloud-based subscription to find the better deal, just know that Microsoft executives have already figured out that their company is going to get paid either way. The real decision needs to be based on the approach that works best for your company's technology landscape.

Summary

There are several factors involved in determining the cost of an ERP system. From a licensing standpoint, there are users, modules, and licensing models. These licenses have been designed to meet the size of the organization, business requirements, critical processes, and desired technology.

Knowing how much ERP software is going to cost requires an initial investment of time speaking with a consultant or partner. There has to be a willingness to share at a high level the business requirements of a company and any special information regarding the current challenges experienced by the business.

The process of sharing this information with a consultant or partner assists each in the creation of an initial "ballpark" estimate based on a system configuration corresponding to the needs of the business. This is not necessarily a "best and final" price. It's simply a starting point for discussion, part of the evaluation process, and perhaps a figure used for budgeting purposes.

For business professionals moving from an entry-level system for the first time or for those who have simply never received an ERP software estimate before, the initial ballpark estimate may create a bit of "sticker shock." It's OK. Although this is a big step financially, this process can help in resetting expectations so that they are more grounded in reality.

In getting past this step, the software evaluation process is more productive when time is spent learning as much as possible about the software, the capabilities available, and how the software may be deployed within the existing software landscape. The software evaluation is less productive when people get stuck on price, try to work out a better deal, and altogether miss the real reasons why they are exploring a new ERP package.

If you develop a reasonable budget for the ERP initiative in advance, then you will be less likely to experience sticker shock. A team with a reasonable budget along with the determination to align the business requirements, current technology landscape, and future state vision can achieve great things.

If there is not a budget for this initiative this fiscal year, then take the information gathered from the ballpark estimate and begin the necessary steps for formulating one for next fiscal year. The information gathered during this process will assist in gaining a realistic expectation for the ERP initiative and will also become a stepping-stone for turning the ERP conversion into reality.

SECTION III

CLOUD VERSUS ON-PREMISES (NONTECHNICAL)

Luck is what happens when preparation meets opportunity.

—Seneca

9
UNDERSTANDING CLOUD
AND ON-PREMISES

For those in accounting and not information technology, the world of ERP can bring several unknowns. For many, the biggest unknown surrounds choosing an on-premises or cloud-based software package.

Since there are several key differentiators, it makes sense to take a deeper dive in understanding the options available in the marketplace. To be more specific, it's important to try and understand why some companies prefer the cloud while others wish to continue using on-premises software.

The ultimate goal is to eventually be using a modern ERP system. Therefore, it is better to have as much information as possible in order to decide which offering best fits the business.

Why Move to the Cloud?

In understanding the modern technology marketplace, the ERP evaluator should know that nearly all new software applications are being developed today on cloud-based technology. The high-tech sector has been rapidly transforming over the last several years, focused on driving innovation to consumers through cloud-based technology, specialized applications (apps), and faster release cycles to deploy system enhancements.

With this innovation, consumers have embraced mobile devices to communicate and access information for both personal use and business use in real-time. That has been pushing digital transformation forward. As these modern systems continue to evolve at a rapid pace, team members have begun to expect a higher level of communication, collaboration, and interconnection from the technical tools embraced in the workplace.

Just by sheer "digital Darwinism," the adoption of on-premises systems and perpetual, license-based products is happening less frequently in the middle market, as there has been an increasing level of expectations on the functionality needed for a growing business (Solis, 2022). In embracing digital transformation, there are several technical benefits associated with utilizing a cloud-based platform, such as accessibility, mobility, scalability, and the ease of maintenance with automatic updates.

With a cloud-based system, a business may eliminate multiple hardware and software contracts, the labor overhead associated with IT staff to support the infrastructure, and traditional downtime associated with updates and upgrades. More importantly, a cloud-based system provides more to the end user than ever before, such as the flexibility of being able to work from home on a snowy day or work virtually from any location.

The technical benefits of a cloud-based ERP system are a no-brainer for startup companies, carve-outs, or divestitures, due to ongoing mergers and acquisition (M&A) taking place in the middle market. In the majority of these business transactions, it is highly likely there will be a time sensitive TSA. With a clock ticking on a TSA, the fastest time to value will be associated with cloud-based applications, including a new ERP system to handle all facets of the business.

In situations in which a company has been around for a while, there may be legacy systems in place that may have not been upgraded or enhanced for several years. The technical debt in these situations may be due to complacency, ignorance, and just being too cheap to invest back into the business with better systems. Whatever the case may be, embracing a cloud-based system is the fastest way to modernize your business software landscape and replace technology debt. However, this may first require a change in leadership or strategic direction to create a new culture with a "growth mindset," which may help "the power of believing that you can improve" and a willingness to embrace the latest in system technology (Dweck, 2020).

In a situation in which a company may already have an IT team in place and maintains a modern infrastructure, there is less urgency in moving to the cloud. However, in these circumstances, moving to the cloud may be more of a migration strategy that will be implemented over an extended period of time as part of a larger technology roadmap. Without significant technology debt, a company has more flexibility and a far greater *runway* for transitioning each of the primary business applications to the cloud.

Whichever business scenario most closely resembles your own, the cloud provides a modern platform, with ease of accessibility, rapid time to value, and the ability to outsource the management and interdependency of hardware, software, and ancillary components. In addition, there are several benefits beyond the end-user experience tied to implementing a cloud-based ERP system.

- Embracing modern technology
- System accessibility and mobile workplace
- Outsource of infrastructure, security, and applications
- No desire for full-time IT team members

Embracing Modern Technology

Once upon a time, the prospect of putting a back-office software package in the cloud was arbitrarily deemed unsafe by most financial controllers and accountants. With cloud applications becoming more prevalent in society—in instances such as online banking, online dating, and fantasy football—eventually the initial excuse morphed into reluctance based on the ongoing costs in comparison to what seemed to be less-expensive on-premises options. In both instances, the procrastination was simply fear disguised as prudence.

Today, the delivery of these applications has become more desirable to businesses and organizations, not only from a back-office perspective but also across departments in the organization. Decision makers today are thinking beyond *old school* departmental scale and considering what is best for the enterprise as a whole, regardless of corporate culture and any political dynamics. The procrastinators are slowly figuring out they're going to have to *get on the bus*. As the SaaS delivery model continues to expand in the marketplace, the delivery of cloud-based applications is becoming more accepted by financial and accounting executives.

Most modern businesses wish to have an innovative business system platform to process their transactions, generate financial reports, and integrate with other business systems. The logical consequence of embracing this approach is having an ERP system that is continuously being updated through automatic upgrades several times per year (depending on the specific ERP product) with limited to no intrusiveness.

With an on-premises system, the deployment of new features has really become a more intrusive process. The level of enthusiasm for coordinating an upgrade is decreasing. The upgrade process includes engaging with billable consultants, scheduling system downtime, coordinating with all the users (running behind on daily transactions), and performing the upgrade.

The prospect of having to plan, approve, schedule, and manage an upgrade with consultants once every couple of years is rapidly becoming a thing of the past. With a cloud-based system, all of that corporate heartburn simply goes away. A good portion of businesses running on-premises systems in the middle market are planning to do this just *one more time* before ultimately moving to the cloud.

With a cloud-based system, businesses will be able to take advantage of the latest and greatest functionality being rolled out across the platform. Examples are dashboards, workflow automation, enhanced reporting tools, and new features and functionality. And because of the cloud, they can do that without the assistance of consultants or necessary downtime. Moreover, as technology continues to evolve, innovations beyond debits and credits will naturally be rolled into these business applications. These are new innovations, such as artificial intelligence, machine learning, robotic process automation, and the internet of things (IoT).

The SaaS-based ERP applications in the marketplace are only scratching the surface of these innovations, but they will ultimately serve to automate routine tasks, increase efficiency, enhance production, and make businesses more competitive in a digital world. The companies embracing modern technology will soon be able to incorporate this functionality into their business systems, and that will help to differentiate them from their competition.

System Accessibility and Mobile Workforce

In the late 1990s, businesses began transitioning from DOS-based data processing to a Microsoft Windows environment to take advantage of certain tools, including Microsoft Word, Microsoft Excel, and Microsoft Outlook. At this point, employees rarely had the option of working anywhere outside the main corporate office. Anyone having remote access was either the owner of the business, an IT staff member providing support, or team members with special privileges. The opportunity of being able to work from home was only for a select few (if any at all).

In the early 2000s, tools such as Citrix and Microsoft Terminal Server paved the way for businesses to implement a remote access strategy (Windows Server Brain, 2022). A remote access strategy provides users the accessibility to authenticate from different locations or devices based on a predetermined location or IP address outside the workplace (Celestix, 2014). A remote access strategy provided a secure and encrypted gateway for users to send keystrokes and screens between workstation and server, including tasks and transactions being performed through an on-premises software application.

Although this approach was bumpy at first because of system latency or the inability to print reports in a timely fashion, this became a new way for team members to access business applications to perform their jobs from different office locations or perhaps work from home. Today, a lot of this technology is widely adopted by data centers and application service providers offering hosting as a less expensive alternative to supporting on-premises environments. These are the same remote-access strategy tools being leveraged by data centers to provide an added layer of security and encryption, more commonly known as platform as a service (PaaS), so that a traditional, on-premises software could be repackaged as a private cloud (Chai, et al., 2022).

With the improvement of technology and connectivity, there was naturally a rise in interest in becoming more mobile. However, the post-9/11 business environment forced a balance between security and productivity. Plus, hardware and software were expensive and, in many instances, big and bulky. With generational change—particularly with Generation X and millennials joining the US labor force—and with the evolution of devices—such as laptops, tablets, and smartphones—the prospect of a mobile workforce increased as the technology became less expensive (Rossier-Renaud & Meier, 2022).

Today, cloud-based applications have grown in popularity—with products such as Salesforce.com and NetSuite—and also there has been the progression of Microsoft Office 365. There has been a proliferation of mobile workers, with employees and team members located in any geography with any device at any time. However, this is only possible if a system is made accessible through the internet.

Beyond a remote access capability, a SaaS system provides the accessibility to log on to the system wherever the internet is available by any type of device, including iPhone, iPad, Surface, MacBook, or personal computer. The application log on leverages an authentication process by username and password so that you may get into this system at the office, a home, the airport, etc. The interaction may be transactional or conventional in terms of consuming data through reports and dashboards, but whatever the case may be, the accessibility offers the quality of being in a mobile workplace.

Outsource of Infrastructure, Security, and Applications

It's often difficult for small- and medium-sized businesses to *keep up on technology*. In managing a software landscape, particularly an ERP system, it will be necessary to stay on top of all product specifications and compatibility of releases, and it will be necessary to have the people on staff trained to maintain all of it. With new releases, patches, and security, there is always a component that may need to be licensed, updated, upgraded, supported, or retired. In this environment, executive management and IT are forced to make decisions and commit dollars on a continuous basis for the ongoing maintenance and upkeep of the infrastructure.

In having an on-premises system without a method for continuous management and oversight, a company risks being unable to keep up on the technology and has potential exposure to many issues.

Cautiously speaking, this will naturally lead to many of the parts and versions becoming outdated and products becoming no longer supported. When this happens, there is not only the potential for incompatibility, but there is also the potential for vulnerabilities in security, hardware breakdowns, and inability for the software to be upgraded to provide new features and functionality.

If a company is willing to invest in a full refresh of all old, complex, and unreliable systems with a "rip and replace" strategy, everything will be new for perhaps a year or two at best (Weldon, 2015). Yet over time, all the pieces will need to be updated, maintained, or replaced again because the cycle of innovation and expiration will continue to repeat. Because of the cyclical nature of this process (and the expenses associated with it), there may come a time when it's necessary to take advantage of an outsourcing model and research and explore cloud service providers and the value they may be able to provide to your business.

For small- and medium-sized businesses, a provider of a cloud-based system would be able to provide the software, a database, an operating system, and all the necessary backend server hardware for a fraction of the cost of a company building everything on its own. And it would be in place without the buyer having the headaches of having to maintain it all. In addition, the provider would be taking on all the responsibility for providing a security layer across the enterprise, so it would be contractually responsible through a service-level agreement (SLA) for maintaining security, encryption, and an element of redundancy for backup in case there was an unexpected act of God, a war, or some other situation beyond the scope of everyday management.

A cloud-based ERP system will bundle software, hardware, databases, operating systems, firewalls, and all ancillary components into a single price point under a single subscription. For this price, there will be no need to purchase and maintain each of these pieces and parts separately or have to withstand the headaches associated with this approach. Outsourcing the applications, security, and infrastructure allows decision makers to spend time on more value-driven tasks to increase the success of the business.

No Desire for Full-Time IT Team Members

Today many small- and medium-sized businesses simply do not have an IT person on their team. With limited budgets, these companies are interested in investing back into the business to generate organic growth, so there is little desire to make a financial commitment in an information technology team to manage infrastructure assets. The investments are naturally being made in sales, marketing, and operations rather than in internal IT resources.

Behind the scenes, a good reason why funds are being allocated toward sales and operations is due to deal makers experiencing "ideal conditions to buy and sell companies" (MacArthur, et al., 2022). With private equity in general, "management is lean and focused" (Barber & Goold, 2007). To be more specific, it's all about EBITDA (earnings before interest, taxes, depreciation, and amortization) as a means to measuring financial performance.

The approach of private equity investors is based on the ability to do more with less by increasing efficiency and throughput in both sales and operations to "increase the value of their investments" (Monterey, 2021). Behind the scenes, this means dealmakers are consumed by controlling costs, and to be more specific, labor costs wherever possible. Being focused in this area means taking a *lean and mean* approaches to business, which leaves little opportunity for having full-time, dedicated IT department employees or even a single IT manager.

To add fuel to the fire, there is no ignoring the fact that the complexity in making computers and software properly run for the business no longer require an army of IT specialists and software engineers. From 1994 through 2019, there has been a vast amount of technological innovation in the ERP marketplace. That includes cloud-based software, but it also includes open-source applications, which are free and developed through public collaboration (Holter, 2020). As these systems became modernized and enhanced, the level of complexity in hardware and software diminished, which inherently led to a reduced cost of ownership, a decline in IT spending, and less dependency on specialized IT skills.

As these systems have become more powerful and highly specialized, they've turned out to be more stable, easier to use, and rather simple to maintain. The average employee has benefited by being able to consume, transact, and report through a web-based experience, or perhaps through working in a mobile environment (on the go) or working virtually (from home). That has contributed to growing work-from-anywhere experiences (Choudhury, 2020). If any support issues were to arise, then an employee would call a partner or the developer, who would provide a support plan to address any issues or answer any questions in special circumstances.

The information technology landscape has become easier to navigate than ever before, which has impacted the entire middle market, whether the business is backed by venture capital or not. Whether it's a lack of budget, fiscal discipline, or the fact that technology continues to innovate, the level of desire for maintaining a full-time IT team has vastly diminished. The IT guy—wearing a hoodie every day and bragging about how he is always having to *save the day*—has all but disappeared.

Why On-Premises Still Makes Sense for Many

Believe it or not, deploying an on-premises ERP system still makes sense for many businesses in the middle market. Many proponents of cloud-based systems believe deploying an on-premises ERP system today is not only a form of heresy but also clearly a means of transacting in the past. However, what works for many businesses may not be the best approach for all businesses, especially if they tend to be a bit larger, have to maintain any type of compliance, need to integrate high volumes of data, or already have a high level of information technology maturity.

For instance, a company located in the upper-middle market may have the resources (people, software, and hardware) to maintain its own infrastructure and sustain it for years. With the right planning and preparation, these companies are able to absorb a new ERP system (or any system, such as CRM, HRIS, proprietary, etc.) within their current software landscape and IT infrastructure. These companies tend to desire having more "direct control and power over the architecture," including the planning and scheduling of upgrades, uncompromising control over their data, and maintaining any customizations to the system (Schultz, 2021). In these instances, the approach is engrained not only into the management style but also the company's corporate culture.

In addition to company size, there are other factors that figure into the on-premises calculation. Businesses that have to maintain specific industry compliance or adhere to privacy regulations have specific needs that directly impact their approach to information technology. These businesses come from several industry types, including health care, education, food manufacturing, life sciences, financial institutions, energy, and government entities, just to name a few. A company in the health-care industry has to maintain compliance with the Health Insurance Portability and Accountability Act (HIPAA), and food manufacturers need to be able be able to track information based on Food and Drug Administration (FDA) compliance (if there is ever a need to recall a product from the marketplace). Whatever the situation, these companies have to maintain compliance and need to be able to not only access their data at all times but also ensure it is secured.

Whatever the case may be, these businesses often build out their own enterprise infrastructure, take advantage of license agreements with big players, such Microsoft and Oracle, and maintain relationships with providers—such as CDW, Trend Micro, or Dell—for all software and server hardware needs. These companies invest into their IT team members (training, certifications, and specialization), the latest software and hardware assets, power and electricity, licensing plans, and internal help desk, and they have the IT asset management software systems to maintain all of it. Furthermore, they take full responsibility for maintaining their own data and all the security, and they have several measures to protect it.

Behind the scenes, there are several characteristics exhibited by businesses that naturally lead down a path toward on-premises deployment of an ERP software system and ancillary systems.

These characteristics include the following:

- Desire to Be in Full Control
- Conservative Approach Toward Systems
- IT Team Maintains a Modern Infrastructure
- Comfortable with a "Best-of-Breed" approach

Desire to Be in Full Control

The companies located in the lower middle market tend to build their businesses more from a bottom-up, grassroots approach while the larger companies tend to manage from the top down, with strong executive leadership driving initiatives. One of the most important roles on the executive team is the chief information officer (CIO), sometimes referred to as the chief technology officer (CTO) or even chief digital officer (CDO). The CIO is responsible for providing leadership and policy for all information technology resources within the organization. The CIO is accountable for all the budgeting, planning, team building, recruitment, resourcing, training, and IT governance and is ultimately responsible for making decisions on the acquisition of infrastructure and software systems (Gartner, 2022).

With the increasing security risks of our ever-changing cyber environment, there is an ongoing threat by hackers or anyone trying to gain unauthorized access to your systems for the purpose of stealing data, creating corporate havoc, committing espionage, spying on behalf of a government, or perhaps making you a target of a larger spamming or phishing campaign. It has been reported by Cisco that "53% of midmarket companies have experienced a data breach" (Cisco, 2018). A company with a CIO has a primary goal of mitigating risk and decreasing the level of exposure for the company, especially when it comes to security and protecting data assets. With so much at stake, the CIO often chooses to maintain full control with on-premises software and infrastructure.

With an on-premises deployment model and security strategy, the CIO is committed to maintaining full control of the infrastructure environment, which includes hardware, security layers, remote accessibility, and the deployment of the features and functionality available in software systems. In maintaining full control and protecting critical data, it is the responsibility of the information technology team to collectively determine when to schedule upgrades, deploy new system capabilities, assign resources to manage the project from start to completion, and progressively roll out these capabilities to the organization and its users.

In building and maintaining this architecture, in-house IT staff members are responsible for future planning, which includes updating, maintaining, and replacing the hardware and all the ancillary components within the infrastructure. These people will need to manage all purchases of software end-user license agreements, all service-level agreements (SLAs), and all annual maintenance renewals. A significant part of the planning is dedicated to the ERP system, which requires corresponding databases, operating systems, and often a dedicated systems manager.

Reporting to the CIO, the systems manager will be responsible for the ERP application, which includes system requirements, product roadmap, partner relationships, third-party providers, customizations, system integrations, reporting, and making sure internal client needs are addressed with resources in-house or with the assistance of a consultant. Managing the ERP system, databases, and operating system provides an opportunity to establish security standards and policy for the purpose of providing extra protection to critical information and data and establishing standards regarding policy and governance.

Being all in on having full control of the information technology and business applications may provide an opportunity for the CIO to sleep at night with peace of mind. In a position with an extremely high turnover rate, CIOs are beginning to leverage more innovative tools because the position demands it. They include artificial intelligence (Microsoft), autonomous databases (Oracle), and leveraging the internet of things ("IoT) as cloud services make their way into on-premises environments. Whatever the case may be, companies can have full control and take advantage of the most modern tools to assist in both ERP systems and security.

Conservative Approach Toward Systems

There was once a time when an on-premises deployment of an ERP system was the only approach available because there were simply no other options. The foundation of modern networking is commonly known as the client/server model (Ingalls, 2021). The software is designed to be installed on a server along with a database with users (aka clients) accessing the system from their workstations. As clients transact within the system, they're essentially *initiating a request* for service to the server within a distributed workload. The ERP software application, corresponding database, dedicated servers, and a number of workstations all belonged to the same network.

In a time when there was only client/server software available in the ERP space, businesses would rely on their information technology teams to prepare the infrastructure for the software installation based on the recommended specifications from the developer. Often near the end of the ERP software evaluation process, a special conversation would be scheduled with the IT manager and the software installation technician (consultant) to discuss all the bits and bytes prior to the installation. It was the responsibility of the in-house information technology team to prepare the environment and configure the backups (tapes or drives) to maintain the system. Over time, the IT department would update the corresponding infrastructure to consume the latest ERP software releases.

However, due to the lasting impact of the great recession of 2008, information technology teams grew smaller in size. That was partly due to the slashing of IT budgets throughout the middle market, partly due to the emergence of reasonably priced cloud options since data centers (private cloud) sprang up all over the country, and partly due to the early adoption of SaaS-based systems. The traditional on-premises approach for deploying ERP systems has over time been seemingly displaced by private cloud and public cloud options. Yet many businesses continue to rely on an on-premises ERP approach because they have been effectively doing it for years. These companies continue to utilize Microsoft products such as Dynamics GP (formerly Great Plains), Dynamics SL (formerly Solomon), and Dynamics NAV (formerly Navision), and they also utilize Sage products such as Sage 100 (formerly Mas 90), Sage 200 (formerly Accpac), Sage 500 ERP (formerly Mas 500), as well as Epicor products.

A good portion of these businesses are owner-managed or family-operated and have a keen eye toward the day-to-day operations, which includes how much money is in the bank at any given moment. These businesses tend to be slow to adopt new innovation. They're mostly staying the course and tend to only spend money when it is absolutely necessary, which can include a new hire, a vehicle, office furniture, or new server hardware. Being old-school in nature also tends to permeate the company culture, including the financial controller, or perhaps bookkeeper, not wishing to make any changes to the ERP system now or in the foreseeable future.

There are businesses located in the upper-middle market that simply have the people, resources, assets, and systems to manage an on-premises environment. They may even take advantage of cloud-based systems or utilize the public cloud providers such as Amazon, Google, or Microsoft. However, their strategy is based on what is best for the business, so they are comfortable managing their own technology needs and software landscape without feeling the pressure to live up to outside opinion or popular thought regarding moving to the cloud. In being selective, they choose to manage their own destiny by putting their businesses first.

At one company, a local director of finance recently listened to a discussion about the possibility of moving from the current, on-premises ERP application to a SaaS-based ERP application. In listening to the options available, the strategic roadmap for these products, and the latest innovations, the director of finance, sitting at the head of the conference room table, said, "Everything is great." The director concluded that there was no reason to disrupt the current environment. Instead of planning a move to the cloud, he indicated an openness to having this very same conversation in a couple of years to revisit the topic.

The fact of the matter is that as technological innovation continues, there are companies unwilling to yield to the pressure of having to be in the cloud. Imagine being in a meeting in which a seasoned IT professional declares to consultants, "The cloud is a rip-off" (Johnson, 2018). These words not only portray confidence, but they are backed up by the speaker staying on top of the technology. The speaker understands that features, functionality, and capabilities will continue to be enhanced, which includes hardware, software, databases, operating systems, etc., and is willing to do what is necessary to maintain them, whether the system is on-premises, through the cloud, a hybrid of both, or even through multi-cloud deployments.

Perhaps in the future, the approach may come full circle. If software, databases, and operating systems can monitor, patch, scale, and update themselves, then why would business information need to be located in data centers to be shared with everyone else? If these systems become autonomous, the value of a shared data center may seemingly decrease. In the years ahead, perhaps there may be a future beyond what business professionals understand to be the *cloud approach* of today. If cloud technology is available for businesses that run in an on-premises environment, then a cloud exit strategy may naturally lead businesses toward bringing applications back in-house. Only the future will be able to tell.

IT Team Maintains a Modern Infrastructure

There are thousands of middle market companies that are simply more mature and often larger in size (either by employee count or annual revenue) than other middle market companies. These larger companies are well beyond startup phase. They are more established and are focused on growth and continued future expansion. These companies have people, processes, and systems backed by a sustainable IT strategy.

The IT strategy is directed by a chief information officer, chief technology officer, or VP of IT, and it is supported by a dedicated IT team. The IT team plays a critical role in managing the IT strategy to serve business in several capacities, with a focused approach and through leveraging the right tools to support the business. A well-constructed IT team will have several types of roles and skill sets in-house, which may include traditional IT operations, project managers, help desk support, and process improvement.

The team members responsible for IT operations are basically managing the day-to-day operations to ensure the system is up and running, including the network, servers and software systems. Project managers are tasked with the facilitation of special short-term projects, such as new system implementations, software upgrades, server migrations, or any IT-related special initiatives. The internal help desk support team will receive, capture, and resolve support requests by team members (sales, finance, operations) to assist the organization in being more productive. Lastly, an IT team may have folks dedicated to process improvement, in which they are tasked with exploring ways for business systems to improve or automate business processes (often this may be a temporary position or an opportunity to leverage an outside management consultant).

With a balanced approach, the IT team is well positioned to execute on a strategy for managing the technology landscape, which includes hardware and software assets, controlling critical data and business information, applying security methodologies and processes, managing vendor and partner relationships, and providing support to the team. In executing upon this mission, the IT team will take advantage of several different technology tools and software applications, such as ticketing systems, IT service management (ITSM) software, collaboration tools (instant messaging, chat rooms, video conferencing, web meetings, etc.), project management software to manage objectives, and reporting tools.

The tools, the team, and the approach are all interconnected and work in harmony as part of the overall IT strategy to maintain a modern infrastructure, which may be scaled at any time to meet the needs of the business. In aligning with the overall business strategy, the information technology team has to keep on top of their game by being comfortable with rapidly changing technology innovations, changes in security, and understanding the growth strategy of the business.

IT leaders will invest in their team members by encouraging professional growth and financially committing resources toward the acquisition of specific product certifications or specialized training for the purpose of supporting and maintaining the latest in technology for the business. IT leaders will advise their team members to be consistently raising their game by participating in technical conferences, user group forums, trade shows, and product expositions to gain insight into product roadmaps and future releases and to network with other professionals supporting similar applications.

In addition to networking with professionals, well-established IT teams cultivate relationships with leading developers (Microsoft, Oracle, SAP, Salesforce.com, etc.), appliance manufacturers (Cisco, IBM, Dell, Lenovo), software licensing houses (CDW, Trend Micro, etc.), and system consultants (Deloitte, Avanade, Capgemini). These relationships serve often as a necessary extension of their technology ecosystem. They provide tools, licensing, configurations, insight, pricing, and assistance when needed. As with other technology-based relationships, they are comfortable leveraging consulting resources for specialized tasks when needed to assist, but these moves tend to be more strategic and short-term rather than long-term outsourcing.

With the information technology team committed to enhancing and supporting a modern infrastructure through timely maintenance, continuous enhancement, and embracement of innovation, a company is well-positioned to manage and support an on-premises ERP system. With this technology framework in place, these companies may spend the majority of their system evaluation focused on the features and functionality rather than basing their decisions on the deployment approach as the primary selling point for the ERP system. Whatever the software evaluation approach may be, with the right leadership, people, and technology in place, it is an entirely reasonable expectation for a team to be able to proactively maintain a modern infrastructure and support the internal clients using these systems to support the mission of the business.

Comfortable with a Best-of-Breed System Approach

As a company grows, it is not always technologically possible or financially realistic to have one software system provide an all-encompassing solution for the business. In many instances, as a company grows and evolves in size and scale, executive management encourages department leaders from sales, operations, HR, and finance to make decisions to increase productivity and achieve gains in efficiency. These department-based decisions often include the procurement and implementation of software systems that provide specific features and functionality needed to execute on their tasks and mission.

The systems implemented by departments may be highly specialized to address a handful of sophisticated business requirements, such as sales orders, work orders, or purchase orders. These software packages may have been either purchased *off-the-shelf* from a partner or vendor or perhaps even written in-house by developers on staff, thus creating a standalone proprietary system. In either of these situations, many of these software applications tend to be older, on-premises legacy systems rather than the latest in cloud-based systems (SaaS).

Aside from department-based decisions, the business may have identified limitations while evaluating ERP systems that market themselves as a single-system solution. Through a software evaluation process, the departmental teams may have determined some of the functionality to be too light in essential areas of the business. Whether because of active choice or increased business complexity, a situation in which there needs to be multiple business applications as part of the overall software landscape is often referred to as a "best-of-breed system" approach (Potts, 2018).

There are companies in the middle market comfortable with the independent nature of a best-of-breed system approach and naturally accept responsibility for maintaining and supporting several software applications to run the business. Beyond accounting and finance, the software landscape may include CRM, HRIS, time clock, expense automation, inventory management, procurement, and asset management. Depending on the industry and the size of the company, the list of subsystems in the software landscape may be significant. With so many systems in place, there has to be a strategy for bringing the data (especially high volumes of data) and critical business information together with the right tools and technology.

In most instances, the business creates system integrations between the ERP system and each of the subsystems in the technology landscape. Ultimately, all the data will eventually roll up to the general ledger, so the system integrations will require considerable design on a white board for the purpose of mapping the data moving between applications and to identify the business action that will "trigger" the movement of data from one application to another. In addition to the design and mapping exercise, the integration will need to be built and configured either in-house or by a consultant, typically using one of a few different approaches.

The first approach usually stems from the integration capabilities available as part of the ERP system, including traditional import/export functionality. If manually importing data is too basic, the ERP system may also provide an application programming interface (API) to be used to communicate with other systems (Freeman, 2019). Integration through APIs is more technical in nature and may require the assistance of a consultant who specializes in scripting code to perform system integrations. Beyond the integration capabilities of the ERP system, the third option is commonly referred to as "middleware," which is developed by a third-party provider to allow for systems to communicate with one another (Onion, 2015). Whichever approach works best for adopting the best-of-breed approach, there is a level of comfort in mapping data from one application to another, such as from a CRM system to the ERP system.

Adopting a best-of-breed software strategy backed by system integration will assist in connecting business functions, automating data from multiple systems (financials, supply chain management, manufacturing, and CRM), and maintaining all these applications as part of a single ecosystem. With the right plan of action, the correct investment in technology, a team of capable information technology team members, and the right partners, this tends to be the preferred approach toward technology for many businesses.

Summary

While cloud-based ERP systems have significantly outgained on-premises software in the marketplace, what is most important is the ability to understand the options available. Each of these options certainly has its benefits, so gaining insight into the characteristics surrounding these approaches makes a lot of sense. Armed with this information, it will be easier to evaluate an ERP system, see how it aligns with the current software landscape, and choose the option that is right for your company.

SECTION IV

THE ERP MARKETPLACE

Destiny is no matter of chance. It is a matter of choice. It is not a thing to be waited for, it is a thing to be achieved.

—William Jennings Bryan

10
ERP SOFTWARE EVALUATION CONSIDERATIONS

The primary purpose of implementing a new ERP software is to improve your business success. The ERP software will unify users, departments, and processes across your business to increase collaboration, facilitate automation, and provide business leaders with information to make better decisions. Once implemented, the ERP system will serve as a platform that may be scaled up and enhanced at any time in the future to meet the growing needs of your business.

The process of scaling an ERP system is based on the ability to continue to roll forward on new versions, add more user licenses, deploy additional features and functionality (modules, granules, packs, etc.), and automate processes so that the application remains aligned with your business. Therefore, the application has to support new lines of business, growing organizational hierarchy (new entities), and more users as they are onboarded to the organization.

The old African proverb "it takes a village to raise a child" represents the importance of interactions within a community and a support system to achieve and sustain positive growth (Morrow-Kondos, 2020). This is also similar to achieving a successful ERP outcome. In order to get to a place where an ERP system is fully functional and optimized, a company must have a dependable ecosystem, which includes the primary software developer, business partners, consultants, and team members participating in the planning, design, implementation, and ongoing support.

The list of potential business applications available in the ERP marketplace may seem overwhelming, particularly because they each have similar brand messaging and expound on the potential of more successfully achieving business goals. However, there are distinguishing characteristics that surround ERP products in the marketplace and their corresponding ecosystems, and those characteristics assist potential customers with the software evaluation process and how to best determine the best fit.

The leading ERP applications in the marketplace consist of horizontal mainstream systems as well as industry-based verticals and microverticals. Outside the general marketplace, there are a select few who choose to embrace home-grown proprietary systems, which can be a good option for some and a living hell for others. In conducting an ERP software evaluation, it is beneficial to not only become familiar with these different product offerings and approaches but to also understand the pros and cons that may naturally come along with them.

Horizontal Mainstream ERP Systems

There are several leading developers in the United States and throughout the world—such as Microsoft, Oracle, SAP, and Sage—that have created ERP software platforms designed for all types of businesses. The ERP software offers features and functionality allowing multiple departments within the business to transact and communicate. These

ERP developers have been creating commercial-off-the-shelf software (COTS) for the middle market for several years.

Each one of these developers is competing for business in nearly every industry sector. Therefore, the mainstream systems offer technical capabilities for all types of businesses, including vertical attributes for service, distribution, manufacturing, professional services, not-for-profit, and public sector. The licensing and subscriptions may be tailored for your business needs so that customers only pay for the functionality needed. Furthermore, if the business grows in the future, additional capabilities may be licensed, turned on, and deployed at any point in time.

These mainstream developers invest millions of dollars into research, development, and user experience to enhance their code for the purpose of reaching the greatest number of customers, and they jockey for position within the Gartner Magic Quadrant (Gartner Inc., 2022). Furthermore, they recruit, develop, and certify partners to support the customer base, and they encourage third-party developers to create specific system enhancements to extend these applications. These ERP software ecosystems offer robust solutions for nearly every type of business.

The short list below highlights both the pros and cons for horizontal mainstream systems, which may be compared to the other types of systems in the marketplace:

Horizontal Mainstream ERP Systems

Pros
- Horizontal functionality with vertical attributes
- Large installed base of customers
- Significant Investment in technology, innovation
- Partners in every geography ready to assist
- Highly accessible certified consulting resources

- Usually publicly traded entities
- Less exposure during downtimes and recession

Cons

- May not be industry-specific enough
- Aggressive sales approach
- Generalized marketing messaging
- Detailed information is hard to find
- No relationship with developer
- Hard to influence changes

In summary, the horizontal mainstream systems have become household names by dominating the marketplace. These developers have the most customers, largest partner channels, highly developed ecosystems, and certified consultants supporting their applications. The mainstream players provide a safe, reliable, and supportable option for potential customers in good times and bad, so there is less exposure to the office of the CFO in choosing to go in this direction.

Vertical ERP Systems (Industry-Based Systems)

There are several niche players in the ERP marketplace serving very specific industry segments rather than appealing to the broader middle market. These developers may not be as familiar as the mainstream horizontal systems but are often recognizable through specific trade organizations or associations. They actively participate in smaller industry-based events and have a strong effect on their targeted audience.

For instance, a business may be a process manufacturer, specializing in the creation and mixing of chemicals to achieve a finished product such as paint, caulking, or sealants. In this scenario, the potential customer may wish to explore a chemical manufacturing system such as Datacor ERP (formerly Chempax) or Mar-Kov CMS (Chemical Management System) instead of one of the mainstream systems.

As necessity often drives innovation, vertical applications are usually born out of a glaring need for industry-based functionality that is nonexistent in the marketplace. An entrepreneur with significant experience and knowledge of a particular industry may decide to build a system from the ground up for his or her own enterprise and then later package the software to similar businesses within the same industry.

In many regards, the vertical option has great appeal to potential customers, especially when the business has specialization and/or government regulatory obligations. In addition, gathering information within familiar industry circles by networking with colleagues with similar backgrounds, experiences, and business requirements is certainly more comforting.

Vertical system developers generate momentum and gain traction at industry-based trade shows, expos, and associations with good-old-fashioned word of mouth. Their experience, qualifications, references, and familiar social circles provide street credibility, thus giving vertical applications a prominent seat at the table of application technology and ERP software.

The short list below highlights both the pros and cons for vertical applications, which may be compared to the other types of systems in the marketplace:

Vertical ERP Systems

Pros
- Industry expertise with leading practices
- Solid customer references
- Strong statement of qualifications
- Alignment with trade associations
- Personable relationship with the developer
- Ability to influence future enhancements

Cons

- Limited customer universe
- Slower release of enhancements
- General support is limited
- Dependent on a thriving industry
- Limited consulting resources
- Exposure to economic downturn

Vertical ERP applications are a great option for many companies since they bring solid industry experience and functionality to the table, which can provide an extremely reliable solution for many years. However, in evaluating the vertical option, keep in mind that this means forming a partnership with a smaller developer and embracing everything that comes with it, such as a limited customer universe, longer upgrade cycles, and a limited support network.

In these circumstances, a fast-growing company may eventually experience limitations from this type of system or encounter support issues by having to rely on a software company with limited resources. Lastly, if there is an economic downturn or recession, then this may have a drastic effect on the longevity of the developer. All of these variables need to be considered when choosing to go down this path.

Microvertical Systems

A micro vertical system represents a hybrid approach combining horizontal and vertical applications. A micro vertical application is based on a mainstream platform—from a company such as Oracle, SAP, or Microsoft—that has been enhanced by a partner to meet very specific needs of a particular vertical industry segment.

These enhancements may consist of customized, user-defined fields labeled for the industry, custom code and scripts running in the background to engineer specific processes or generate formulas, and industry-based reporting templates. There are several examples of micro vertical applications in the marketplace serving particular industries, such as mill and lumber processing, craft breweries, distilleries of spirits, auto restyling, and dairy farming.

Micro vertical systems are frequently born from a single, successful large ERP implementation, which required several specific enhancements and customizations for the customer in one of these industries. These enhancements to the mainstream application are then repackaged, bundled, and branded for another business in a similar industry by the partner that created them. In having this experience and intellectual property (IP), the partner can market the solution at targeted events, trade shows, and associations and to potential customers all over the world.

In many cases, the micro vertical system approach offers a mainstream software system with industry-based attributes, which brings together many of the characteristics from both worlds.

Microvertical Systems

Pros

- Horizontal functionality with vertical IP
- Industry expertise with best practices
- Solid customer references
- Strong statement of qualifications
- Alignment with trade associations
- Personable relationship with partner
- Ability to influence future enhancements

Cons

- May not be Industry-specific enough
- No relationship with the developer
- Limited customer universe
- General support is limited

- Limited consulting resources
- High-priced for lower middle market
- Exposure to economic downturn

Implementing a micro vertical system is a great option for many businesses because it offers the benefits of the horizontal mainstream application with industry-specific functionality. In having the best of both worlds, it would seem as though nothing could go wrong.

However, if the particular industry experiences any type of market disruption, government regulation, or economic downtown, the partner may choose to no longer enhance or support this code. Furthermore, if it sells the IP to another provider, the customers may be at the mercy of a new provider's corporate strategy.

Whatever the situation, the original partner can simply recalibrate and focus on selling and supporting mainstream horizontal systems. In this situation, the lone survivors will be on their own in having to find another developer to enhance the application (after acquiring a source code release from the original partner), and the lone survivors may not only pay someone else to learn the code but also enhance it. Or they can move to another software system.

Best-of-Breed—Horizontal Mainstream ERP Integrated with Vertical System

As you grow up in life, you are often told that "you can't have your cake and eat it too" (Know Your Phrase, 2022). It's an old English proverb indicating you cannot have two incompatible things at the same time. On the contrary, a best-of-breed solution is predicated on acquiring the best type of solution for different areas of the business and integrating those solutions so that they are compatible with one another.

In this scenario, a business acquires a mainstream ERP system for the purpose of tracking all financial aspects of the business (remember, everything rolls up to the office of the CFO). In addition, a vertical system would handle all of the operational aspects of the business. In order for these systems to communicate with one another, a system integration will need to be performed between the applications.

For instance, a business in the hospitality industry may leverage a mainstream ERP system for handling all the back-office transactions while leveraging a vertical reservation software system for the purpose of booking rooms for each of the properties. These two systems can be integrated so that the data has a single point of entry and flows through the entire system.

Depending on the two systems and their popularity in the marketplace, the integration may already be pre-built, so customers may adopt it immediately. However, in most instances, the system integrations will need to be performed by in-house employees or by a skilled consultant using a middleware product.

The best-of-breed approach is widely utilized throughout the middle market, mostly by necessity and maturity. A mainstream ERP used in conjunction with a vertical application offers the following attributes.

Mainstream + Vertical = Best-of-Breed

Pros

- Strong financials management (mainstream)
- Strong operations management (vertical)
- Ability to deploy products with the most features
- More flexibility between departments in adoption
- May replace systems by department

Cons

- Investment in IT department (FTEs)
- Investment in systems integration
- Manage multiple vendor relationships

- More complex technical environment
- Issues may lead to "finger-pointing"

A best-of-breed solution makes a lot of sense for mature companies residing in the middle market. These companies are able to take advantage of the functionality offered by both a mainstream ERP software system and a vertical operational system through system integration, which also means less exposure to economic volatility or recession.

The environment will be more complex and will require more resources to manage. The management of multiple systems and vendor relationships may also require a larger annual budget, but this tends to be a reasonable solution for lots of middle market businesses.

Homegrown Proprietary Systems

Without going into a full history of ERP software, the development of homegrown systems was more prevalent in the past, definitely more so than today. In going back as far as the late 1990s and early 2000s, most ERP systems were in the process of transitioning from DOS to a Windows environment, and the marketplace slowly adopted to the change in technology because this commitment required the acquisition of new (and at the time very expensive) software, hardware, databases, and operating systems.

The sellers of the mainstream systems of the era were in a race to add whole-product feature sets (financial reporting, fixed assets, human resources management, etc.) of functionality, processes, and capabilities in each new release to try to differentiate themselves from the competition. At the time, many of the leading ERP products were designed for larger businesses such as SAP, Oracle, JD Edwards, PeopleSoft, and Lawson. Meanwhile, other developers—

such as Great Plains, Solomon, and Platinum—designed their systems for small- and medium-sized businesses.

Whether because of perceived gaps in the functionality of that ERP software or because of the seemingly high price of that software, many small- and medium-sized businesses chose the option of creating a homegrown system as their solution. A homegrown proprietary system is predicated on having either in-house development resources or reasonably priced outside consultants to develop a software package from the *ground-up* to meet all the business requirements and thus become a perfect fit for the business.

In situations in which software development is the core competency of a business, the outcome has a better chance of being successful. At the epicenter of this approach, your team of developers has to create a system offering both robust financial and operational capabilities, the ability to be enhanced or upgraded in the future, and usability for team members.

Pros
- Functionality specific to the business
- Less expensive to maintain
- Ability to influence future enhancements
- Control of the source code
- Pride in ownership

Cons
- May not be able to be enhanced
- Exposure to turnover of developers
- General support is not available
- Limited roadmap for scale
- Exposure to economic downtown

With technology and modernization, the ground-up development has become the least-common approach for deploying new ERP software. There are several reasons why homegrown systems have become less popular, including usability, functionality, upgradability, and supportability.

The mainstream systems have filled the functionality gaps of previous years and now provide more innovation and automation. The pricing for the licensing has become more competitive, less expensive, and easier for small- and medium-sized businesses to embrace. The homegrown approach is more realistic and sustainable for addressing very specific operational aspects of the business—which may be considered to be proprietary—rather than attempting to create an entire ERP software package.

Summary

In forging a path to evaluate ERP software, it is extremely beneficial to know the market each product represents, the types of customers they have been designed to fit, and the environmental conditions surrounding them. Just as there are several ways to slice an onion, there are several different approaches to ERP software that may be implemented and adopted.

Each type of ERP software package has its pros and cons, which needs to be considered as part of the system evaluation process. Beyond any features and functionality, the software developer must have a dependable ecosystem consisting of the primary software developer, business partners, and consultants that are able to assist clients with design, implementation, and ongoing support.

It's imperative for the ERP software to sustain the needs of the business through years of growth, change, and maturation. That's why it's important to note that the characteristics that distinguish each of these ERP packages may impact the business either in the near term or perhaps several years down the road, and those considerations eventually tie back to the ERP software decision of today.

SECTION V

ERP ARCHITECTURE

I squeeze oranges every morning to make juice.

—Utada Hikaru

11

THE LINEAR ERP PROCESS

Whether companies are small, medium, or large, they all have the common interest and desire to consistently generate revenue. Obviously, all businesses have their own unique characteristics and mission, so revenue generated may be used for investing back into the business, paying investors, compensating family members, or perhaps funding special causes.

Regardless of the situation or industry, the lifeblood for any business is to produce new sales, which are invoiced and paid for by the customer to generate revenue. Once a company has generated revenue, then investors, bankers, vendors, and team members will be able to get paid.

In selling products or services to a customer, there is a linear process that goes through several stages, from the beginning through completion (Pieroux, 2017). When a customer places an order, the next step is to fulfill the order (product is provided, shipped, or a service has been completed) so that an invoice may be generated for payment. Examples include a distribution company shipping a product from its warehouse, a manufacturing company building or assembling

135

a product, or a professional services firm performing a project or job. This process is referred to as "order to cash" (Wong, 2022).

The order-to-cash process has existed since the beginning of commerce, when the primary goods of a marketplace were cotton, salt, spices, and tea. Today, successful businesses that consistently generate revenue follow an order-to-cash process in some form or fashion, either manually or through system automation.

In circumstances in which order to cash is a manual process, team members are naturally dependent on physical touch points to capture everything happening with sales orders through the various stages of fulfillment. In these scenarios, constant alignment meetings are necessary to determine open activities with team members using large "catchall" spreadsheets. To make matters worse, *manual workflow* may become vulnerable to any number of internal obstacles tied to specific individuals, such as bad habits, poor judgment, political bureaucracy, and the ever-so-popular having to wait on one person with all the knowledge to fix everything.

In situations where the order-to-cash process requires manual intervention, information is scattered. There is increased reliance on using nondigital tools, such as using a paper traveler (job paperwork), emailing spreadsheets among multiple team members to list orders to be fulfilled, using dry-erase boards to illustrate stages in the work-order process, or daily meetings for team members to discuss pending orders.

In developing system requirements and evaluating a new ERP system, the order-to-cash process should be viewed as the primary business requirement to be addressed with systems automation. With a modern ERP system, the order-to-cash process is mapped into the foundation of software so that it may be configured to provide process automation very quickly, creating a rapid time to value.

As an illustration, the order-to-cash process flows in a straight line, as referenced below from left-to-right, and it exists in nearly every business or organization for the purpose of generating revenue.

ERP
Order to Cash
Order Entry ⇨ Fulfillment ⇨ Invoice ⇨ Cash Application

The automation of the order-to-cash process in the ERP system will increase efficiency and collaboration by eliminating the need for manual steps, ancillary spreadsheets, and wasted time on meetings and constant last-minute fixes. In an effort to increase production and efficiency within a business, the automation of order to cash provides the main justification to move to a new system. Ultimately, this can be the fundamental difference between a business *limping along* or *making it happen* on a daily basis.

In addition to order to cash, there is another process in the business that automates the sales cycle. It's called lead to order. In software terms, the lead-to-order approach represents traditional sales force automation (SFA) for driving new business through a sales pipeline, which is most often tracked with a customer relationship management (CRM) system. With lead to order, a business has the ability to track the sales lifecycle with the customer from "cradle to grave," which includes leads, opportunities, product quotations, and finally, a sales order (LEADTO, INC., 2020).

Lead to Order
Sales Force Automation: CRM
Lead ⇨ Opportunity ⇨ Quote ⇨ Order

Depending on the line of business or industry, the sales cycle may take minutes, hours, days, months, or in some circumstances, even years to achieve. Regardless of the length of time, a closed-won opportunity in CRM triggers the order-to-cash process as a quote becomes an order. Once the order is fulfilled, the client will be invoiced for payment, and the company will be able to recognize the revenue, which will be reported in financial reports and executive dashboards and charts.

In taking this a step further, the combination of lead to order and order to cash creates an end-to-end process through any organization known as lead to cash. As Swati Sinha, senior director of product marketing at Reltio, once wrote, "Lead to cash is arguably the most important customer-centric process in an organization, starting with the customer's intention to buy, and ending with revenue recognition" (Sinha, 2020). The lead-to-cash process officially aligns several departments—including sales, marketing, operations, delivery, accounting, and executive management—through a single data entry point spreading through the entire organization.

Lead to Cash: CRM and ERP
Lead ⇨ Opportunity ⇨ Quote ⇨ Order Entry ⇨ Fulfillment
⇨ Invoice ⇨ Cash Application

Due to the nature of team-based processes and the tradition of businesses making software decisions by individual departments, the lead-to-cash process is often taking place through a two-system experience. The CRM software and ERP software by themselves represent disconnected applications, separate silos of information, and duplicate data entry points for team members.

For example, a CRM system such as Salesforce.com, Dynamics 365 for Customer Engagement (formerly Dynamics CRM), or Zoho CRM provides sales force automation (SFA) tools and technology for the sales and marketing departments. On the other hand, the order-to-cash process may be owned by the operations and accounting departments in using system applications such as Dynamics 365 Business Central or Sage 200.

At the lower end of the middle market, it is normal to see a business using an entry-level accounting system, such as QuickBooks, along with Saleforce.com for CRM. Without any third-party middleware, these systems are not integrated. Therefore, there will be a significant gap in the lead-to-cash process, which once again necessitates duplicate entry, additional paper-based processes, spreadsheet-driven reporting for tracking purposes, and perhaps extra people to bring all the data and information together.

Traditionally speaking, the sales department is led by a vice president of sales while the accounting department is led by the CFO or the financial controller. Although part of the same corporate team, these are two departments with separate leaderships, agendas, and approaches to execution. With separate teams, it's no surprise to find a company embracing separate CRM and ERP systems as part of its software landscape.

In spite of this situation, the CRM software and ERP software may be integrated to automate lead to cash, thus keeping these departments separate but the data flowing forward through this critical business process. In scenarios where CRM and ERP systems are integrated—whether through a middleware product, scripting through an API, or even using a "plug-in"—this is referred to as a "best-of-breed-technology" approach for achieving an interconnected enterprise (Bly, 2020).

As alternatives to a best-of-breed-technology approach, there are several ERP software packages in the marketplace that offer accounting and sales force automation functionality, thus keeping lead to cash under a single umbrella. Most notably there are Oracle NetSuite, Dynamics 365 Business Central, and SAP Business One, all of which provide both ERP and CRM capabilities in a modern, single software package.

Whether the single-system approach or the best-of-breed approach is adopted, the automation of the lead-to-cash process can be vital. The process naturally connects team members across departments through an organization. Team members need to work together in interdependent roles, essentially becoming an extension of one another to deliver a product or a service to a customer.

With the right tools in place and the willingness of team members to adopt this functionality, the software will increase efficiency, escalate productivity, and create a happier work environment. Furthermore, the integrated harmony achieved from each department working together will enhance the customer experience, which is especially important in an ultracompetitive environment.

System Integration—Automating Lead to Cash and Beyond

If there are several business systems residing in the existing software landscape, a portion of the ERP system evaluation process has to focus on understanding the integration capabilities or potential limitations of bringing data into the new system. Through these conversations, there may be a need to include technical resources from your team and a technical consultant to discuss this topic in more detail.

As previously mentioned, system integration provides the ability to bring data from multiple business applications into the ERP system to establish unification through a single point of entry. The automation of lead to cash with "CRM and ERP integration is relatively common" (Jenkins, 2020).

An ERP system with robust APIs offers a technical path for data to be authenticated and imported on a scheduled basis (hourly, daily, weekly). Once critical data moves from one system to the other, system integration eliminates separate silos of information contained in multiple business applications.

As a product offering, cloud-based middleware is often referred to as platform as a service (PaaS). It offers out-of-the-box adaptors and connectors for several leading mainstream business applications.

These PaaS tools provide the consultant or perhaps in-house employees technical resources with a visual workbench showing the objects—such as customers, accounts, and items—located in software systems and databases available for mapping purposes. Through the workbench, these objects may be mapped, tested, and published into production between systems so that data moves between systems on a scheduled basis without the need for any manual intervention.

With regard to leveraging API or PaaS software, if system integration is a part of the business requirements, odds are that one of these tools will be needed to be a part of the overall system configuration. Please be aware this will entail additional licensing that will go along with the traditional users and modules, thus increasing the overall software investment.

In addition to the increase in software costs, anticipate needing more professional services as well. The system integration process will require a reasonable amount of consulting hours to perform the project, thus adding more complexity to the overall implementation beyond the base deployment of the standard features and functionality of the system.

In centralizing the ERP system and rising above a state of duplicate data entry, anticipate each of the proposed system integrations to require necessary planning and development. A technical consultant will be able to create the needed architecture for a path that enables the data to reach the ERP system.

It will be important for the consultant to understand how data flows through the organization, including how it originates and how it proceeds through each critical business process, such as lead to cash. In gaining insight into the flow of data and the process touchpoints through the organization, the consultant will have the goal of identifying the business action or "trigger" to move data between systems, such as a new order landing into the ERP system.

With the necessary planning up front and the creation of these systems integrations as part of the ERP deployment, teams will no longer have to enter critical business data into multiple systems. The elimination of duplicate entry saves valuable time in the workday, minimizes the chance of making errors, and allows team members to focus on higher-value tasks to be more productive in the workplace.

During the ERP software evaluation process, it may be tempting to let the topic of system integration become larger than necessary and inadvertently slow the process down. Quite often in the ERP software evaluation process, the potential customer desires *to see* the system integration.

In demonstrating the features and the functionality of the ERP, it is highly unlikely that the partner will be able to show the system integration. Providing a demonstration of the system integration as part of the software evaluation process would essentially constitute a project in and of itself. It is just not possible to build an integration for each prospective customer based on every unique software landscape. However, it is reasonable to ask whether the consultant has performed a specific integration with a common business system or business process to gain insight into the consultant's experience.

A technical consultant with significant experience will be able to speak to the design process, the mapping exercise, the testing, and the volumes of data that may be integrated between systems. Meeting the technical consultant should provide a level of confidence into this portion of the project and firm understanding of the positive impact these integrations will provide to your team.

The partner should be able to explain the tools available for integration purposes. The tools can range from setting up basic template-based import utilities, leveraging APIs, licensing third-party middleware options, or confirming if there is a nominally priced, off-the-shelf plug-in available. The technical consultant ought to be able to speak to the design and mapping process for each one of these options in more detail.

If, however, the topic of system integration is still a bit murky, it is essential to recognize it is commonplace today for data to be transmitted between systems. Those systems might include ERP software, banking systems (reconciliations), procurement systems, invoicing systems, CRM systems, point-of-sale systems, e-commerce platforms, payroll systems, and so on. The list goes on and on. Since most developers and providers want their platforms to be adopted by as many customers as possible, most have developed APIs or created plug-ins to provide businesses a method for accessing and utilizing data.

Once system integration with the ERP is established, a business is able to connect information from multiple sources—thus eliminating the dependence on spreadsheets—and is able to achieve a level of data integrity that had previously not existed. With data integrated into the ERP, a business will be able to report on several critical data points, including sales from multiple channels, special projects, cost of sales, cost of labor, etc.

Believe it or not, there are thousands of businesses in the middle market still needing to leverage system integration. In taking this a step further, it may be of assistance to describe a hypothetical situation in which system integration and the unification of systems could enhance the business and make decisions better and faster.

Multichannel Distributor Example

Assume a multichannel distributor is selling its products to big-box retailers and to individual consumers over the web. In order to run the business, it is highly likely it will need a CRM package for tracking the sales lifecycle and relationships with the large retailers (business to business). Plus, there may be an e-commerce system used for processing sales orders over the web (business to consumer). There may also be a purchasing system, warehouse management system, and shipping software package. Lastly, in the back office, there may be a separate entry-level accounting software to perform daily journal entries and run financial statements.

In this example, the multichannel distributor has several disparate systems coexisting within the software landscape. They are tracking multiple sales channels without a clear system of record for managing the business. With disparate systems and separate silos of information, there is an immediate reliance upon manual processes and dependence on spreadsheets to fill in all the cracks that appear in managing the business. In this situation, it takes longer to report sales to management, close the monthly books, and generate an accurate financial statement for investors. This example is all too common in the middle market.

What is notable in this situation is that each department needs access to the same strand of data and information. In selling a product, the sales manager wants to know how many units will be sold this month and how many have been sold this quarter and year-to-date. In the warehouse, the operations manager has to manage the amount of product in inventory so that orders may be fulfilled to meet customer demand. Down the hallway, the finance department wants to know the exact same information for budget, revenue, and financial reporting purposes. If there are multiple systems in place, the opportunity for all this information to be compiled, managed, and reported accurately is diminished.

In the multichannel distributor example, the mapping of the system integration would allow for the access of data points between CRM software and an ERP platform and between e-commerce and an ERP platform. The figure below represents four integrations that may be created to centralize the sales information, automate processes, and create an environment wherein reporting becomes a lot easier for the team.

CRM Contacts ←→ ERP Accounts/Customers

CRM Quotes ⋯→ ERP Sales Orders

E-commerce Customers/Orders/Product/Price ⋯→ ERP Invoicing

CRM (Account History) ←⋯ ERP Sales History/Payments

While the example above is simplistic, and there may be several software packages needing to be integrated, these integrations would be the first to be created because they are the highest priority. Additional integrations may be established over time so that the ERP system becomes the overall system of record.

But Wait—There's More

Companies in the middle market may have any number of software systems, depending on their industry, sales channels, and relationships. In sticking with the distribution example, a middle market company may have grown to include a standalone point of sale for cash-and-carry orders, an e-commerce engine for online sales, a web portal for partners to place orders, and an electronic data interchange (EDI) to receive orders from big-box retailers. Whatever the software landscape, the major mainstream ERP packages, along with one of the integration toolsets, may be used to integrate with these systems to form a single solution.

Here is a sample list of industry-based systems that may need to be integrated with an ERP system as part of a best-of-breed approach.

Sample List of Industry-Related Systems
- **Manufacturing**—product lifecycle management, CAD design, configure/price/quote (CPQ)
- **Distribution**—e-commerce, electronic data Interchange (EDI), configure/price/quote (CPQ)
- **Health Care**—medical billing and invoicing, electronic health records
- **Life Sciences**—laboratory information management system (LIMS), quality management system (QMS)
- **Retail**—point of sale (POS), e-commerce, electronic data interchange (EDI)
- **Software**—e-commerce, software license key generator, revenue management
- **Construction**—project management, time and expense, certified payroll

- **Professional Services**—project management, time and expense
- **Government Contractors**—project management, time and expense
- **Not-For-Profit**—donation management, event management, and membership management
- **Public Sector**—municipal government software, utility billing

Special Note: Agriculture, construction, oil and gas, legal, and transportation are industries that rely heavily on operational systems to perform their business. In many instances, a mainstream ERP system may not be able to provide as much operational functionality as an industry-based vertical system. Although sometimes hard to find, these specialized operational systems handle unique requirements, such as crop management, compliance management, case management, authorization for expenditure (AFE), maintenance management, and fleet management. Businesses in these specialized industries may first need to deploy an operational software before evaluating ERP software.

Summary

Most middle market companies follow the linear order-to-cash process, so adopting a software package that automates this key business process is critical to the success and perhaps the survival of the business. Furthermore, the order to cash process is most likely a part of a much larger lead to cash process.

Depending on the software system landscape, the lead to cash process may require the integration of one or more systems. That is why taking a best-of-breed approach toward the ERP software evaluation and overall technology strategy yields tremendous results.

When it comes to evaluating a new ERP system, the integration of these critical business systems as a means of automating critical business processes has to be a primary part of the system requirements and a focal point during discovery meetings. The implementation consultants have to understand the key business processes, the data flows, and the technology in place so they can create a roadmap for performing these integrations.

Once the integrations are in place, they will have an immediate impact. The process of duplicate entry and the need for managing so many static spreadsheets will be eliminated. When this happens, team members will become more productive by spending time on valuable, forward-driven tasks and activities.

Imagine a future in which data and information from the various systems of the software landscape all roll up into the ERP system to automate critical business processes. When this happens, the ERP package can become a system of record and the single point of truth, real-time data can be used for strategic planning and analysis, and businesses can make better decisions to execute on the growth strategy.

Have patience. Wait until the mud settles, and the water is clear.
Remain unmoving until right action arises by itself.

—Lao Tzu

12
THE LAYERS OF ERP AND THE CORRESPONDING LEVEL OF COMPLEXITY

In evaluating a new ERP software system, the term "scalable" is an adjective often used to describe how the functionality may evolve over time, based on the needs of the business. To a chief financial officer or any decision maker, it is reassuring to know that as the business grows, so will the software, thus eliminating concerns of "growing out" of the ERP any time soon (or having to again go through the evaluation process any time in the near future).

In the Meaden & Moore article "What Layer of Functionality Do I Need in My ERP System?", Scott A. Holter highlights "ERP systems can generally be characterized as having 3 layers" (Holter, 2016). While the subject of the article is based on manufacturers evaluating ERP systems, Scott A. Holter clearly distinguishes the layers of complexity in ERP systems and appreciates the importance of scalable functionality designed to support different business models.

The term *scalability* represents the layers of functionality available in the system and the extent to which it may be deployed based on the business's corresponding requirements. For a company located at the lower end of the middle market, the software may be deployed in a basic fashion, to establish the foundation for the system. For companies perhaps larger or more complex, the ERP software may be deployed to include the foundation and include ERP transactions or quite possibly advanced ERP transactions (Holter, 2016).

In the most simplistic of terms, an ERP system is analogous to a tree growing in a forest. A tree develops from its roots, over time a trunk emerges, and branches grow. As the tree continues to develop, the trunk and the branches become bigger and stronger over time. Once fully grown, a tree provides benefits to the surrounding ecosystem, including the creation of oxygen, soil stabilization, providing a home for wildlife, and raw materials for humans to build future homes (Tiles, 2013). In less-than-technical terms, an ERP system may be built from the ground up by putting the "foundation" in place and extending the functionality at any time to provide the features and functionality essential to the business.

For a small company in the lower middle market, once the foundation is in place, the system may be scaled to include more functionality (ERP transactions) and greater complexity (advanced ERP transactions) as needed over time. The adoption of an ERP system should yield a reasonable amount of confidence in using the financial platform for several years, with the ability to grow at any time in the foreseeable future.

With the larger companies having more complexity, there is a need to deploy functionality from each of these layers in order to attain the capabilities needed to run the business. For instance, a company in the hot dog cart business named Doggie Dog Inc. is a manufacturer needing the ability to track several bills of materials, which are comprised of all the assemblies and parts required to construct a finished item. In this situation, the ERP software system will need to offer capabilities in financial management, supply chain management, and manufacturing.

Layer 1— The Foundation	Layer 2— ERP Transactions	Layer 3— Advanced ERP Transactions
Financials	Supply Chain	Any One or More
Multientity	Sales Orders	of the Following*:
Financial Reporting	Invoicing	Manufacturing
Budgeting	Purchase Orders	Project Accounting
Banking Solutions	Receivings	Revenue Recognition
(ACH)	Landed Cost	E-commerce
Accounts Payable	Inventory Management	Multicurrency
Accounts Receivable		HR/Payroll
Fixed Assets		System Integration

The figure above represents the Layers of ERP software:
*Special Note: All potential advanced ERP transactions should each be considered a layer of complexity on its own. For instance, in addition to the Foundation and ERP transactions, a software company may need several types of advanced ERP transactions, such as project accounting, revenue recognition, and system integration. In this circumstance, the ERP would essentially have five layers of complexity.

Layer 1—The Foundation

As mentioned earlier, all financial management activities roll up to the office of the chief financial officer. ERP software is designed in a similar fashion, with the purpose of automating all financial operations and financial reporting, coupled with application security and controls to maintain regulatory compliance. All data and corresponding attributes in the ERP systematically roll up to the general ledger so that costs are properly accounted for, and information is accurately reported. This is also why new chief financial officers or controllers often replace existing entry-level systems with a new ERP system as the first order of business upon joining a new company.

The base functionality of an ERP system offers enhanced financial management capabilities, which go well beyond the abilities of a standard entry-level accounting software. Often referred to as "the foundation" (or sometimes "the platform"), the base system offers tighter security, more controls, the ability to run multiple companies, and robust reporting tools. From an accounting perspective, the capabilities include financial management, financial reporting (financial statements), and basic budgeting, which is comprised of general ledger, accounts payable (money owed vendors), and accounts receivable (money owed by customers), with the ability to take advantage of electronic banking (automated clearing house (ACH)) and fixed asset management.

Used together, these capabilities provide the system launching point, which may be scaled up over time to include more features and functionality. In taking the "giant step" from an entry-level accounting software to an ERP system, the company provides auditors, bankers, and potential investors with more confidence in working with your team because those parties understand these systems have controls in place, accessible audit trails, and better reporting functionality for providing insight into the business. Once the foundation is in place, a company is well-positioned to do even more with the system in the future.

Layer 2—ERP Transactions

In deploying the second layer of functionality, businesses begin to take advantage of traditional ERP transactions beyond financial management into automating standard processes. For instance, with ERP transactional functionality, order to cash may transition from a manual process to an automated one. With this functionality, you are going outside the accounting department and potentially into sales and operations, which creates a unifying effect on the team, naturally enhances collaboration, and begins to eliminate repetitive data entry from the corporate culture.

To get more granular, the second level of the system often represents supply chain features and functionality, which are used for capturing a *sequence of processes* needed to produce and distribute a product for a customer. In software module terms, the functionality includes sales orders, invoicing, purchase orders, landed cost, inventory management, bills of materials, and kitting. Purchase orders are aligned with accounts payable while sales orders are tied to accounts receivable, so there is automation with the back-office accounting features.

Often these capabilities are associated with distribution companies, but sales orders and purchase orders provide nearly the majority of middle market companies with process automation to create efficiencies regardless of using the inventory capabilities. For instance, not-for-profit organizations may sell books, videos, and CDs, which are all kept in inventory. There are several types of middle market businesses that may take advantage of this functionality.

With the second layer, the ERP software is automating processes, aligning multiple departments, expanding into operations, and beginning to report meaningful metrics for gauging the pulse of the business. In addition, static processes once outside of the system—based on old-fashioned paper and email pushing of items such as requisition requests and expense submissions—can bring additional employees into the system through workflow to increase productivity. These features may be deployed in an initial ERP implementation or may be considered part of a future-phase project. Whatever the case may be, ERP transactions are a game changer for a business trying to get to the next level.

Layer 3—Advanced ERP Transactions

With the foundation and ERP transactions in place, the third layer acts as a natural extension of the ERP, providing multifaceted functionality, thus giving companies the ability to leverage the system for growing and expanding the business. Advanced ERP transactions provide more forward-thinking, proactive planning and very specific capabilities to increase business success. The utilization of advanced ERP transactions expands the software system from finance and operations into more complex processes and procedures based on a specific line or lines of business.

Prime examples of advanced ERP transactions include manufacturing, project accounting, revenue recognition, e-commerce, and multicurrency. Each one of these advanced ERP transactions consists of multiple modules or functionality with multiple touch points throughout the ERP software system.

For instance, manufacturing may include materials requirements planning, production scheduling, assemblies, and demand planning modules to turn raw materials into a finished good. While project accounting touches several parts of an ERP system with project budgets, realization, utilization, time and expense, and invoicing to track and report on specific transactions allocated to a project.

Other examples include revenue recognition (fair value of contracts, deferred revenue, and waterfall visualization reporting) to maintain revenue recognition standards as part of the ASC 606 accounting standard. In addition, functionality in e-commerce (business-to-business (B2B) or business-to-consumer (B2C)), in handling web portals to place orders in the system, or in checking on account balances and making payments would also be considered advanced ERP transactions.

In moving into the third layer of the system—depending on the industry, number of lines of business, and company size—a business may take advantage of one or many of these system capabilities all within a single ERP package. The functionality available with advanced ERP transactions is beneficial to companies in the manufacturing, distribution, professional services, high-tech, and e-commerce sectors. The features and functionality assist with planning, production, time lines, and regulatory compliance and are fully integrated with the rest of the ERP system. Once again, taking advantage of this functionality assists with efficiency, productivity, collaboration, and better decision-making throughout the enterprise in an effort to consistently grow the business.

Advanced ERP Transactions with Unique Inter-Connections

Going beyond advanced ERP transactions, whether they be based on preference or necessity, there may be a precondition requiring more interrelated functionality from the system. Although completely different from one another, both HR-payroll functionality and system integration are highly specialized, requiring significant design, planning, configuration, and testing before deploying into the ERP system. Due to the level of sophistication, it will be wise to consider the deployment of HR-payroll and system integration as unique inter-connections of the ERP system.

In either circumstance, HR-payroll and system integration may be an extension of the foundation (layer 1), a part of a system that includes ERP transactions (layer 2), or perhaps an addition to a system performing advanced ERP transactions (layer 3). While each of these levels builds off one another, HR-payroll and system integration can be beasts that stand on their own two feet and may be a part of any type of system configuration.

Depending on the company, line of business, size, and people running the organization, one or both of these capabilities may be "in play" for the ERP implementation, or possibly they may not be in play at all. The significance is, once again, acknowledging and accepting the level of effort needed to deploy this functionality and to manage it on an ongoing basis. All too often these capabilities are underestimated by the client as part of the broader scope of the implementation.

Payroll and Human Resources

When it comes to HR-payroll, middle market companies embrace one of two approaches: "We absolutely have to process payroll in-house," or "We are completely outsourcing our payroll to a vendor." It is more popular to outsource HR-payroll to leading providers—such as ADP, Paychex, Paylocity, and Paycom—as a means to saving time, forgoing in-house stress, and being in compliance with government regulations. However, HR-payroll has options. The process may be brought "in-house" to be a part of the ERP system, or it perhaps may be a standalone system as part of the software landscape.

To dig a bit deeper, when bringing HR-payroll "in-house," depending on the system solution, this functionality may be a part of the ERP system architecture as modular-based functionality and licensed as part of the overall system. However, HR-payroll functionality may also be brought in-house through a separate, disparate system, often referred to as a human resources information system (HRIS) or human capital management (HCM) system. The former would be a part of the ERP system implementation, while the latter would be more of a system integration exercise. The purpose of this section is to focus more on the HR-payroll functionality being deployed as part of the ERP system to provide a framework for how this may impact an implementation.

Regardless of industry, labor costs tend to be the largest expense of most businesses. However, in choosing to deploy HR-payroll functionality as part of the ERP system, there is often a significant business case made for embracing this approach, which corresponds with the daily execution of the business and may be a part of the corporate culture. For instance, if the people assets are comprised of a combination of day laborers, seasonal employees, hourly employees, and salaried employees (who perhaps receive a high rate of garnishments), then these situations lead toward bringing HR-payroll in-house. Generally speaking, entities in construction, agriculture, trucking, nonprofit, and public sectors are more likely to bring HR-payroll in-house versus, say, manufacturing, distribution, professional service, high-tech, and life sciences sectors.

In deploying HR-payroll as part of the ERP system, the base functionality may be deployed to include several capabilities, including applicant tracking, onboarding, benefit management, employee self-service, direct deposit, and tax filing. As a special note, many of these capabilities may be available as part of the system configuration, but there also may be third-party provider enhancements developed to extend the base HR-payroll functionality. Once again, there are many providers in the marketplace that have developed both on-premises and cloud-based payroll and human resources management systems. There are a lot of options in this area, so look to the partner to provide more detailed information on the possibilities available.

The prospect of taking HR-payroll in-house is also a reflection of departmental structure and the team members responsible for performing these internal processes. In some instances, human resources and payroll responsibilities may be within a single department while in other circumstances these are two separate teams on the organizational chart. When human resources and payroll are separate departments, there may be less incentive to work together, which may create a complicated situation during the ERP system evaluation. In these situations, it may require executive management to assist in sharing a vision for a single system solution.

Assuming that strategic alignment between the human resources and payroll teams may be achieved through the ERP software evaluation processes, then there will be a much greater chance for collaboration through the deployment. With internal alignment as part of the methodical approach—along with assistance of a highly skilled consultant—the rollout of HR-payroll functionality requires significant planning, care, and execution to ensure a positive outcome. In deploying HR-payroll functionality, failure is not an option.

If employee payroll checks are not distributed on time, or withholdings are incorrect in some form or fashion, there is a mission-critical problem. There is nothing less desirable than having a line of people outside the door waiting for their payroll checks. Some may even bring their kids with them so that they can jump up and down on the office furniture while they wait. This is truly a situation worth avoiding.

With HR-payroll, the processes need to be mapped and designed into the ERP system configuration. The employee data will need to be migrated, and the specialized reports will need to be created. The functionality will need to be tested by performing several payroll "dry runs," and the users will need to be trained on the functionality so that they may perform the payroll run on their own. With all the planning, configuration, testing, and training in bringing HR-payroll "in-house," anticipate this being an additional layer of complexity to the ERP software implementation.

System Integrations

It is easy to underestimate the impact of the system integrations. However, taking advantage of this approach will align systems and also touch several departments by automating the sequence of processes to digitally transform the business. There are still thousands of businesses in the marketplace with leaders who either do not understand that integration is achievable or simply prefer to live in the dark ages. Herein lies the opportunity to no longer be one of them and to have critical data from disparate systems rolled up into an ERP software system.

In moving forward with system integration as part of the initial ERP deployment, there has to be a cohesive strategy to ensure that the planning for the unification of systems is managed as part of the software landscape. As mentioned earlier, there are different integration tools or middleware options available to assist with the data mapping, each with varying levels of complexity. Ultimately, the goal will be to achieve integration between the ERP system and any number of other systems already existing within the software landscape, such as CRM, e-commerce, expense management, and payroll.

Once again, system integration creates the opportunity for automating the flow of data from multiple sources into a single ERP system, thus creating the unification of disparate systems and eliminating silos of information. The benefit of the integration is the achievement of a natural flow of data and information within the existing software landscape, thus eliminating the need for rekeying data into multiple systems. In addition, the establishment of system integrations tends to be welcome by all department teams because it removes time-consuming and redundant processes, enhances the ability to report on key metrics, and leverages other technology investments.

With any system integration, there needs to be a formal design session or sessions between client and consultant comprised of business stakeholders and information technology professionals as well as functional consultants and developers on the consulting team. The integration planning session provides a great opportunity to use the conference room whiteboard to illustrate the data mapping, landing spots in the application, and triggers (business actions that are either data-driven or event-driven) for building these system integrations. With all the primary stakeholders in place, this will assist in ensuring the data is being mapped correctly and the triggers are all agreed on before moving forward with the build-out of each integration.

Unless there are team members on staff with a significant background in system integration, the developer from the consulting team will need to build the system integrations, using the middleware as the platform. The middleware product will provide adaptors and connectors for each of the applications and provide a virtual workbench for creating these integrations so that actual scripting may be kept at a minimum. Once built, the integrations will need to be tested in a nonproduction environment by the client, with any necessary adjustments taking place before the software is put into the production environment.

Once established, the system integration will authenticate the data to ensure only the right information is brought into the system, with any exceptions being pulled to the side for review and/or correction. The integration may have a dozen, thousands, or tens of thousands of transactional records, so the information has to be validated, thus eliminating the opportunity for bringing bad data into the system. In addition, the low and high volumes of data may be transferred between multiple systems as either one-way or two-way integrations.

Regardless of the approach, the data will be moved based on a predefined trigger in the system, which may be based on a specific time or action. The integration of data can range from *nice to have* all the way to *business critical*, but either way, this process is an absolute game changer. Journal entries may be uploaded in the general ledger, sales orders can go into the invoicing module, or a multilevel BOM can go into a bill of materials module on a scheduled basis, such as weekly, daily, or hourly intervals.

The system integration approach works for a business deploying a financial foundation, ERP transactions, or advanced ERP transactions so that all parts of the business have the opportunity to reap the benefits of a single point of entry and the unification of business systems. In dedicating a reasonable amount of time to planning, developing, and testing, system integrations will naturally add a layer of complexity to the overall ERP implementation.

Summary

While each middle market business is unique, ERP software has been developed and designed to reflect the complexity needed to run all types of businesses, regardless of their size or industry. This is made possible by the layers of features and functionality that have been designed for scale.

A growing middle market business can adopt the capabilities of an ERP system to manage financials, operations, supply chain, manufacturing, e-commerce, projects, human capital, and reporting. These capabilities are best illustrated as layers consisting of the foundation, ERP transactions, and advanced ERP transactions.

In understanding these layers and the capabilities they represent, team members evaluating a new ERP system can associate business requirements with specific features and functions. This means the layers of functionality needing to be deployed determine the amount of complexity in the ERP implementation.

The amount of ERP complexity needing to be deployed will differ by business. One company may only need the foundation while another may only need the foundation and ERP transactions. And another may need the foundation, ERP transactions, and advanced ERP transactions.

In taking things up a notch, there are several businesses that need multiple types of advanced ERP transactions, such as project accounting and revenue recognition. In addition, payroll, human resources, and system integration may be added to anyone of these system configuration scenarios, which would add several additional layers of complexity.

The business requirements and strategic vision assist in determining the capabilities needed in a new ERP system. The layers of capabilities determine the level of complexity of the deployment. With this information, business professionals can head into ERP software evaluation grounded in reality and cannot play the "we are a simple business" card.

SECTION VI

BALLPARK ERP COSTS

Don't count the days; make the days count.

—*Muhammad Ali*

13
THE LEVEL OF EFFORT
TO IMPLEMENT AN
ERP SYSTEM

"We are a simple business" is a statement frequently broadcast during ERP discovery meetings and conversations. Company executives quite often believe their company's business model is *simple*, which presupposes that the implementation should go very quickly and be relatively easy.

Although a tremendous oversimplification, this statement serves as a starting point in the dialogue between the prospective client and consultant to discuss the current environment, pain points, system limitations, and the opportunity to understand the desired future ERP system. The natural dialogue of the discovery conversation will assist in uncovering both standard and complex business requirements and in identifying any advanced ERP transactions needing to be deployed in the new system.

Advanced ERP functionality is highly specialized, usually involves elements of compliance, has an increased level of transaction detail, and handles information shared across departments and multiple employees. Believe it or not, just about every industry has some form of complex business requirements.

The questions being asked by the consultant during the discovery meetings will assist in driving the conversation from a high-level dialogue into specific details. The consultant digging deep into the business requirements should assist in removing any illusions by the client as to the simplicity of the project. That deep digging should also lead to the careful acceptance of the effort it will take to implement the system.

As an example, a high-tech company sells software licensing, implementation services, and support plans each as a separate line of business. From an ERP perspective, you can quickly assume this will require financial management, project accounting, and revenue recognition functionality.

In deploying both project accounting and revenue recognition, there will be a need for additional discovery meetings and conversations, extended design and planning sessions, meticulous system configuration, testing of specific-use cases, and thorough training for users before those functions are ready to use.

Moreover, the implementation for any advanced ERP capability will need to be led by a senior consultant proficient in that particular topic. Often referred to as a *subject matter expert*, this consultant will have a professional résumé consisting of industry and implementation experience in areas such as manufacturing, project accounting, or revenue recognition.

In using this example, a standalone financial management system will take less time to implement than an ERP system needing financial management (foundation) and supply chain deployment (ERP transactions). Furthermore, a company requiring capabilities in financial management, supply chain (purchase orders, sales orders/invoicing, and inventory), and project accounting (master projects, budgets, tasks, time and expense) will require an even greater level of effort.

In circumstances in which one or more types of advanced ERP transactions are necessary, such as project accounting and revenue recognition, one must assume the project will require more time to implement (increased design, setup, configuration, and training to the end users of the system). In these deployment scenarios, the implementation will have a significant increase in project scope, time line, and budget.

As mentioned earlier, just about every industry has some form of complex business requirements, and ERP software has been designed to handle these needs. However, it takes time to set up and configure the ERP system to properly meet these needs. The figure below helps to illustrate the type of functionality that may be needed across several major industries.

There is a direct correlation between the level of complexity needing to be built into the system and the time it will take to implement it. All too often, there is an assumption that this work may be performed in a quick fashion or that it may even be left to resources in-house. Both are common misconceptions, often leading to disastrous results. These approaches should be avoided at all costs.

An experienced consultant or ERP software provider will be able to determine the number of hours or days needed to perform tasks required for the design, setup, configuration, training, and go-live cutover support. In addition, following the discovery meetings, the consultant will be able to provide a preliminary implementation estimate, which may be used by decision makers within the company to understand the budgetary expectation and financial commitment.

On a side note, there will always be lower-cost alternatives out there. These lower-cost alternatives can be smaller shops looking to add new customers or independent consultants looking for their next plum gig. Whatever the case may be, be leery of going down this path. Often the consultant providing the lowball estimate is also the weakest alternative, which may have dire implications down the road. How would you like it if you caught a consultant "googling"

High-Level Industry Examples with Advanced ERP Functionality*

Industry	Financials	Supply Chain	MFG	System Integration	Project Accounting	Revenue Recognition	E-commerce
Service/Retail	√			√			√
Distribution	√	√		√			√
Health Care	√			√			
Life Sciences	√					√	
Manufacturing	√	√	√				
Professional Svcs	√	√			√		√
Energy	√			√		√	
High Tech	√			√	√	√	
Not-For-Profit	√	√		√	√		√

*Special Note—These checkmarks are not meant to be definitive statements. Rather, they are to serve as general examples to assist in illustrating the potential complexity of ERP systems across major industries. Each business is unique and has its own set of business requirements. For example, a life sciences company may manufacture its own products, or a professional services firm may maintain inventory items. All situations will need to be evaluated based on the actual needs and requirements.

for the answers to your questions? An experienced consultant will have the answers to your questions based on first-hand experience.

Being grounded in reality and having the guts to accept what it takes to deploy an ERP system leads to a path of success. In taking the low road and trying to circumvent the process—by searching for low-cost providers, exploring cheap workarounds, or forgoing the necessary functionality to artificially keep the price point down—executives can lead their companies to undesirable results. In the ERP software journey, it is not only essential to recognize what is needed to implement this functionality, but also it is necessary to have the courage to accept it.

There Is No Way to Cheat on the Time It Takes to Implement an ERP System

As pointed out earlier, one of the best skills of accounting professionals is the ability to cut costs. Cost cutting is engrained in the accounting culture and is often a way to show executive management an immediate impact toward helping expand the bottom line. The cost-cutting mindset shines brightest nearing the end of the ERP software system evaluation. Before making a final decision and signing the contract, executives find that the price of a new solution becomes the biggest priority.

Going through the discovery process and having a project-scoping conversation provides the consultant with the information needed for generating a detailed estimate for the implementation. With a time-and-materials project approach, the implementation estimate typically lists a number of hours (or days) to perform the project. These hours are based on experience with similar projects of roughly the same size and scope and a professional understanding of the level of effort needed to perform all the necessary tasks, including planning, design, setup, configuration, report writing, system integration, testing, and training.

Taking the proper approach to performing the project tasks will take time, and understandably, time is money. Therefore, it only makes sense to try to reduce the number of hours, thus lowering the corresponding price point. The easiest behavioral sign (also known as buying sign) is to look for ways to make reductions in the overall price point before making the final decision to move forward.

Assuming this is the case, before deconstructing the implementation estimate, trust in the relationship being forged with the consultant to understand that the information being presented is based on professional experience and the amount of complexity being built into the system. The partner providing the estimate has a professional obligation to dispense a realistic budgetary number based on the level of effort, which also takes into consideration any unforeseen variables or unplanned challenges faced during the project.

If the goal is to collect estimates from multiple consultants to compare pricing, be wary of the consultant who is estimating far less than the others, as that consultant is likely trying to *buy the business* rather provide a fair price. Business professionals repeatedly fall for this maneuver since achieving the immediate reduction costs in comparison to the original (and likely more realistic) estimate garners an immediate *hero effect* and financial satisfaction. However, these situations potentially lead to the worst possible results, unfinished implementations, and potentially career-affecting circumstances.

Aside from shopping around as a means of cutting costs, the tactic of taking a *line-item-veto* approach to the implementation estimate may have adverse effects during the project—for possibly months or even years later. Cutting corners on project resources, taking shortcuts on the design or configuration, or not appreciating the importance of the team being trained can have a direct effect on the outcome.

Another backward scheme for saving money is by planning to bring in independent consultants, short-term contractors, or temporary workers at a lower hourly rate to save dollars on primary consulting resources. This corporate mercenary approach often backfires as well. These types of outside workers have no incentive to impact the long-term success of the business, they bring zero continuity to the team, and they have a professional agenda that will never align with the corporate mission.

In getting back to basics, the hours estimated for the ERP implementation directly tie back to the business requirements, processes, industry, and people using the system. It will take time, with multiple phases, and it will require a significant amount of effort by members of your team and the time of a consulting firm. Why would anyone wish to avoid taking the necessary time to get this done right by trying to cheat on the actual time it takes to implement a system?

Everything done well in life takes time—and often more time than you may have initially presumed. As a business professional and a leader, this is an opportunity to self-reflect on other life experiences, whether they are personal or professional. If this is the first time on the ERP software journey, perhaps reflect on the effort it previously took to renovate a house, learn to ski, or cook a meal for your family on Thanksgiving. All these special projects require planning, resources, and time, and frequently they take longer than expected. Why would the ERP implementation be any different?

If there is still a burning desire to save money on the implementation, then there is one highly productive approach that will not sacrifice the critical aspects of the project. As French writer Voltaire once said, "With great power comes great responsibility" (Voltaire, 1996). It will be well within your power and responsibility to expect your team to raise the level of its game for the implementation. The best way to save money is to have your team step up to be lean, mean, and focused on achieving the overall objective.

In more specific terms, team members need to dedicate a reasonable amount of time and effort toward the project each day, including being prepared for meetings, staying on top of assigned responsibilities and tasks, and being able to deliver on agreed-upon deadlines. Team members will consistently need to be "in the moment" with focus and full attention, whether it is participating in the training sessions or in user- acceptance testing.

In reality, when the home team raises its game during the implementation, it assists in ensuring that the consultants stay on track with the budget and that billable tasks are taken away from the consultants' to-do list. It's simple arithmetic. When the client does more, the consultant does less. If the consultant does less work than initially planned, then the client saves money on the implementation.

With the right level of effort and attitude by the project team, there are plenty of the ways to save money through the implementation and beyond. There is no way to cheat on the time it takes to do the implementation correctly. However, the more the project team is willing to take on, the more will be the cost savings and the more enhanced will be the user adoption of the ERP.

An investment in knowledge pays the best interest.

—Benjamin Franklin

14

ERP SOFTWARE:

OUT OF THE BOX ($), CONFIGURABLE ($$), OR CUSTOMIZABLE ($$$)

As your company reaches an evolutionary period in its growth, the capabilities of the entry-level accounting system become stretched beyond its limits. Using multiple spreadsheets to reconcile data from disparate systems is a time-consuming and inefficient way to track business performance. When this happens, it is clearly the right time to transition to a more robust ERP system, which offers features, functionality, and the capabilities needed to help growing businesses.

The majority of ERP products available in the marketplace are most often distinguished by their application accessibility and architecture, such as on-premises or cloud. However, there are other ways to classify ERP systems, such as whether they have been designed for the greater marketplace, such as a horizontal mainstream ERP system, or designed for a specific niche, such as an industry-based vertical ERP system.

Looking primarily at the horizontal mainstream ERP system, there are several software packages in the marketplace worth evaluating. These ERP software packages have been designed for customers of all size types, including SMBs, middle market, and enterprise-sized companies. Furthermore, they are designed to scale for businesses experiencing growth and increased complexity.

In the LNS Research article "Understanding Out-of-the-Box vs. Configured vs. Customized," Matthew Littlefield highlights the need for "a common way" to differentiate systems to help "eliminate confusion" (Littlefield, 2015). While the subject of the article is based on manufacturing management software, Matthew Littlefield's terminology is applicable to ERP software.

ERP software can be identified as representing one of three options: out of the box, configurable, or customizable. These classifications are similar to the more familiar comparison of small, medium, or large. These labels directly refer to the intended market, size of business, and capabilities available.

For instance, Microsoft is one of the leading developers in the middle market offering several ERP systems as part of its product portfolio to customers, including Dynamics GP, Dynamics SL, Dynamics 365 Business Central, and Dynamics 365 Finance & Supply Chain. In taking a closer look from both ends of the spectrum, Dynamics GP is a horizontal, on-premises, out-of-the-box package for SMBs and the lower middle market. On the other hand, Dynamics 365 Finance & Supply Chain is a horizontal, cloud-based, highly customized package designed for the top end of the middle market and for enterprise-sized businesses. These are strong solutions meant for two different types of potential customers.

The leading ERP software developers have built a portfolio of products designed for the needs of the customer to capture as much market share as possible. These products have been designed with customers in mind based on the type of business, the number of employees using the system, and annual revenue. A company that has $5 million in revenue and twenty-five employees is better served exploring the functionality of Dynamics GP instead of Dynamics 365 Finance & Supply Chain. On the flip side, a company with over $500 million in annual revenue that is growing exponentially year-over-year needs to evaluate Dynamics 365 Finance & Supply Chain rather than Dynamics GP.

With so many options and several products available in the marketplace, the key is understanding how the systems have been designed to determine which ERP software options should be evaluated. Just as these ERP systems have been packaged and marketed to provide solutions to lower and upper ends of the middle market, the level of effort to set up and deploy each one of these systems naturally corresponds to how the system has been designed.

Out-of-the-Box

An out-of-the-box (OOTB) system instantly provides a significant number of features and functionality far beyond an entry-level software package. With an OOTB system, there is minimal need for advanced design, configuration, special customization, or a high-priced software developer. The OOTB system provides predefined roles for end users (CFO, controller, accounts payable clerk, etc.), preconfigured reports and dashboards, traditional accounting and business management functionality, and standard business processes—all conveniently baked into the system to manage the day-to-day business.

In working with a consultant through the implementation process, there will be several options on how to perform tasks in the system, such as paying a vendor, printing a check, or running an aging report.

With the capabilities immediately available in the system, the time spent with the consultant may be focused on deploying the options that work best for the team and automating processes that are impacting the business.

With an OOTB system, small-to medium-sized business will have approximately 85 percent to 90 percent of the functionality immediately. Obviously, no system is 100 percent perfect. Customers can choose to invest in light customizations or modifications to narrow any gaps. However, "workarounds" tend to be less expensive. One example is exception-based reporting used to find the "needle in the haystack."

Although there are significant features and functionality available in an OOTB system, a detailed implementation process is still required for a successful deployment. Along with an upgrade in technology, a significant amount of cultural change, and the desire to be successful, there has to be a commitment of time, consulting dollars, and personnel resources dedicated to the success of the project.

The implementation will include the necessary time for planning, analysis, design, system configuration, data migration, report writing, and training for the end users. However, please be aware that the time line for the implementation of an OOTB system will be approximately three to four months from project kickoff all the way to going live, which is a significantly shorter time span and less expensive than the larger ERP software options.

System Type: Out of the box

Target Market: Small and medium-sized businesses / lower middle market

Size in Annual Revenue: < $50 million

Implementation Timeframe: Three to four months from kickoff to going live

Reasonable Budgetary Expectation: Starting at $100,000-plus for software and professional services

Product Examples: Sage Intacct and Microsoft Dynamics GP

Configurable

On the surface, a configurable system shares several similarities with an OOTB system, including hundreds (if not thousands) of features and functionality available to a customer on day one. However, the configurable ERP application offers a more robust and extensible toolset, which is designed to allow for the addition of further capabilities and functionality. With this extensibility, a configurable ERP system offers the ability to add a greater level of personalization, which may be used to automate sophisticated business processes, create script-based extensions to capture industry-based information, or perhaps take advantage of precoded, microvertical intellectual property available through the partner channel.

A configurable system may be personalized to the business needs and conditions of the customer rather than having to force the customer to adapt its needs to the system. Examples of system personalization include user roles being modified, adding user defined fields with labels to capture relevant business data and demographics, changing existing entry screens or creating entirely new screens, or producing unlimited reports and dashboards. Furthermore, there are flexible workflow tools available, so a business may automate tasks and business processes based on specific actions taking place in the system, such as initiating approvals, triggering reorder points, and distributing reports to executive management.

A configurable ERP system performs well with medium-sized companies, including carve-outs from larger enterprise-sized companies, start-up ventures and private-equity-backed businesses with an accelerated growth strategy. These companies may come from a variety of different industries, such as service, distribution, manufacturing, high-tech, life sciences, or professional services.

In these circumstances, the business evaluating ERP software systems requires financials and operations functionality to increase efficiencies and throughput, or it may have microvertical industry requirements requiring personalization of the system. A configurable system takes approximately six months to implement, requiring more analysis, planning, design, consulting, internal resources, and financial commitment than an OOTB system.

System Type: Configurable

Target Market: Middle market / medium-sized businesses / private equity-owned / venture-based

Size in Annual Revenue: < $500 million

Implementation Timeframe: six months from kickoff to going live

Reasonable Budgetary Expectation: Starting at $250,000 for software and professional services

Product Examples: Oracle NetSuite and Microsoft Dynamics 365 Business Central

Customizable

Designed for the large-enterprise-sized businesses, a customizable system offers OOTB functionality, which may be modified and extended, similar to a configurable system, but it offers a robust toolset to enhance and personalize the application across multiple levels and departments. In addition to traditional finance and accounting functionality, a customizable system has been designed for the global enterprise with significant operational ERP capabilities, including retail, supply chain management, manufacturing, transportation, and warehouse management capabilities.

In addition to financial management and operational capabilities, a customizable system provides the ability to design and build the system to automate complex business processes, perform intricate formulas and calculations, execute multilevel workflows for approvals, and generate quantifiable operational metrics. With this high level of system flexibility, customers may adopt all the functionality they need, whether developed through the implementation, through embracing industry-based microvertical solutions developed via a partner channel, or through working with an authorized independent software developer specializing in system enhancements.

Beyond providing traditional functionality designed to manage the day-to-day business, the product developers for these systems are actively incorporating the latest in application technology and innovation into these products with intelligent analytics, machine learning, artificial intelligence, cognitive services, and the internet of things (IoT). With these highly advanced tools, the ERP system will automatically apply algorithms to data, naturally automate repetitive tasks, and provide an environment for faster decision-making, continuous improvement, and predictable analytical outcomes.

With larger potential clients in this market and a highly customizable system, global consulting firms, including the "Big Four" and several prominent firms dedicated to the middle market, have seized on the opportunity to develop intellectual property to enhance these platforms, personalize these systems for particular industry verticals, or develop functionality to address a very specific business case. On the client side, a system of this magnitude will require dedicated resources to support users, understand the technology, and gain alignment between the IT strategy and the ERP product roadmap.

System Type: Customizable
Target Market: Upper middle market / enterprise-sized businesses
Size in Annual Revenues: > $500 million in revenues
Implementation Timeframe: twelve-plus months
Reasonable Budgetary Expectation: Starting at $1 million-plus for software and professional services
Product Examples: Oracle ERP Cloud, Workday, Microsoft Dynamics 365 Finance & Supply Chain

Summary

In using the original example, a company with $5 Million in annual revenue should not waste any time gathering information or evaluating Dynamics 365 Finance & Supply Chain because it has been designed for much larger companies. Alternatively, a company with $500 million in revenue growing exponentially year-over-year can easily leave Dynamics GP out of the evaluation entirely because it will be too difficult to scale beyond the OOTB functionality. Whatever the size of company, if the evaluation includes an OOTB system versus a customizable system, one of these options simply does not belong in the discussion, and a reputable ERP partner will provide this feedback immediately.

The leading ERP software developers have built a portfolio of products designed for the marketplace but with intentionally dissimilar customers in mind. Obviously, there is always a chance of going up and down market as each product is individually sold to new customers and circumstances change.

In deciding which ERP systems to explore as part of a formal evaluation, it's most advantageous to invest precious time with the options that best align with the size of the business and contain functionality that will be the most impactful. Ultimately, choosing which ERP options to evaluate in more detail requires aligning the size of your company and growth trajectory, gaining comfort with increasing technology investment beyond previous thresholds, and managing the impact of cultural change across the business.

"D'ye see him?" cried Ahab; but the whale was not yet in sight.

—Herman Melville

15
HOW TO BUDGET FOR THE ERP IMPLEMENTATION

In starting the software journey, CFOs, financial controllers, and accounting managers want to know how much an ERP is going to cost before committing to making a change. Armed with a traditional product-centric mindset, these professionals often search online for countless hours, scouring numerous websites in a time-wasting effort to find this nonexistent information.

When it comes to ERP software, there may be generic software pricing available online either posted by software developers or ERP industry bloggers with references to $99 per user per month or other high-level information. However, when it comes to cost of an ERP implementation, this information is not available, or it may be completely inaccurate.

According to KBV Research, "The global ERP software market size is expected to reach $70.3 billion by 2025" (KBV Research, 2019). With such a huge market, the ERP software space is dominated by global high-tech titans such as Microsoft, Oracle, and SAP.

From an implementation standpoint, there is a vast array of trained and certified specialists ranging from local mom-and-pop resellers to, regional consulting firms, national resellers, and Big Four accounting firms, such as Deloitte and PwC.

Since the ERP software market is clearly a big business that is based on sophisticated technical and financial capabilities, providers routinely avoid sharing implementation estimates online for public consumption. Although this approach may seem frustrating, these firms specialize in personalizing the pricing to each customer and try to avoid having misinformation published on the internet.

Unfortunately, searching on the internet typically leads mostly to doomsday stories of failed ERP implementations and references to lawsuits. With the help of the internet, many have learned about the failed ERP implementation for the jewelry retailer Shane Co., which played a role in its filing for Chapter 11 bankruptcy protection in 2009 (Kanaracus, 2009).

Whether small or large, consulting firms and value-added resellers follow a consultative sales approach because they are solution-driven organizations. They understand that the capabilities of ERP software have to align with the unique business requirements of each client. This alignment ultimately determines the level of effort needed to deploy the ERP, and it will be used to create an implementation estimate.

Without having previous experience evaluating ERP software, many business professionals familiar with low-priced, entry-level accounting software inadvertently have unrealistic expectations as to what an ERP deployment costs. With so many big-time players in the game and with the huge market space, it's safe to assume moving to an ERP system is a big step in terms of both technology and financial commitment.

Rather than blindly walking into an uncomfortable "sticker shock" situation, it would be certainly beneficial to have the ability to anticipate the cost of the implementation as early as possible. Having a reasonable expectation of the cost commitment of the ERP implementation provides an amount of confidence, and it eliminates a potentially awkward situation of having to tell a consultant you cannot afford the ERP.

The goal here is to shed light on the information that is impossible to find—and to help business professionals from having to ask the uncomfortable question: "Will this cost $50,000, $500,000, or $1 million?" Having a reasonable expectation of ERP software implementation costs in advance will not only assist having an open dialogue regarding business requirements with a consultant, but it will also assist in being able to prepare a necessary budget for this financial commitment.

The goal here is to align the high-level business requirements with the layers of complexity in the ERP software. Connecting the functionality needing to be deployed in the system (financials, supply chain, manufacturing, etc.), the size of the company (small business, medium-sized business, global enterprise) and the type of software packages available for that sector of the ERP market (out of the box, configurable, and customizable) will assist in providing insight into a reasonable budgetary expectation and help to avoid any embarrassing surprises.

Now this exercise is only intended to set a reasonable expectation and is not supposed to replace a detailed estimate based on actual requirements, unique elements to the business, or any special circumstances. The goal here is to anticipate the "ballpark" to develop a budgetary figure without having to piecemeal this information through websites and multiple vendor conversations. Here is the basic formula:

**{Type of Application} (# of Layers) x (Hourly Rate)
= Ballpark Implementation Estimate**

In explaining this formula, it may make the most sense to work our way backward, beginning with billable rate. This is always a topic of consternation with CFOs, financial Controllers, and accounting managers, who are never pleased to be discussing billable rates for consultants. However, in order to generate a ballpark implementation estimate, it is a necessity to consider the hourly rate as the backbone of the formula.

The standard billable rates for consultants in the local marketplace will fluctuate based on the size of system and geography. Large cities—such as New York City, Chicago, San Francisco, and Los Angeles—tend to be more expensive than middle market towns—such as Seattle, Denver, Dallas, and Charlotte. Depending on where you are located, the market will impact the standard hourly billable rate.

In the example below, you are beginning with a standard billable rate of $200 per hour, which is low in most locations (in large cities, $250 is a more accurate rate). If you are unsure of the going hourly billable rate for ERP consultants in your area, ask one of your professional contacts you trust within your network. That person may be able to provide insight without your having to contact a consultant directly. (As a side note, always be leery of consultants with the lowest rates because they often have the least experience and limited knowledge. And they often achieve the least desirable results.)

In addition to requiring a standard billable rate, an estimate needs to assign each layer of complexity of an ERP system with a block of consulting hours for performing the system design, setup and configuration, data migration, report writing, and training. Each one of these necessary activities correlates to each layer of functionality and is critical to the successful deployment of a system. As each situation is unique, this provides insight into the level of effort necessary to be successful.

Lastly, the size your business determines the size and scale of the ERP system that is necessary to implement. A small business may leverage an out-of-the-box system, a medium-sized company a configurable system, and a large-enterprise-sized company a customizable system. These ERP systems have been designed to meet the needs of each size of company and scale for growth, so it is important to be realistic about the size of the company and explore the right-sized solution.

Example 1
Target market: Small- and medium-sized businesses
ERP system: Out-of-the-box
Assume a __minimum__ of 250 hours per layer of complexity

Assume a minimum of 250 hours to deploy each layer of complexity within the ERP system. Once again, the hours reflect each layer of the deployment, which is comprised of analysis, design, setup, configuration, data migration, and end-user training.

Out-of-the-box assumption: billable rate of $200 per hour (adjust hourly rate as needed)
Layer 1—Financial management = $50,000 deployment ($200 x 250 hours)
Layer 2—Financial management + supply chain = $100,000 deployment ($200 x 500 hours)
Layer 3—Financial management + supply chain + manufacturing = $150,000 deployment ($200 x 750 hours)

A small- to medium-sized company wishing to evaluate an out-of-the-box product will spend fewer dollars than on a customizable system. With this approach, it's entirely realistic to have a budgetary expectation of approximately $50,000-plus for implementing a financials-only business management system. However, plan on adding $50,000 for each additional layer of functionality needed. For example, a lower middle market manufacturing company leveraging an out-of-the-box system will need to plan for a minimum of a $150,000 system implementation (for three layers of functionality).

Ballpark Hours Estimate to Implement Out-of-the-Box System for SMB*

Industry	Financials	Supply Chain	MFG	Project Accounting	Revenue Recognition	Hours
Service/Retail	√					250
Distribution	√	√				500
Health Care	√					250
Life Sciences	√	√				250
Manufacturing	√	√	√			750
Professional Services	√			√		500
Energy	√				√	500
High-Tech	√			√	√	750
Nonprofit	√	√				500

*Special Note: Figure does not include system integration or e-commerce

Example 2
Target Market: Medium-sized businesses
ERP System: Configurable
Assume a <u>minimum</u> of 500 hours for each level of complexity

A configurable system requires additional design, setup, configuration, and planning compared with an out-of-the-box system. The hour assumption for each level of complexity within the system would be at a minimum of 500 hours for deploying each level. The 500 hours of the deployment would be comprised of analysis, design, setup, configuration, data migration, and training.

Configurable assumption: billable rate of $200 per hour (adjust hourly rate as needed)
Layer 1—Financial management = $100,000 deployment ($200 x 500 hours)
Layer 2—Financial management + supply chain = $200,000 deployment ($200 x 1,000 hours)
Layer 3—Financial management + supply chain + manufacturing = $300,000 deployment ($200 x 1,500 hours)

Although more expensive than an out-of-the-box system, a configurable system is designed to provide more functionality and is geared for businesses striving to execute on a faster growth strategy and compete at a global level. In most instances, a company requiring this functionality needs to utilize the financial and operational capabilities of a system. (If a medium-sized business needs financials only, it should consider an out-of-the-box software package and save on the implementation.) With this approach, it's entirely realistic to have a budgetary expectation of approximately $200,000-plus for implementing the configurable system.

Ballpark Hours Estimate to Implement Configurable System for Medium-Sized Business*

Industry	Financials	Supply Chain	MFG	Project Accounting	Revenue Recognition	Hours
Service/ Retail	√					500
Distribution	√	√				1,000
Health Care	√					500
Life Sciences	√					500
Manufacturing	√	√	√			1,500
Professional Services	√			√		1,000
Energy	√				√	1,000
High-Tech	√			√	√	1,500
Nonprofit	√	√				1,000

*Special Note: Figure does not include system integration or e-commerce

Example 3
Target Market: Upper middle market / large / global / enterprise
ERP System: Customizable
Assume a <u>minimum</u> of 2,500 hours for each level of complexity

A customizable system is incredibly complex and requires a significant amount of design. For instance, the system design phase of the deployment may require several weeks and multiple consultants, which will take significant billable hours. The hour assumption for each level of complexity within the system is at a minimum of 2,500 hours for deploying each level. The 2,500 hours of the deployment will be comprised of analysis, design, setup, configuration, data migration, and training.

Customizable Assumption: Billable Rate of $200 per hour (adjust hourly rate as needed)
Layer 1—Financial management = $500,000 deployment ($200 x 2,500 hours)
Layer 2—Financial management + supply chain = $1 million deployment ($200 x 5,000 hours)
Layer 3—Financial management + supply chain + manufacturing = $1.5 million deployment ($200 x 7,500 hours)

The leading customizable ERP systems have been designed for the Fortune 500 and the largest businesses in the world. However, in an effort to gain market share, there is no line set in stone between the middle market and the enterprise space. There will forever be a willingness by developers and partners to come downstream and provide ERP capabilities to the upper end of the middle-market. With the vast amount of system capabilities and the amount of design needed to configure the system, it only makes sense to move in this direction if your company plans to utilize the operational capabilities of the system.

Ballpark Hours Estimate to Implement Customizable System for Large Companies*

Industry	Financials	Supply Chain	MFG	Project Accounting	Revenue Recognition	Hours
Service/ Retail	√					2,500
Distribution	√	√				5,000
Health Care	√					2,500
Life Sciences	√	√				2,500
Manufacturing	√	√	√			7,500
Professional Services	√			√		5,000
Energy	√				√	5,000
High-Tech	√	√		√	√	7,500
Nonprofit	√	√				5,000

*Special Note: Figure does not include system integration or e-commerce

In utilizing the operational aspects of a customizable system, the implementation will automatically be three or more layers deep, including the foundation, ERP transactions, and advanced ERP functionality. Therefore, the cheapest, most bare-bones implementation would be in a ballpark of $1.5 million. Unfortunately, this number may realistically be only a starting point for a budgetary expectation, as there may be a need for a larger footprint with sophisticated system integrations, scripting by developers for customizing unique aspects of the business, and perhaps specialized third-party products.

Keep in mind, if the business requirements are based on the financial and supply chain aspects of the system, it may make more sense to explore a configurable system at a lower price point rather than going all-in on a customizable system. In the dot-com era, many small businesses exhibited hubris by choosing to implement enterprise-sized customizable systems. They believed they were on a path of achieving accelerated growth and would easily outgrow out-of-the-box and configurable ERP software. However, as with the Shane Co., it was simply too much to handle both in functionality and financial commitment.

There are many businesses needing customizable ERP software, but it requires being all-in from a technology, operations, and cultural standpoint. Customizable ERP implementations pose more challenges, require more consultants, demand a tremendous level of teamwork, and require a greater financial commitment. Achieving a successful ERP implementation for a project of this size is a major accomplishment.

Summary

Most professionals care about being prepared for conversations, meetings, and presentations—no matter the location, setting, or subject matter. Exploring ERP software options should be no different.

Having a reasonable expectation of the financial commitment assists in the overall ERP evaluation experience. It reduces the probability of being "blindsided" by the costs from a potential vendor; it eliminates embarrassing internal situations with executive management and direct peers because of having to ask for more money; and it removes the temptation of compromising the implementation in order to lower the price point.

More importantly, having a reasonable expectation provides confidence in establishing a realistic budget for the ERP implementation. With a realistic budget in place, business professionals can be confident in the ERP software evaluation process and spend more time focused on the actual solutions to the current business challenges being experienced and addressing the business requirements and strategic vision.

SECTION VII

SELECTION OF ERP SOFTWARE AND IMPLEMENTATION CONSULTANT

Definition of Evaluate: (1) to determine or fix the value of (2) to determine the significance, worth, or condition of usually by careful appraisal and study

—Merriam-Webster

16
HOW TO EVALUATE ERP SOFTWARE

With a broad understanding of the varying applications available in the ERP marketplace, it's imperative to evaluate a shortlist of ERP software systems by using a straightforward approach to gain the best result.

The evaluation approach will need to incorporate features and functionality and also appraise the long-term sustainability of the business application.

The vast majority of CFOs and financial controllers spend an inordinate amount of time reviewing system capabilities, such as how a system handles debits and credits, the processing of accounts payable transactions, and generating reports—often finding themselves somewhere deep "in the weeds." Although this traditional approach is based on the best of intentions, it places way too much emphasis on addressing the requirements of today without careful consideration for the needs of tomorrow.

A delicate balance has to be incorporated into the software evaluation to purposely select an ERP system that will provide the most value over the longest period of time. In doing so, the ERP software evaluation needs to look beyond the application and carefully consider several characteristics and environmental conditions that may prove to be beneficial years down the road. There is a way to strike this delicate balance.

The ERP software evaluation needs to be conducted as if the company is making a long-term investment.

As with the acquisition of any asset, you want to collect as much information as possible to formulate an informed decision before making the investment in an ERP software system. A reasonable approach is to borrow from Philip Fisher's "scuttlebutt method," here applied to the ERP evaluation process.

Philip Fisher was an American stock investor and author of *Common Stocks and Uncommon Profits*. In his book, he outlined a technique called, "scuttlebutt method" as the basis of researching everything about a company before investing in it, including executive management, market competition, customer and employee satisfaction, research and development, and sales performance (Fisher, 1996). With this information, analysis, and evaluation, one can make better informed decisions to invest in great companies. Even well-known professional investor Warren Buffett referred to the scuttlebutt method as "an important investing technique" (YouTube, 2019).

By using a modified "scuttlebutt" approach to the ERP evaluation, one may begin to see the much larger picture by evaluating and analyzing the most impactful characteristics, which create a connection between the developer, the product, and the customer. By simple alignment, one will notice that these characteristics are significant and that they may eventually impact your business more than the actual features and functionality of the system.

In making this investment, you want to achieve the best results over the longest period of time possible. In creating a shortlist of software packages to evaluate, use the opportunity to investigate the following criteria:

- ✓ Usability
- ✓ Research and development/innovation
- ✓ Product roadmap
- ✓ Scalability
- ✓ System integration
- ✓ Developer ecosystem
- ✓ Partner channel
- ✓ Corporate longevity

Usability

It is important to assess the degree of usability for ERP software. Team members are going to log into the system each morning, process transactions, upload data, generate reports, and make business decisions based on the information being presented to them. These ERP system users are going to essentially live in the software application all day, each day, and they will have to rely on it for recording all aspects of the business pertaining to their role within the organization.

In order to encourage interaction between team members and the ERP application, there has to be an intuitive navigation promoting an elegant look and feel and ease-of-use so the users will be able to adapt to a new system and continue to use it in the future. The user experience should have a natural process flow, including cascading menus, ad hoc query analysis tools, colorful dashboards, accessible shortcuts to frequently traveled areas, and the ability to search on all types of information.

The process of moving from a legacy system to a more robust application can be hard on team members having to change from a familiar interface and personal processes to a new screen with more features and automation. If the team becomes frustrated or resistant to change, then this will affect user adoption and ultimately the success of transitioning to the new system. ERP software with a high level of usability will naturally assist in the level of user adoption among team members and the success of the implementation.

Research and Development/Innovation

There are several leading developers in the marketplace, but to be continuously competitive, they need to invest significant capital into research and development (R&D) to continue to innovate their ERP products. Innovations through R&D drive system improvements, new technologies, and more customer-focused capabilities into the application, which in turn provides more value to customers.

Innovations from R&D lead to new system releases containing features and functionality and also improvements, enhancements, and new capabilities for both finance and operations. Beyond features and functionality, these innovations are quickly heading into a new era of digital abilities, including artificial intelligence (AI), robotic automation, predictive analytics, and blockchain functionality.

The process of researching actual R&D is not always easy. If the ERP software developer is a publicly traded company, this information is typically located on the annual report. However, with small software developers, this may require asking for this information. Although they may not provide an actual number of dollars being invested into R&D, the answer should provide enough insight not only into the level of commitment, but also how dollars are appropriated for R&D.

As a potential customer, confirm that a portion of the dollars you will spend on licensing is being reinvested into future innovations of the ERP application. By having this conversation, if it seems as though this commitment is lagging or unimportant, this should be an immediate cause for concern.

A developer making significant investments into research and development will ultimately yield innovative solutions to complex issues today and tomorrow. The best way of gaining insight into the future of an ERP system is to research the level of dedication by the developer in the area of R&D.

Product Roadmap

In moving beyond research and development, the leading ERP developers will communicate the strategic direction of the application through a product roadmap. The product roadmap offers a high-level visual summary of future releases and system enhancements based on a near-term time line so that customers may plan to take advantage of these capabilities in the months and years ahead.

New product features can potentially assist growing business in several ways, such as making the application more user-friendly, providing easy-to-use tools for automation, and offering more insightful report and business metrics. There may also be new features assisting the business in the areas of finance, sales, operations, or compliance.

A particular application may already be light on functionality in certain areas, such as inventory management or project accounting. These areas may clearly need updating and require better functionality.

Being able to clearly articulate the product strategy and long-term vision goes a long way with customers. It provides customers with an opportunity to understand where their product is going so that they may discuss, plan, and strategize as part of managing the current system or choose to deploy new features in the future. Would you get on a train or an airplane without knowing where it would be going? Of course not. So why would you embrace a new ERP system without knowing where it's going in the future?

As part of the system evaluation, request a copy of the product roadmap or get a list of the new features soon to be released to the customer base. As part of the evaluation, take the opportunity to gain insight into the strategic direction of the ERP application and the capabilities coming in the future.

Scalability

Scalability is a characteristic used to describe the ability of the ERP system to grow and manage the increasing demands by the customer over time. A scalable ERP system will be open, flexible, and accessible, and it will be able to adapt to the growing and changing needs of the business. The way a company may use the system today may be minor in comparison to the way it may need the system to function in the future.

The system platform has to be able to address immediate financial and accounting needs, such as financial management (general ledger, accounts receivable, accounts payable, and bank reconciliation) and financial reporting. However, as the business grows either organically or through acquisition, the ERP software will need to support a wider range of capabilities, such as supply chain management, manufacturing, revenue recognition or project accounting.

On a similar note, there may only be a handful of team members needing user licenses today, but perhaps through growth, there may be dozens of users needing access to the system in the future. More users and functionality mean more transactions. The ERP software system will need to handle increased volumes of sales, orders, warehouses, bills of materials, projects, and report generation.

In evaluating and researching ERP software systems, it will be imperative to identity any technical limitations of the system because these boundaries may affect your business in the future. One example of a limitation may include an on-premises system that will never be accessible through the cloud. Another example would be a cloud-based ERP system that only works with a single web browser. One more example would be an ERP system with poor APIs for system integration, thus reducing the ability to communicate with other critical business systems.

The ultimate goal is to fully embrace the ERP software system that provides financial, operations, and integration capabilities to sustain the business as it grows for the next ten-plus years. The only way this will be possible is by embracing a scalable ERP software system today that will continue to provide advantages for tomorrow.

System Integration

A new ERP system has to be able to communicate with the other business systems that already exist within your software landscape or with other applications to be implemented in the future. These may be traditional packaged solutions or homegrown developed systems handling critical areas of the business, such as e-commerce, point-of-sale, or, most often, customer relationship management systems.

The primary objective is to avoid a situation in which data from one system has to be manually entered into the ERP software system. The application needs to provide a toolset with the ability to import, authenticate, and post information into the ERP software system. Depending on the business, there may be hundreds, thousands, or hundreds of thousands of records needing to be brought into the ERP system on an hourly, daily, or weekly basis.

Additionally, there may be a business process requiring the flow of data between multiple systems. For instance, the integration between ERP accounts and CRM customers. As mentioned earlier, the lead-to-cash process begins in CRM and finishes in ERP. However, with two-way integration, the ERP will be able to push the final order and corresponding payment history back to the CRM system. The new ERP system either needs to handle this type of process automation or leverage a strong middleware product to achieve one-way or two-way system integrations.

For whatever reason, the topic of system integration is usually near the end of the ERP software evaluation process, when in fact it really needs to be front and center. The ability for the ERP software system to communicate with other business applications will have the most impact when it comes to speed, efficiency, throughput, and production. Ultimately, the data being integrated will most likely represent new sales orders and the ability to generate profits and recognize revenue as quickly as possible.

Developer Ecosystem

Whether evaluating a mainstream horizontal system or vertical ERP system, these applications serve as software platforms offering thousands of system capabilities. However, to be fair, there is no single ERP software that can possibly do everything you need. Depending on the current requirements or to support future growth, there may be a need for a specific feature, toolset, or application that may be industry-related, regulatory-based, department-specific, or process-driven. In these situations, a developer ecosystem becomes critical.

The leading mainstream and vertical ERP software developers recruit, cultivate, and organize a community of independent developers for the intended purpose of creating extensions to their platform. In meeting core competency standards and achieving required certifications, these individual software developers design and package their own intellectual property (IP) for a global market,

There are literally hundreds of examples of independent software developers in the marketplace, specializing in areas such as sales tax automation, expense management, accounts payable automation, e-commerce, budgeting, and planning (just to list a few examples). These *third-party* developers may have designed their applications to work with only one particular ERP product or perhaps several different applications.

The developer ecosystem also serves as a community with a shared goal of providing specific functionality to assist customers with unique or complex business needs. The developer ecosystem not only strengthens the ERP product, but it also impacts the overall satisfaction of the customers using these systems.

There is a lot to learn by exploring the ERP developer ecosystem. The size, stature, and depth of the developer ecosystem speaks volumes about the ERP product. In addition, the developer ecosystem opens the gateway to learning about impactful features that may help your business. Most importantly, exploring the developer ecosystem provides a great opportunity for assessing the strength of the community you may soon become a part of.

Partner Channel

A channel partner is a company in a working relationship with a software developer to market, sell, and implement software in supporting customers. Within the ERP industry, channel partners are commonly referred to as value-added resellers or VARs for short. A VAR (or the industry preferred term, *partner*, referring to partnering with the developer and with the client) has sales, technical sales, developers, and implementation consultants on staff to introduce the ERP product, align the system capabilities with the prospective customer business requirements, and deploy the system through an implementation project. Once implemented, the partner then provides ongoing service to the customer through an agreed-upon support plan.

The mainstream ERP developers have hundreds, if not thousands, of channel partners both nationally and on a global scale. There are many vertical ERP players with channel partners as well, although not as many as the mainstream players. In either case, the primary goal of the partner is to establish a relationship with prospective customer to sell, implement, and provide on-going support with respect to the ERP software system.

Over the years, the ERP partner channel has taken many twists and turns. Once dominated by small partners in local geographies, the ERP industry has grown significantly through the early twenty-first century and has become more specialized due to technology, innovation, and complex accounting standards. The once-dominant mom-and-pop-sized resellers have been unable keep up with sales expectations, rising salaries, and technical certifications, so many have chosen to *cash out* and be swallowed up by larger regional, national, and global VARs.

As a matter of continuous growth, ERP product developers proactively and strategically attract, recruit, and grow their partner channel. ERP developers seek highly skilled resellers that align with their ecosystem and have a proven track record of achieving customer success. The success and growth of the partner channel directly impacts the growth and market penetration of the ERP developer and leads to a growing number of customer-success stories.

Why is this information important in selecting a new ERP system? It is important to recognize there are three members of the ERP transactional relationship: the developer, the partner, and the customer. On the other hand, there are two members of the direct personal ERP relationship: the partner and the customer.

At any point in the future, your company may experience unforeseen circumstances or tough situations through internal or external forces that will require the assistance of a partner to provide help. When these situations arise, it will be highly undesirable to discover you are running on an ERP product that is not widely supported or, even worse, you discover you cannot find anyone to provide the necessary assistance.

Also, as with any relationship, through the passage of time, people change, circumstances change, and consequently relationships may change as well. There are a lot of successful relationships between the partner and the customer. However, like any loving relationship over an extended period of time, it may ultimately end in a separation.

Without a reseller community to provide necessary support, your company will be at risk, or at the very least take on unnecessary exposure for an unspecified period of time (picture yourself alone on an island needing to be rescued). These unfortunate circumstances may lead to mission-critical situations.

In tough situations, the best place to turn is to a robust partner channel to identify new partner options and potential candidates to provide ERP software support. With numerous options available, you will be able to convert an unfortunate situation into a relationship with a new partner and decrease the level of exposure.

Before purchasing an ERP software system, one should have insight into the depth and breadth of the partner channel supporting a particular product. Selecting an ERP product backed by a strong partner channel should provide added confidence to the customer. If you're ever in need of assistance, there will be a partner able to assist you in your ERP journey.

Corporate Longevity

The global technology industry grows primarily through two different strategies: innovation and financial transactions. On the innovation front, the technology industry continues to mature in the areas of cloud computing, internet of things (IoT) devices, and artificial intelligence due to increasing customer adoption. On the financial transaction front, technology companies are rapidly growing through merger, acquisition, and divestiture (M&A&D).

When it comes to financial transactions in the technology and the software industry, the amount of deal volume has not only increased, but the overall deal value is getting larger (PwC, 2022). These "tech and talent" deals offer software companies with a significant opportunity for revenue growth, the acquisition of talent (team members/developers), assets (products and customer lists), and the ability to obtain intellectual properties (IP) (Krikhaar, et al., 2018). These acquisitions provide software companies with the ability to expand product offerings to existing customers and to add more capacity to grow into new markets.

Whether growing through new innovation or by financial transactions, when software companies provide better solutions to address complex issues, they generate value for customers. The software companies creating the most value will endure while the others will disappear over time. The same paradigm holds true when it comes to ERP software systems.

Since the beginning of new millennium, with only a bit of a drop-off during the Great Recession, there has been significant dealmaking in the ERP software industry. Among several notable deals, Microsoft acquired Great Plains Software (2001), Axapta (2002), and Navision (2002); Oracle acquired JD Edwards (2003), PeopleSoft (2004), and NetSuite (2016); and Sage acquired Adonix X3 (2005) and Intacct (2017).

These mainstream ERP players have been around for several years and have thousands of middle market customers globally with highly developed software platforms. These mainstream ERP players also have the added pressure of being publicly traded organizations. Being publicly traded means companies have to provide earnings guidance on quarterly performance to Wall Street analysts and return dividends to shareholders.

Outside of the publicly traded high-tech firms in the ERP space, there are several ERP developers backed by private equity. Today, there are about a dozen dominant private equity firms that specialize in the software area of the high-tech segment. These private equity companies acquire software companies with the goal of "re-vamping" them through a process of optimization, which includes increasing sales, enhancing operational efficiency, and often making changes to the executive management team (Gottfried & Cooper, 2018).

In addition, there are small software companies that may be owner managed, usually by an entrepreneur trying to build a software company on an ideal, goal, or vision. In the ERP space, these developers tend to be more focused on industry verticals than on trying to compete with the mainstream horizontal developers. However, in order for these companies to grow and continue to be relevant, they will eventually need to bring investors in from the outside, which may ultimately lead to being in a financial transaction.

With so much growth in the technology industry sector, there is only one true measure of "corporate endurance," and that is survival (Davis, 2014). In order to establish corporate longevity, a company needs to create value for customers on a consistent basis with innovative solutions to complex issues.

If you are about to spend tens of thousands of dollars on a new ERP software system, wouldn't you be more comfortable purchasing it from a developer with established corporate longevity? Before purchasing ERP software, it may be a good idea to understand more about the software developer, such as ownership, business structure, management team, previous experience, and corporate direction. Basically, try to understand where in the hell this company is going to be in the future.

Do the homework by researching these companies. If the company is public, then read the annual report to shareholders. If the company is privately owned, search for articles in trade publications or periodicals reporting on business news, such as the *Wall Street Journal*, *Barron's*, or *Forbes*. Follow the company through social media outlets such as LinkedIn and Twitter.

By taking the time to conduct research and gather information, you will be able to become familiar with the corporate communications, announcements, and general dialogue taking place in the market. All the information gathered through this research should either create a level of comfort or potential concern. The bottom line is that you are investing in the software company behind the ERP software application you are about to adopt, and you need to be confident it is going to be around for a long time.

Summary

A new ERP software system will bring tremendous value to a business by helping to increase success by performing daily transactions, automating processes, gaining efficiency, boosting productivity, and saving valuable time. This new ERP software will become the epicenter of all financial transactions, sales orders, and business activities. But for just how long? Without a crystal ball, it is difficult to see into the future.

There is clearly tremendous change and dealmaking taking place throughout the software marketplace, and that dealmaking is beyond the control of anyone on the outside. However, as a potential buyer of a new ERP software system, it absolutely behooves you to not only evaluate a product you are about to embrace, but also where it comes from and where it may be potentially going in the future. If the software company disappears or a product is sunset, or if there is nobody to provide support on a platform, you are strictly out of luck.

The best way to approach the ERP software evaluation is to equate the acquisition of software to making a long-term investment. In borrowing Philip Fisher's scuttlebutt method, you carefully consider the ERP application from all possible angles. You can gain insight into the current state of the usability, scalability, system integration and product roadmap aspects of the ERP application. You can also evaluate the potential future, such as research and development (innovation), partner channel (support), and corporate longevity (staying power). You are exploring aspects affecting your business today and in the future.

As a CFO, financial controller, or any business leader, you wish to operate as effectively as possible and minimize your exposure. The best way to accomplish these goals during the ERP software evaluation is by thorough alignment of the developer, the product, and your company. The right ERP system will be utilized for many years, or perhaps the entire lifecycle of the company. With this approach, the CFO and financial controller may only have to go through an ERP software evaluation perhaps once or perhaps twice in a full career, which only strengthens processional success and legacy.

The evaluation of a partner is just as important as the selection of the software.

—Unknown

17
SOFTWARE DEVELOPERS WRITE CODE WHILE PARTNERS IMPLEMENT IT

An ERP software system is a complex application consisting of several interdependent parts. It takes expertise and know-how to manage the rollout of an ERP software system. Unless your company is already experienced in deploying ERP software, your team most likely lacks the professional experience, the necessary time, and the skill sets to self-implement it. In this situation, you will need an ERP implementation partner or consultant (value-added reseller) to provide the necessary assistance.

ERP implementation partners field a team of software consultants with business knowledge, communication skills, technical proficiencies, problem-solving abilities, and first-hand experience with complex projects. More importantly, the leading implementation partners have already established a path, or "implementation methodology," for each project, which assists in guiding clients along the ERP journey.

The ERP implementation methodology is based on the client and the partner working together through all phases of the project. Through each step of the journey, each team will have responsibilities for the implementation, which requires everyone to understand what is truly expected from one another. In order to achieve this level of collaboration, a partner has to be proficient in communication (written and verbal), project management, and change management.

Unfortunately, during the ERP software system evaluation, the concept of client and partner working together often takes a back seat. Most businesses and decision makers primarily focus on the features and functionality and put less emphasis on how the system is going to be deployed or supported. They have their checklist of requirements in hand, and they simply want to know whether the software can handle it or not.

The ERP evaluation process needs to be more than just about the software. The client needs to assess the partner as well. The overall success of the project will ultimately come down to how well the client and partner are able to work together through the implementation, and the level of ongoing support will determine the long-term success of the business relationship.

From software evaluation through system implementation, the partner's goal is to build a long-term strategic relationship with each client to achieve the status of a trusted adviser. The partner can provide insight into how the ERP system will perform daily transactions and also handle the most complex business issues. With experience, technical skills, and implementation methodology, the partner can help clients turn their strategic vision of embracing a new ERP system into a reality.

Unfortunately, there are situations in which the relationship with the implementation partner is actively undervalued. It may be due to hubris, inexperience, or underestimating the overall impact a partner may bring to the success of the implementation. Regrettably, it usually has more to do with reluctance to spend money on the proper resources to achieve the best solution. Decision makers who consider ERP software a commodity (rather than a utility) simply prefer taking the least expensive approach to get the job done.

Once a decision maker treats the procurement of ERP software as a commodity, that decision maker will typically pursue several channels to save money or to get *the best deal possible*. This approach ultimately leads to poor choices, such as considering in-house resources for a do-it-yourself (DIY) implementation, engaging short-term, independent contractors (mercenaries), or working directly with the developer on the implementation (Psst! Software developers specialize in writing code and not performing implementations).[1]

The good news is that the majority of CFOs and financial controllers understand the importance of forging relationships with partners, consultants, and advisers to assist in bringing specialized experience and expertise to their organization. When it comes to ERP software applications, it will take expertise from the outside to really help a business excel, so the goal is to find the best implementation partner available.

---

[1] One important channel worth mentioning is the purchasing of the software and implementation services directly from the software developer. With a "sales-first" software organization, a direct sales representative is incentivized to sell software licensing to ensure a quota is met. With the constant pressure to sell, the sales representative will be willing to "cut a deal" on the licensing and provide a low-priced, fixed-bid implementation. The direct sales representative does not care about your implementation because there is no incentive to see your team be successful. While basking in the glory of winning a special discount or special incentive through your "negotiation" and getting "the best price," you have just placed all the heavy lifting on the backs of your own team. Without an experienced implementation partner to assist, your team will likely have to self-implement the ERP system with limited guidance from the developer's professional service team. These ERP implementation missteps often lead to unfortunate consequences down the road that affect the business and team members. If the implementation goes bad, you will feel isolated, frustrated, and angry. This is a hard place to be because when you started this process, the goal was to make things better for the company.

There are several ways to evaluate a potential ERP software partner. Being focused on basic statistical information is useful. Ask questions such as these: How many years have you been in business? How many clients do you have? However, these data points are not enough information when it comes to forging a relationship with an ERP partner for the purpose of increasing your business success.

Going beyond basic information, you should be able to find an ERP implementation partner candidate with experience delivering solutions and perhaps local consulting resources (in your region). However, when it comes to ultimately selecting an implementation partner, these factors may have appeal at face value but should not be the differentiators in determining which partner to engage with on the project.

There are several criteria worth exploring, and they assist in truly evaluating and selecting the best ERP implementation partner. In order to get the necessary information, you will need to "peel the onion" to do the necessary research to discover which firm is the best fit for the ERP implementation and for building a successful long-term business relationship.

As Chad Ergun, CIO of law firm Davis Graham & Stubbs, noted at a monthly meeting of The CFO Leadership Council, "The most successful companies tend to approach their vendor selection with an open mind, a clear understanding of their goals, and a desire to view their software vendors as partners" (Ergun, 2019).

In working toward establishing software vendors as partners, there are several items to consider during the evaluation process to make the best selection possible:

- Critical mass (size, stability, and leadership)
- In-house technical know-how
- Business knowledge and industry experience
- Knowledge assets
- Proven track record

Critical Mass–Size, Stability, and Leadership

According to Merriam-Webster, the definition of critical mass is "a size, number, or amount large enough to produce a particular result" (Merriam-Webster, 2022). There are several valued-added resellers, or partners, in the market that are making the necessary investments to build critical mass in these times of significant change. These partners focus on their core business with the technical readiness to be able to execute so that they can provide clients with the best results.

An ERP partner has to plot a course through the daily challenges of business, such as growing revenue through marketing and sales, continuously recruiting and hiring talent, and demonstrating strategic leadership. However, as a value-added reseller in the ERP space, there are constant technical challenges as well. With technological innovation, software has become less expensive, which has impacted margins; products are continuously being enhanced, changed, or repackaged; and team members have to constantly be learning new skills and competencies.

With continuous change, there has been a shift of ERP partners in the marketplace. There used to be many small *lifestyle* partners and value-added resellers in the market. These partners were focused on generating revenue to self-sustain the business instead of trying to grow the business. In the past, these partners generated a significant *book of business* in their backyards but could not keep up with the changes in the marketplace (technological innovation, certifications, customer satisfaction, etc.). A lot of these lifestyle partners have fizzled, sold out, or are still out there holding out hope that they may someday be acquired.

The partners who have been able to exhibit a significant amount of leadership by adapting to the ever-shifting environment–such as navigating economic turns, embracing technical innovation, and making strategic technical investments—are the folks you are going to want to meet. These partners place an emphasis on recruiting top talent, being open to making strategic acquisitions, using best practices on implementations, and forging long-term relationships with clients.

It is fair to say that a successful relationship with an ERP partner may indeed evolve into a complex business partnership. The most highly successful ERP implementation partners have grown their business to include complementary service offerings in areas such as business intelligence, e-commerce, corporate performance management, and customer relationship management. These complementary capabilities provide even more value to clients beyond ERP software to enhance the long-term strategic relationship.

Furthermore, with advances in technology, communication, and logistics, companies in the middle market have been pursuing global growth opportunities more than ever before. Therefore, it makes considerable sense to select one of the leading accounting firms and IT consultancies that represent several ERP products but that also have significant resources across the United States and internationally.

The first criteria to evaluate in an ERP implementation partner is critical mass and the ability to deliver strong results in several areas over a long period of time. These partners bring considerable consulting resources to bear, not only through the implementation but also in perhaps assisting in other areas of complexity in the future. Just like an army, a reputable partner consulting firm has the organization in place, the leadership, and multiple consulting resources, and it also is driven with the purpose of assisting its clients.

In-House Technical Know-How

When you formally engage with a partner, you want to have confidence in the individual consultants working with your team since you will depend on them to bring the technical know-how to get the job done. These consultants need to have experience, skill, and the expertise to provide the necessary assistance during the ERP implementation and for system support in the future.

At the very root of the partner organization, the consulting team members should reflect the necessary roles of an ERP implementation, which include project managers, application consultants, technical specialists, and software developers. The level of participation of each of these consulting team members will fluctuate from project to project. However, just as with any sports team, these are the playmakers on the field needed for the ERP software implementation.

In addition to having the right role players, these team members need to be trained and certified in their craft. Using the example of an application consultant, these individuals should have participated in the necessary training classes designed for the purpose of understanding and using the software, including setup and configuration of the application. Furthermore, at the conclusion of the training, the application consultant should have received a passing grade on a formal exam to achieve the software certification or certifications.

Similar to application consultants, the application developers need to be certified in programming for the purpose of extending the capabilities of a business software application. The application developer needs to be trained and certified in the application programming language and the underlying database architecture of the ERP system. The application developer can enhance the application for clients by writing code to exist within the software application, which may be maintained for the duration of the system's lifecycle.

In all these areas, as with any team, there will be both junior and senior members, so there will always be varying degrees of skill and experience. Lighter tasks will go to junior members while more sophisticated activities will be assigned to senior members. For example, senior-level consultants have the ability to communicate effectively and interact with the primary stakeholders and senior management of the client to understand the company, the industry, and any political implications within the organization.

In putting the roles, certifications, and tenure to the side for a moment, it is important to know whether the partner relies on full-time employees or independent contractors. Small ERP partners simply cannot afford to employ all the consulting resources needed to perform the tasks required in a complex implementation, so they have to backfill projects with contractors. These ERP partners maintain a personal network of independent contractors all over the world, which they may use on any given project to tackle the most seemingly difficult tasks or custom programming needs during the ERP implementation.

The partners choosing to grow their practice in-house with full-time employees instead of contractors or offshore resources should be highly regarded during the evaluation process, especially if they have application developers on staff. The application developers are truly specialists, with the ability to address complex business issues in the system, create sophisticated system integrations, and truly personalize the system for clients. These resources increase team credibility, especially at a time when so many small, value-added resellers in the marketplace are outsourcing this work.[2]

To connect the dots for you, a partner should have a team of consultants made up of full-time employees with very specific roles, and they should be trained and certified in the ERP software application. More importantly, since these consultants work as a team, they are able to communicate with one another effectively, they

---

[2] Choosing to work with independent contractors or partners who rely on independent contractors can naturally lead to special issues or unforeseen circumstances. For instance, it is unlikely the consultant you work with during the implementation will ever be available after the project is complete. Independent contractors get paid to perform specific tasks, and once those tasks are completed, they move to the next job opportunity. If the project takes longer than originally anticipated, this will create a stressful relationship, and they may simply choose to move on. An independent contractor has no incentive to create a lasting relationship with the client. Once the independent contractor moves to the next project, he or she may be gone forever.

work within the same organized framework, and they are aligned with the goal of bringing their client live on a new ERP.

The technical know-how of a partner is a key differentiator in the evaluation process, so plan to ask questions about the partner consulting team to learn as much about the people and resources you may be working with in the future. If you discover there may be several independent contractors or perhaps multiple partners, then you may consider finding another partner with more in-house technical know-how. The partner consulting firms with the finest in-house technical know-how will be best positioned to navigate the ERP implementation and assist their clients in getting the most out of the system.

Business Knowledge and Industry Experience

Over the last several years, the vast majority of professional service firms in the United States—which includes lawyers, accountants, and consultants—have proclaimed themselves industry focused. These professional service firms have decorated their websites in an effort to highlight each of the industries they serve, promote the professional bios of their industry practice leaders and experts, and exhibit industry-focused thought leadership and industry-focused special events.

When a prospective client reaches out to a professional service firm, the client assumes the firm has experts in given areas of concentration, such as corporate business transactions, compliance, credits and incentives, or ERP software systems. Prospective clients presuppose the firm's experts have deep and wide knowledge in these areas, but the prospective client also wishes to know that the professional service provider understands the nuances of an industry. There is a delicate balance between business knowledge and industry experience in serving clients.

Today there are many ERP partners boasting about their ability to provide consulting resources to clients in specific industries and sectors. Although there are many benefits to *speaking the language*, it is extremely beneficial to be working alongside consultants with experience serving clients from multiple industries, such as service, distribution, manufacturing, health care, nonprofit, and public sector.

Consultants serving clients in multiple industries gain a considerable amount of business knowledge, which is an incredible asset for their clients to draw on. These consultants have a high degree of technical skills, significant experience, and situational insight, and they will be extremely effective in deploying ERP software systems for clients in a wide range of industries.

On a financials-only implementation, a partner with consultants having experience in multiple industries brings a significant amount of value to the client because of their ability to see conditions and situations with "freshness" and have the capacity to think "outside of the box" (Guha, 2014). Because there are so many similar interchangeable processes across industries, such as record to report, procure to pay, and order to cash, these consultants bring innovative ideas to their clients during the ERP deployment.

However, as the ERP implementation transitions from the financials into operations, there will be a need for more specialized consulting resources to play a larger role on the team. In these situations, it will be important to leverage consultants as subject matter experts in areas such as manufacturing, revenue recognition, and project accounting. Therefore, it's important to be mindful that more sophisticated system solutions require a greater need for consultants with applicable industry experience.

As you revisit the ERP blueprint, the foundation may be deployed by consultants with considerable business knowledge while the more complex layers of the implementation will require industry experience. In everyday life, this approach is no different than visiting a primary care physician when you are sick or ill but making an appointment with a specialist if there is a more specific medical condition.

The ERP partner with consultants having industry experience will be able to assist in very detailed phases of the implementation. When it comes to the deployment of manufacturing, project accounting, e-commerce, and revenue recognition, it will be absolutely necessary to work with consultants having relevant industry experience in order to achieve a successful result.

However, it is also important to understand that industry experts have limitations too. Consultants with industry expertise are purely focused on a very specific area of the implementation. It may be harder for the industry expert to see the bigger picture in the deployment of an ERP system, thus requiring the specialist and the generalist to collaborate as a team.

In performing research on ERP partners, strive to get past the decorative facade of industry focus in order to discover the true experience and backgrounds of the consultants working with your team. The best firms and IT consultancies will have a blended team of consultants with significant business knowledge and consultants with industry experience working hand-in-hand.

If the partner plans to staff your ERP implementation project with consultants offering a balance of business knowledge and industry experience, odds are you will be in really good hands. These are the partners able to serve their clients through the ERP implementation and provide support in the years ahead.

Knowledge Assets

Accountants often track and measure tangible or physical assets on a balance sheet, such as stock, equipment, machinery, or property. However, the measure of an ERP partner needs to go beyond the number of consultants and clients. It should extend to an assessment of the partner's ability to cultivate, develop, and deploy "knowledge assets" (Kaplan, 2017). The knowledge assets tapped by the consultant will have a direct impact on the ability to achieve a successful ERP implementation.

Knowledge assets are the amassed intellectual resources within an organization that are used to create value for management, employees, partners, and clients and become a driver for growth and sustainable success. These knowledge assets have had their origin in difficult, challenging, and complex situations in which important lessons have been learned, and that learning has evolved into standard procedures and successful processes. Ian MacMillan, management professor at The Wharton School of the University of Pennsylvania, has said, "Strategic knowledge assets are the pieces of knowledge that make a difference in your ability to compete and prosper" (MacMillan, 2015).

In evaluating prospective ERP partners, the most common examples of knowledge assets are best practices, intellectual property, implementation methodology, data migration templates, and user training guides. In addition to these examples, other notable knowledge assets include thought leadership, published articles, and blog posts on detailed subject matter, all of which provide insight into the skill and expertise of the ERP partner.

The leading ERP partners deploy knowledge assets in a structured fashion; they are woven into the greater sequence of activities taking place during the implementation. As part of the deployment strategy, these knowledge assets are used repeatedly to save time, reduce costs, and successfully manage the project as a company goes through an extremely transformative process.

When a company chooses to fundamentally change the way the business operates and influence the culture of the organization, there will be an element of disruption in going from long-standing manual business processes toward adoption of new processes and automation. To the uninitiated, there are a lot of unknowns for a company taking this significant step, which is why a partner with strong knowledge assets has a better chance of putting systems in place for the purpose of achieving this goal.

For instance, in leveraging best practices and intellectual property, an ERP partner may have already developed software code for a specific industry (microvertical) in the market. Well-developed code or scripts will assist in bridging any potential gaps on the new ERP software platform by leveraging specialized reports, visual dashboards, complex formulas, and personalized, user-defined fields on screens. These personalized features may address several client needs automatically.

Perhaps not as all-encompassing but also extremely valuable, an ERP partner may have a library of software code originally developed for previous clients for very specific business needs that can be reused (all or a portion) for new potential clients. When code becomes widely embraced by several clients, the ERP partner may potentially brand the code as a product or an "accelerator" that may be used on future ERP implementations, including your own to save time or increase the speed of the project (Bridgwater, 2018).

One of the best ways to save time through the ERP implementation is with partner-developed data migration templates. These templates are necessary for the purpose of mapping data from the legacy software to the new ERP system. The objective is for the accounting team to place its critical business data from the legacy software in a specially formatted spreadsheet that can be easily imported into the new ERP system.

Although this sounds simple, the data migration can be an extremely meticulous and time-consuming process. The data migration templates have been developed by the partner to save time, minimize errors, and bring critical business data into the new ERP system. Ultimately, the data-migration-template approach will assist in ensuring data integrity, minimizing business disruption, and increasing efficiency.

In transitioning from data migration to user adoption, the best way for team members to get up to speed on new ERP software and transacting in its environment is through a personalized training strategy and documentation. The training strategy and documentation are knowledge assets developed by the ERP partner to provide the information necessary for your team to prepare for the software transition.

The training documentation may consist of a syllabus, manuals, detailed lesson plans, and hands-on exercises covering the course subject matter and system processes. All these materials may be tailored to be based on the client roles in the system and business processes. Since adults learn through different styles—such as visual, auditory, and kinesthetic approaches—the training strategy needs to encompass step-by-step walk-throughs, detailed instruction, and the opportunity to perform tasks in the system. These materials will accommodate the training model that works best for a partner's clients (on-site with the client, designated training center, online, or a combination of options).

The largest and most important knowledge asset developed by a partner is the ERP implementation approach and methodology. The ERP methodology is a framework of best practices, guidelines, and procedures for the purpose of ensuring a successful implementation.

You may find several ERP partners with very similar implementation methodologies, such as define, discover, design, develop, deploy (Altuit Inc., 2022). Or discovery and planning, design, development, testing, deployment, and ongoing support (Booth, 2021). Or Microsoft's Sure Step methodology: diagnostic, analysis, design, development, deployment, operation (Skelton, 2018). But there are a few points that need to be made.

The ERP partner needs to maintain an implementation methodology that can be illustrated and carried out through action rather than just a payment of lip service to an invisible process. All the consultants and team members should follow the methodology through meetings, written and verbal communications, and documents to provide the client with a framework and overall structure. In addition, the implementation methodology has to be modified and personalized for each client based on the amount of complexity designed into the implementation, the skill sets of the client, and the projected time line. There cannot be a *one-size-fits-all* approach to the implementation.

During the ERP system evaluation process, there will be an opportunity to become acquainted with several partners and their professional service offerings. While taking the opportunity to become familiar with the partner, plan to gain insight into knowledge assets the partner has developed and can deploy during the implementation. A lot of this information will be available during the software demonstrations and presentations, through the partner's website and blog articles, or by simply asking for sample documents and presentation slides. It will be your responsibility to review and familiarize yourself with this information because these knowledge assets will serve as a differentiator between the firms you are evaluating. These are the tools that will ultimately provide structure and guidance through the implementation, save time, reduce errors, and lead to a successful experience.

Proven Track Record

A track record is the total sum of an organization's past successes and failures, which can show how well they have performed in the past and provide an indication as to how well they will perform in the future. Through the software evaluation process, you may meet with several potential partners with relevant experience. However, the partner you want to engage should have a proven track record.

A proven track record demonstrates how much a partner is dedicated to the success of its clients, how good its team is at performing its jobs, and how strong is its commitment to a long-term relationship. The ultimate goal here is to not simply understand what the partner has done in the past but also to understand how the partner will be able to assist your company in accomplishing the strategic goals of today and tomorrow.

By engaging in conversations and discussions with potential ERP partners, you can begin to investigate their track records by strategically requesting more information. In breaking this down further, the primary request is for the partner to provide real examples of successful implementations with high customer satisfaction, excellent technical support, and training and continuing education opportunities.

The partner may provide a statement-of-qualifications document to offer a narrative into past performance, highlighting its strengths, skills, and accomplishments. However, you must keep in mind that this is a document created with the intended purpose of trying to win business. On the other hand, a statement-of-qualifications document can be tremendously valuable since it may be used to initiate the dialogue into how the partner serves its clients over time, and it might be used as a basis for asking very specific questions.

Whether the partner plays the statement-of-qualifications card or not, request a short list of client references to speak with to gain insight into definitive customer success stories. These references should have comparable characteristics to your business, which may include being in the same industry, experience moving from an identical system, or business processes that are similar to yours. On a side note, requesting to speak with a company *just like us* tends to be unrealistic and unproductive unless the partner specializes in delivering microvertical solutions (example: forestry software). In reality, even if the partner has a client just like you, the company background, corporate culture, and technology landscape will be entirely different. (And if that company is a competitor, its representatives will probably be unwilling to speak with you.)

If a client reference believes its system needs are being fulfilled by the partner through understanding, know-how, experience, and skill, it will certainly be an advocate on the partner's behalf and have the willingness to share positive experiences with an absolute stranger. Partners with several clients they can use as references are willing to share familiar company names or logos and online video testimonials, and provide the contact information of past clients to assist in highlighting each partner's past accomplishments.[3]

By having direct conversations with references, you will be able to become more familiar with the partner, gain insight into the level of satisfaction its clients have experienced, and confirm that the partner is properly representing its performance. If a partner has happy clients, odds are that it is a firm exhibiting accountability, reliability, time lines, and good service.

In addition to exploring client references, another way to research a partner's track record is by examining the customer-support options available and what's included with them. Here you can explore the resources dedicated to support (local, onshore, or offshore), the methods of communication (phone, email, live chat, etc.), technology used to promote troubleshooting (ticketing system, knowledge base, web portal, etc.), and corresponding SLA (support metrics, measurements, escalation, etc.).

Post-implementation, your team will typically have questions, concerns, system issues, and technical problems that will need to be resolved, so partner support will have to be dialed in. For instance, a user may receive an unfamiliar error message and not understand its meaning. A team member may get locked out of the system by forgetting the login and password credentials. Perhaps a member of the accounting team has trouble processing a transaction. Whatever the case may be, when this happens, there needs to be a reliable resource

---

[3] A reputable partner respects the time of its valued clients and holds meaningful business relationships in the highest regard. A partner needs to request permission from its client before handing out the client's contact information to a prospect. With so many ERP conversations leading to no decision, it makes sense for the partner to let the dialogue naturally reach the formal proposal stage before accommodating reference requests to ensure the prospective client is not wasting the time of its valued clients. (If having a reference really matters early in the evaluation process, simply request a case study or client testimonial video from the partner and move on with the evaluation. You will be able to get references before signing any contracts.)

to contact and get assistance from in a reasonable amount of time with the expectation of obtaining a resolution.

There will also undoubtedly be times when your team will unexpectedly run into issues with the system, or there may be special extenuating circumstances or deadlines within the business, or even worse, periods of unforeseen severity (economic recession, pandemic, Mother Nature acting up, etc.). If your partner is not committed to providing dedicated support, it may take days for calls to be returned. On the client side, this can lead to missed deadlines, frustration, and perhaps a fractured relationship. It will be absolutely necessary to have a partner ready to provide *air cover* in the form of service, support, and issue resolution when it is needed the most.

In addition to exploring the customer support methods of the partner, the potential client can have a conversation that can naturally lead to the investigation of training and continuing education opportunities offered by the partner. Here you are researching the availability of formal training classes and the consistent delivery of particular activities, such as special events, presentations, and webcasts that are educational, informative, and valuable to system users. The training and continuing education opportunities assist end users with daily performance, increasing skill sets, and gaining knowledge about new features and functionality.

A partner with a successful training strategy will offer multiple options for clients to develop knowledge and skills with respect to the ERP application, including training in-person at the client site, at a designated training center, or over the web using remote technology. The learning experience should be enhanced by course materials developed and distributed by the partner, which should include a syllabus listing the items being covered as part of the class, hands-on exercises, and tests based on specific-use cases in the system.

A partner with a training facility should absolutely be viewed as having a key differentiator. A training facility offers the client the most productive environment for learning without common office distractions, such as email, the crisis of the day, personal interruptions, or general nuisances. Partners offering regularly scheduled training classes provide clients a resource for growing team member skills and onboarding new team members to the system's capabilities. The importance of training to the success of the ERP implementation should not be taken for granted but rather viewed as a critical factor in the partner evaluation process.

In addition to training classes, the partner needs to consistently deliver educational and informative content through in-person special events, technical presentations, and webcasts. These events may cover *tips and tricks*, industry trends, product roadmaps, and introductions to new products and service offerings. While many partners try to deliver content, the best are delivering valuable content to customers on a consistent basis with easy-to-understand formats.

It just takes doing a little bit of homework to measure the track record of prospective partners, which includes asking questions, requesting more information, and following up on client references. With good investigative tactics, you may discover a huge separation between one partner and the rest of the competition. Once again, the track record of the partner provides a strong indication of future performance. Ultimately, the goal is to select the partner to not only assist you through the ERP implementation today but also provide the service and support needed in the future.

Summary

As ERP software mentor Jim Auer said throughout his entire ERP career, which spanned over two decades, "People buy from people." Therefore, the evaluation of a partner is just as important as the selection of the software.

During the evaluation process, the appraisal of the partner needs to be comprehensive and all-encompassing. That begins with the way the consulting team has been built, its technical chops, its industry experience, its special tools that are leveraged, and its demonstration of a proven track record with clients.

All it takes is allocating a little bit of time and research to investigating the potential partner's background by asking questions and requesting more information. In addition, make the effort to follow up with client references. Ask these references direct questions regarding the partner and their first-hand experience with implementation and ongoing support.

The partner you select will work with your team hand in hand by applying leading processes and technical competency to deploy functionality needed to grow your business. The partner will be your guide on the ERP journey and help to turn your strategic vision into reality.

No risk it, no biscuit.

—Bruce Arians

18
HOW TO FORMULATE A
FINAL ERP DECISION

When it comes to reaching a decision point on a new ERP software system, you may need to reflect on the original drivers for this initiative, encapsulate all the information gathered through the process, and incorporate all the careful planning. It began with a strategic vision and the fundamental desire to increase team productivity, but it was solidified by a need to embrace a system that will grow with the business into the future.

In moving from strategic vision to requirements gathering, you should take the time to understand the current challenges by working with team members to identify the "as-is" processes for the organization and each of the departments. The current-state analysis yields specific business requirements from each department, and it identifies manual processes needing automation and time-consuming spreadsheets that have to be eliminated.

With the assistance of several outstanding resources, you recognize the leading ERP providers based on the requirements gathered. Independent research can be gathered from advisory companies such as Gartner (www.gartner.com), Forrester (www.forrester.com), and IDC (www.idc.com). They offer executives reliable market intelligence and detailed research on the leading ERP software systems. These resources provide an incredible amount of relevant information on market leaders, emerging technology trends, industry perspectives, and C-level insights into the particular systems worth evaluating. A decision maker can build a strong business case for undertaking the ERP project based on the information provided by these resources.

In exploring these potential options, invest time in speaking with several partners and consultants regarding the strategic vision and the system requirements. Share with them the highest priorities and biggest challenges. They are best positioned to match the business requirements with the ERP software. Furthermore, they will be able to personalize the product demonstrations so that your team has a better opportunity for gaining familiarity with the *look and feel*, navigation, features, automation capabilities, and pricing.

Through this process, a clear leader may emerge as the best ERP software fit for the business. Taking the time and effort to investigate the various configurations available (user counts and module options) for this system will ensure the initiative meets budgetary expectations.

Armed with as much information as possible, go the extra mile by speaking with client references and professional colleagues to gain insight into the ERP journey from someone who has already been through it. Speaking with client references almost always provides an enlightening experience. Reach out to professional contacts in your network who can offer other essential viewpoints, experiences, and candid feedback that you may not get anywhere else.

Lastly, internal examination may be performed with well-known methods, such as T-Charts (pros versus cons), cost-benefit analysis, or SWOT analysis. With all that information, there is an opportunity to carefully weigh the options in several different ways in order to make a final decision. The good news is that for many, this is the beginning of the ERP journey.

The bad news, however, is that, even getting to this point in the process, there is still no guarantee of moving forward. The reality is that many ERP initiatives lose momentum, stall out, or simply die on the vine. This happens for several reasons, many of which are due to internal influences that, while perceived as business constraints, are just excuses. (It's not the right time. We had a bad quarter. We need to define our processes first. And on and on.)

Too Many ERP Software Initiatives Lead to No Decision

As a decision maker or project influencer, you will have to deal with these pressures or perceived business constrains in order to execute on the ERP strategy. Although a company may need a new ERP software system and a team may have done all the necessary research, it may not be enough. In order to move forward, there needs to be alignment with executives, primary stakeholders, and several team members to steer past any internal influences, business constraints, and straight-up excuses.

Here is where you may be put to the test. Although all situations and circumstances are different, the fact remains that when it comes to making big decisions, everyone encounters obstacles, unique situations, or different personalities. Through determination, the willingness to exhibit diplomacy, explaining the benefits, and spreading excitement through the workplace, a leader can ultimately gain the support needed to move this project forward. As the old proverb from the 1600s goes, "Where there's a will, there's a way" (Grammarist, 2022).

Here are a handful of highly effective steps to follow in decision-making:

- Become an ERP evangelist—share the vision
- Include team members in the decision-making process
- Get buy-in from middle management

- Work closely with the executive sponsor
- Make a call

Become an ERP Evangelist–Share the Vision

Take it upon yourself to *spread the good news* by sharing the vision of moving to a new ERP software system with the team. Clearly communicate how this decision will benefit everyone by saving time, eliminating manual processes, and getting rid of all those nasty spreadsheets.

In daily conversations with team members, take the time to describe how modern ERP software has more features, functionality, automation, integration, and colorful dashboards. Also, emphasize how modern software systems assist everyone in saving time and increasing individual productivity.

Provide examples in which other companies have taken advantage of technology so that team members can conceptualize how they may benefit personally with more work-life balance and professionally by gaining new software skills. The team needs to understand that where there is personal growth and business growth, there is opportunity for achieving the highest levels of success.

As the evangelist, forge a connection with as many team members as possible and share the enthusiasm in moving to a new ERP software system. As team members understand the benefits for themselves and the company, they will become more supportive of this transition and excited about it.

Include Team Members in the Decision-Making Process

The implementation of a new ERP system will have a cultural impact on the business and the team members using it. These are the people counted on each day to get the job done by using the system to process orders, create invoices, make payments, perform journal entries, and generate reports.

These team members are performing tasks within multiple levels of the organization, with varying degrees of responsibility and skill level. When their feedback is welcomed and their voices are heard, team members are more inclined to adapt to change rather than resist it. If team members are not willing to embrace the new software, then this whole project may turn out to be a waste of time and money.

There are several different ways to gather honest feedback from employees and team members so that they have a voice in the decision-making process. There are several techniques—such as using a suggestion box, sending out employee surveys, and forming steering committees—each of which provides a positive channel for communication.

Businesses have used suggestion boxes for over a hundred years to gather comments, questions, and special requests from employees. Whether it is a physical box or a more modern email inbox, the feedback and comments can be directly routed to management for follow-up. In this case, you can establish an ERP suggestion box to uncover special business requirements, current pain points, and lesser-known business processes so that management may incorporate these items into the ERP software evaluation process.

In addition to a suggestion box, surveys are a tremendous way for gathering information on employee perceptions in the workplace. The simple action of sending a survey to team members sends a positive message that their feedback is valued and is being considered by management. Here you can send a survey with questions regarding an ERP software to gauge the aspects of the system and implementation that people feel are the most important.

A survey will be able to reach everyone on the team and unearth concerns, such as whether the new software poses a threat to anyone's job or whether training will be provided so that everyone will be able to use the new software system. The data gathered from the surveys can be consolidated, aggregated, and addressed by management so that all employees not only have a better feeling toward the initiative but also believe they play a key role in its success.

Another way to include team members in the decision-making process is by forming an ERP steering committee. The ERP steering committee should be comprised of senior executives, department managers, key team members, and information technology representatives for the purpose of choosing the primary objectives. The ERP steering committee will be able to provide a foundation for prioritizing business requirements, create an internal roadmap for the strategy, and communicate directly with team members. The interaction between the steering committee and team members will help to get everyone aligned during the software evaluation and implementation process.

A new ERP system will impact the everyday lives of team members, so it makes a lot of sense to include them in the decision-making process. Incorporating multiple channels of communication throughout the organization significantly aids in the success of this project, and more importantly, it gets folks on board with moving forward.

Get Buy-In from Middle Management

All businesses have a hierarchy and structure for making decisions. In the middle market, the organization chart typically has an owner/ president/CEO, CFO, vice president of operations, and perhaps a vice president of sales at the top. There may be middle managers at the next level below who are in charge of sales orders, purchasing, and inventory.

While middle market companies have traditionally purchased software by department, a modern ERP software system can unify multiple divisions within an organization. Since the goal of the ERP initiative is to cross departmental boundaries and eliminate separate silos of information, there needs to be buy-in from middle management.

As middle managers are nestled in between the executive team and the employees, they are in a unique position to be able to support special initiatives or potentially take a hardline *torpedo* stance against them. Therefore, a careful approach is needed to gain the necessary buy-in on the ERP initiative.

With middle managers, it is important to be candid, straightforward, and to the point when discussing the ERP initiative. When presented with detailed information on the needs and the benefits of a new system, middle managers will reach the right conclusions on their own and understand why this needs to be done.

Furthermore, plan to break down the larger ERP initiative into much smaller portions so that there is a more manageable commitment of time and resources and to alleviate any concern of massive change. If you take the time to explain the activities, goals, and objectives for their departments, middle managers will be able to envision a realistic path for achieving successful results.

Lastly, incorporate the thoughts and feedback from middle managers into the ERP initiative. A top-down approach to the initiative often leads to resistance. By having an open dialogue and demonstrating the willingness to listen, middle managers will be indispensable in gaining acceptance and full cooperation.

Middle managers have the ability to be positive, negative, or even indifferent to the ERP initiative. You need for them to be positive, proactive, and playing a key role in the strategy and execution. In order to proceed with the ERP initiative, it will be important to carefully craft a strategy to work with middle managers to gain their participation and essential buy-in.

Work Closely with the Executive Sponsor

The one person ultimately responsible for the strategic vision and direction for the ERP project is often referred to the as the executive sponsor. The executive sponsor is the person giving the final approval on project funding and furnishing a signature on the contracts for the software and its implementation. The executive sponsor needs to play an active role in the ERP initiative from the beginning of the evaluation process through the implementation of the project—from kickoff to going live.

Whether the executive sponsor is the owner, president, CEO, or CFO, this person is responsible for maintaining the strategy of the organization, owning the business case for the project, and managing potential costs, risks, and benefits of the ERP implementation. In addition, the executive sponsor provides leadership in establishing alignment with other executives, middle managers, and team members to ensure this initiative supports the culture and values of the organization.

As noted by the role in the organization, this is a person with a demanding job requiring plenty of time management to play an active role throughout the organization. In this regard, the stakes are no different. In order to keep things moving forward, the executive sponsor often has to rely on the most dependable subordinate to play an active role in the ERP initiative.

Assuming the executive sponsor is the CFO, the financial controller will play a key role throughout the ERP software evaluation processes. The financial controller will most likely be organizing the meetings, conversations, demonstrations, and requests for pricing. The financial controller will work closely with the CFO throughout the entire process to ensure strategic alignment.

When it comes to making the final decision, there is a strong chance the financial controller will have to ask the CFO to provide a signature on the contracts. This process is indicative of the close working relationship between the CFO and the financial controller and their mutual desire to perform their responsibilities as effectively as possible so that the company reaches its full potential.

The executive sponsor will be able to navigate ebbs and flow of the ERP initiative, including providing direct communications, interactions at all levels of the organization, and overcoming any potential challenges. The executive sponsor will ultimately provide the final approval to move forward on the ERP initiative.

Make a Call

Business decision makers are responsible for making choices that affect the organization and the team. Most decision makers got in their position by exhibiting leadership and making difficult choices throughout their career, whether by executing on strategy, operations, or tactics to achieve positive results.

However, there are still many leaders out there who are simply afraid to make big decisions. They are waiting for the right situation, better timing, or a more favorable economic climate, or they simply become discouraged by perceived business constraints.

As French writer and activist Voltaire once wrote, "The perfect is the enemy of the good" (Dominguez, 2013). Whatever the situation may be, if you are waiting for a perfect set of circumstances in anything in life, then nothing will ever get accomplished. Instead of falling into this trap, stay focused on getting things done.

Here is where you need to relax, revisit the goals and priorities of the project, and have confidence in your resources, including your team members and the assistance of experienced consultants. Tap into your inner "eye of the tiger" (Survivor, 1982) to visualize success and "make a call" (Willink & Babin, 2015).

Once you make a call, you can confidently move forward by signing contracts and mobilizing your team for a hard but rewarding project that will take your business to the next level.

Summary

The process of decision-making is never easy, even for the most highly experienced professionals. There are always going to be fear and anxiety over potentially making a mistake, going down the wrong path, or having to take responsibility for an unforeseen corporate disaster.

However, the delays and excuses associated with not moving forward with a new ERP software system usually tend to be based on old-fashioned procrastination. Even worse, there are times in which procrastination is proudly portrayed by decision makers with an aura of prudence that is a total sham (Ridler, 2019).

As legendary football coach Bill Walsh eloquently wrote in his book *The Score Takes Care of Itself*, "Do all the right things to precision, and the score will take care of itself" (Walsh, et al., 2010). When you do all the right things during the ERP software evaluation process, there is a greater chance the final decision will lead to achieving the desired results.

Always remember that it is usually better to do something rather than nothing at all, including when it comes to moving to a new ERP system. The best leaders gather the information needed, ensure there is alignment with people and resources, and then exhibit decisiveness in making the decision to move forward.

If perhaps the decision turns into a mistake, then this becomes a corporate-world lesson and an opportunity for professional growth. With a little bit of time and effort, things have a way of working themselves out.

More often than not, the right decision will be made, and the company, team, and culture will ultimately benefit from it. There is nothing better than being able to play a key role in leading your company through significant growth and change by implementing innovative solutions that increase business success.

You have brains in your head. You have feet in your shoes. You can steer yourself any direction you choose.

—*Dr. Seuss*

19
THE MOST COMMON ERP
TRAPS TO AVOID

It takes a lot of effort to generate enough momentum to bring your team through a full ERP system evaluation. There will be several meetings and conversations for the purpose of defining requirements, getting introduced to ERP consultants and partners, participating in software demonstrations, and ultimately reaching a final decision to move forward.

Although the vision of eliminating time-consuming tasks, automating processes, and gaining real-time insight into the business has been a catalyst for the initiative, it may not be enough to finish it. While the ultimate goal may seem to be within grasp, it can all slip away at the end by getting sidetracked for a number of reasons, including timing, budget dollars, or indecision.

Believe it or not, there are several potential self-inflicted issues that lay the foundation for indecision. As Admiral Ackbar proclaims in the movie *Return of the Jedi*, "It's a trap!" (Star Wars: Episode

VI—Return of the Jedi, 1983). These potential self-inflicted traps are easy to recognize and should be avoided as much as possible.

Here are the most common traps to avoid in the ERP software evaluation process:

- Being cheap
- DIY ERP—reluctance to outsource
- Everything has to be compared apples-to-apples
- Waiting for the right time
- No decision

Being Cheap

The effort to manage and control business costs is responsible and normal. However, there are times in which a business can and should spend money, especially when it comes to increasing efficiency and productivity. It is safe to say that in moving to a modern ERP, this is no time for being cheap.

Being cheap can affect the success of the ERP initiative in several ways, including settling for a mediocre software package over a slightly more expensive, robust software package. Another way of being cheap is purchasing the right software package but then skimping on the necessary number of user licenses and software modules. In this circumstance, there is less functionality being deployed to the least number of team members possible.

On the ERP implementation front, being cheap can affect the success of the overall project. The insistence on removing critical tasks from the implementation to lower the overall price point can drastically affect the outcome of the project. The removal of necessary activities such as project management, user acceptance testing, data validation, user training, or go-live cutover support can each negatively affect the chances for a successful implementation.

It is fascinating to watch experienced business professionals believe they are *heroes* for being cheap, especially when they are proactively compromising the ERP initiative. It is one thing to be a tough negotiator to get a fair price on software and a reasonable billable rate on professional services. It's another to simply be cheap by throwing the necessary software and critical steps of the implementation overboard.

If the game plan is to save dollars on the ERP initiative by cutting corners in every conceivable way possible, then do not expect a successful outcome. Saving a few bucks by cutting back on software or skimping on critical aspects of the project only leads to future headaches and troubles. In the long run, being cheap can eventually become very expensive.

Whether it's ownership, executive team members, or the finance department trying to cut corners, it simply shows a lack of commitment to winning. Seriously, don't be cheap here; be cheap somewhere else. Before beginning the process, put together a reasonable budget for the initiative and stick to it. The dollars spent on a robust ERP system along with full implementation creates a path for achieving success in business.

Reluctance to Outsource—Do-It-Yourself ERP

There are businesspeople and decision makers reluctant to outsource special projects to consultants. Perhaps the mindset is based on the culture of the organization, lack of knowledge, a bad previous experience, or just being cheap. Whatever the case may be, these businesses have a do-it-yourself mentality and believe an ERP implementation can be performed in-house.

After meeting with several consultants and solution providers, the decision maker might purchase the ERP software as a single transaction but choose to perform the implementation in-house. The decision maker might proclaim with confidence, "We have a person on our team who is going to implement the system for us. She's done it several times. This person is going to do the work. We'll call you if we need any assistance."

There is no doubt there are a lot of people with tremendous skills and experience with the demonstrated ability to own several tasks of the implementation. However, to entrust one person on the team to run a project of this magnitude is not practical and is unrealistic. There are several moving parts that require multiple skill sets, technical specialties, and professional experience. There are no do-it-yourself YouTube videos for this type of project.

The DIY ERP lead person will have a huge amount of work to do. Without manpower, the lead person will need to be the project manager, subject matter expert, data migration specialist, and trainer all in one—from initial kickoff to going live. In addition to having to do all the heavy lifting, this person will have to be direct, demanding, and fully committed to assigning tasks to peers, colleagues, and perhaps managers. Good luck telling management there are gaps in their business processes.

Furthermore, the DIY ERP lead person will not have the benefit of a proven deployment approach, methodology, or any project structure based on best practices to keep the project on track within a reasonable time line. This approach will only lead to a failed implementation, long-term heartburn, and an unrealized vision. As Mr. T says in the motion picture *Rocky III*, "My prediction? . . . Pain." (Stallone, 1983).

Real example—health-care industry (startup): The executive team and private equity investors believe they can save thousands of dollars by having the controller perform the ERP implementation. After all, the controller previously worked for an ERP reseller, so he is qualified to deploy the new ERP system.

The idea of engaging with any consulting resources to assist is a complete afterthought. After a few months, the controller decides to pursue another opportunity (probably looking for something less stressful), thus leaving the company with a less-than-functional ERP system.

With the system unable to perform a simple check run to pay vendors, the departure pushes the company into a mission-critical situation. Desperate to pay vendors in a timely fashion and to have a fully operational system, the executives and investors finally engage a consulting firm to assist with carrying out daily accounting activities and with performing a full in-place system implementation.

The reluctance to outsource served up real-life negative consequences, which proved to be tremendously more costly than having the implementation performed correctly in the first place. Putting good people into a bad system is a recipe for disaster.

It's hard enough for a company to be successful. There is no reason to self-inflict such a painful situation on the business. Get over the reluctance to outsource and focus on the core business. Engaging with a partner or consulting firm and working with experienced consultants provide the best chance for success.

Everything Has to Be Compared Apples-to-Apples

It is important to understand the licensing and pricing structure for each product and service offering as part of the ERP system evaluation. Unfortunately, many decision makers try to analyze software products and services through an *apples-to-apples* comparison as an orderly means for determining the best solution. The goal is to visually compare similar products and solutions on a spreadsheet by placing all the software and service values in rows and columns to capture as much information as possible.

However, when software pricing is presented by a partner or a developer, it is based on the entire system configuration. All software licensing models and pricing are going to differ in some form or fashion, so trying to break this information up into user types, price-per-user license, separate modules, and their functionality can become cumbersome. Furthermore, the ERP system may have a bundled pricing, basic or advanced functionality (with licensing prerequisites), and special discounts available.

In addition, all ERP implementation partners are different when it comes to skills, experience, resources, geography, methodologies, and billable rates. While there are no too partners alike, they all have a common dislike to have their time wasted. When it becomes apparent partners are being compared with one another, the best-performing partners may decide to withdraw from consideration instead of becoming "column fodder" due to the higher rates of their highly experienced consultants (Apollo, 2019).

In trying to break up all the information gathered into a detailed comparison, you can become focused on making micro-comparisons on minute details. The more granular this endeavor becomes, the less value it brings to the process. The goal of making an apples-to-apples comparison often turns into "analysis paralysis" (Chen, 2021).

Instead of getting lost in the matrix, remain focused on the personalized aspects of the original strategic vision and the detailed business requirements. If you participated in all the meetings, demonstrations, and conversations, you and your team should be able to make a clear choice on the right approach for moving forward. Save the apples-to-apples approach for the used car lot. How do you like them apples?

Waiting for the Right Time

There is an old English proverb: "Good things come to those who wait." It means that people with the ability to practice patience and work hard will eventually attain their goal (PoemAnalysis.com, 2022). While this approach works well in a lot of areas of human development and professional growth, this is not necessarily the best approach for achieving rapid success in business.

Unfortunately, there are a lot of decision makers waiting for the right time before moving to a new ERP system. In these situations, the reasoning may be based on either real or perceived internal business constraints, such as fiscal budget limits, restrictions due to the time of the year (busy season, holidays, etc.), physical limitations (servers, hardware, social distancing, etc.), or environmental influences (recession, war, etc.). These limits of discomfort may be characterized as internal (budget, timing, and any physical limitations) or external (environmental influences).

In tackling internal examples first, remember that due to the continuous nature of business, you already deal with these types of limitations, constraints, and circumstances on a daily basis. New orders are placed, transactions need to be processed, month-end close happens every four weeks, detailed reports need to be generated, and decisions have to be made in a timely fashion. These are all examples of actions that are already taking place each day within these limitations.

From an external perspective, just looking over the past twenty years, there have been economic recessions, industry bubble bursts, terrorist attacks, stock market flash crashes, super storms, tumultuous political elections, bank bailouts, and a global pandemic. These events each have had an effect on the economy. These external influences often decrease the willingness to take on special projects and corporate buying decisions.

When you experience limitations in life, whether personal or professional, you need to embrace the words written by best-selling author Marie Forleo, "everything is figureoutable" (Forleo, 2020). When you face obstacles, challenges, and limitations each day, there is always a means by which a goal can be accomplished. This is where you place good old-fashioned tools, such as ideas, wisdom, and creativity, into action.

If the concerns are budgetary, then set a preliminary budget for the software and implementation project. The best approach is to take the preliminary ballpark estimate from the ERP partner and multiply it by 1.5. (If the ballpark estimate is $100,000, then multiply by 1.5 and get an internal estimate of $150,000.) Use the internal estimate and not the ballpark estimate for the budget for funding for the project. It is always better to ask for more on the front end so that there are no budget issues on the back end.

When there are concerns about timing, create a time line for the project. The ERP consultant will provide a preliminary time line, such as three to four months or four to six months for the project, based on the functionality being deployed. Use the calendar software of your preference, such as Microsoft Outlook, and pick a go-live date that works best for the schedule. Once there is a date in mind, then simply work backward, navigating around seasonal business peaks, month-end closings, holidays, and vacations. Provide the team members with enough time to perform their daily tasks and responsibilities plus perform work on the ERP project.

In regard to physical limitations, such as hardware and multiple locations, cloud-based tools and technology may provide a remedy. If there are infrastructure limitations, then servers can be *spun up* in the public cloud through Microsoft, Google, Amazon, or any private cloud data center. If people are located in separate offices, there are several remote access tools available as well, such as Microsoft Teams, Google Hangouts, and Zoom. Through all these cloud-based resources, team members may be aligned and software systems may be deployed without any physical limitations.

Lastly, when it comes to environmental influences, obviously there is a level of sensitivity to businesses directly affected by recessions, powerful storms, the price of oil, or global pandemics. These are situations that create challenges for businesses and require patience, resolve, and perseverance. However, there will always be macro and micro political, social, and economic factors that are beyond your control. So, unless the business is directly impacted by one of these events, they should not affect the ability to make decisions.

Examples of Twenty-First Century External Influences:

- Early 2000s recession (2001)
- Dot-com bubble
- 9/11 terrorist attacks
- Great Recession (2007–2009)
- Sub-prime mortgage crisis
- US housing bubble
- Automobile industry crisis
- $700 billion banking bailout
- The post-crisis bull run (2010–2021)
- COVID-19 pandemic (2020–2021)

There will never be a right time to move to a new ERP, so stop waiting for it to happen. Get started now by putting ideas, creativity, and wisdom in motion. Create a fiscal budget and time line, take advantage of tools and technology, and stop worrying about the outside world. With the right amount of time and proper financing, there should be confidence in moving forward and turning the ERP project into your finest hour.

No Decision

The phrase "no decision" has one specialized meaning in the sport of baseball. It refers to a starting pitcher exiting a game without achieving a win or a loss (Baseball-Reference.com, 2022). However, it is a term frequently used in the software business too. In this case, a business begins to evaluate new ERP software systems, dedicates significant time and energy to it, and then, for whatever reason, the process simply leads to no decision.

Getting to a no decision is perhaps a consequence of many different circumstances, some of which may in fact be well justified, such as C-level turnover, raising capital, recession, etc. Yet when the reasoning is just a business cliché—such as "the timing is bad," "we had a slow quarter," or "we are going to just push this out a year"— then procrastination is being superficially disguised as supposed prudence (Ridler, 2019).

In spite of any momentum generated by discovery meetings, software presentations, or excited team members, procrastination can come about because of fear of making the wrong decision. In the evaluation of ERP systems, when there is no decision, there is a waste of time and money and the ruination of an opportunity to seize upon valuable momentum.

Instead of being fearful of making a big software decision and pushing the decision out to sometime in the future, an executive might find that the best place to begin is by making a smaller decision first. Moving forward with smaller, easier steps first will assist in maintaining a level of momentum and generating excitement.

For example, it may be a good idea to engage a consultant for a proof of concept (Singaram & Jain, 2018). A proof of concept incorporates aspects of the design and client data so that the client can test an ERP system. Taking the time to gain more familiarity with the system in advance may assist in creating a level of comfort, alleviating any concerns, and identifying any perceived gaps in the software. All of this may be achieved before committing to the purchase of the software or going through with a full implementation.

Another approach is to take advantage of a design-first engagement. A design-first engagement is an approach based on the carving out of the initial phases of the implementation into a separate project. The initial phases of an implementation are focused on the system design and the creation of a project plan. This process will assist in creating a detailed roadmap for a phased deployment approach and ensure corporate alignment on the project. Similar to a proof of concept, a design-first project may be performed prior to committing to a software purchase or full implementation project.

In these examples, you are making much smaller, easier decisions first rather than making one big decision, or even worse, no decision. By taking these smaller steps first, there is an opportunity to build a cadence with a consultant, move the project forward with the team and organization, and begin to see positive results. Smaller decisions naturally create momentum, provide confidence, and lead to the courage to successfully make a big decision in the future.

Summary

As mystery writer Raymond Chandler wrote, "There is no trap so deadly as the trap you set for yourself" (Chandler, 1953). It is best to have a keen awareness of these potential ERP traps so that you can plan to navigate a path to avoid them.

Once again, being cheap, trying to compare everything to the lowest common denominator, waiting for the right time, trying to do it yourself, or making no decision are all everyday ERP traps. Over time, the implications of these traps can have a detrimental effect on the business, especially as team members turn over, the marketplace evolves, and technology improves.

Meanwhile, the business will continue to deal with old, stagnant processes, half-implemented systems, or the same antiquated system from years ago. When these traps happen, they self-inflict harm on the organization, and that can stand in the way of a successful outcome for many years.

All of these traps can be avoided with the right approach and the planning of a reasonable fiscal budget, allocating the proper amount of time, and dedicating the necessary resources from the team. The big question is whether there is a willingness to avoid these traps.

SECTION VIII
THE ERP IMPLEMENTATION

Individual commitment to a group effort—that is what makes a team work, a company work, a society work, a civilization work.

—*Vince Lombardi*

20
A SUCCESSFUL ERP JOURNEY REQUIRES LEADERSHIP, ACCOUNTABILITY, AND TEAMWORK

The ERP journey is based on the effective navigation of technology, business processes, and people. During the ERP evaluation, it is natural to get caught up in software features, functionality, and pending costs. However, you can spend an insufficient amount of time preparing your own team members for the effort they need to contribute to the project for it to be successful.

As with any organization, there needs to be executive sponsorship at the top along with designated team members playing critical roles throughout the project. The team members on the project team need to include a project team leader and several subject matter experts representing technology, finance, and any of the departmental groups involved in the deployment, such as supply chain and manufacturing.

In addition to the project lead and the subject matter experts, there will be several team members who will have to play a critical role in the implementation by testing the system and actively participating in the training sessions. These are going to be the people using the new system each day, so they have to play a proactive role in the implementation.

While the level of participation for each team member will vary through the project, the true path to success is through leadership and accountability. *New York Times* bestselling author Kevin Kruse defines leadership as "a process of social influence to maximize the efforts of others to achieve a common goal" (Kruse, 2013). Whether leadership is exhibited by the president, CEO, CFO, or financial controller, the executive sponsor of the ERP implementation has to set the tone by preparing team members for the digital transformation that lies ahead. It begins with communicating a clear vision and approach so that people can comprehend the level of commitment to improvement.

The executive sponsor has to exhibit leadership by establishing realistic expectations with the team, including meeting in-person to discuss the goals and objectives of the project. The executive sponsor needs to ensure everyone understands so that there is agreement and commitment. The conversation should include addressing the amount of time needed to be dedicated to the project, the increase in daily workload, and the expectation of taking personal accountability for performance and execution. Team members have to understand the level of effort necessary for making a significant contribution to the project, and they need to accept responsibility for accomplishing these business goals.

Furthermore, in order to achieve the goals and objectives for implementing a new ERP system, team members will need to be action-oriented, and they will have to bring a positive attitude. There has to be a willingness of the team members, regardless of title, to learn and grow through the implementation.

When everyone on the team is working toward a common goal, team members are dependent on one another to perform and execute the best way they can. This means actively working on assigned tasks, having an openness to making mistakes, and being thoughtfully engaged in project meetings.

While several team members may be excited at the opportunity to take things to the next level by increasing efficiency, enhancing collaboration, and becoming more productive in the workplace, there will always be some critics on the team. Ultimately, this process is going to mess with somebody's "comfort zone," so it makes sense to be ready for negative attitudes and potential resistance (Walsh, et al., 2010).

To take this thought a bit deeper, when it comes to participation in any transformation, people naturally bring *human elements*, such as skills, talent, drive, and raw emotion to the game. These human elements need to be embraced. When human elements are not embraced, there is a diminished chance for success. As Michael Hendrix has said, "The biggest hurdle to an organization's digital transformation effort is people" (Hendrix, 2020).

You may have to accept that there will be team members with deeply ingrained, bad organizational habits. Or they may simply dislike anything new or unfamiliar (neophobia). Whatever the case may be, once identified, a potential negative situation has to be transitioned into a positive one as soon as possible, or it can become disruptive to the team and the overall success of the project.

There is nothing worse than a team member spreading negativity, sucking momentum from the project, and creating distrust on the team as it works toward accomplishing a strategic business objective. These people could be essentially on the brink of sabotaging the success of the project. If a team member is not willing to play a productive role in the software implementation, that team member may need to be moved off the project (or possibly be removed from the team).

Most *naysayers* are usually acting out on one of the following emotions: fear of the unfamiliar, job insecurity, or general stubbornness. Whatever the case may be, once identified, the negative emotions can be overcome with reason and positive reinforcement. Given a chance, even the least enthusiastic of team members can eventually be won over.

When it comes to fear of the unfamiliar, it is only natural to have anxiety over anything new, especially if a team member has been comfortable operating with the status quo environment for several years. This is the same emotion a person experiences when going to school for the first time, moving into a new home, or having to meet new people. The good news is that although it may feel uneasy at first, over time people adapt and adjust to the changes and become more comfortable in situations.

Team members need to understand that the same paradigm shift will also take place within the new ERP software environment. They just have to be willing to make the effort and allow a reasonable amount of time to experience the benefits.

If the issue is job insecurity, people have to understand there will never be a guaranty that anyone will be able to work at a job as long as desired. However, it is unlikely the ERP software package is going to downsize a position. If anything, the ERP system will assist team members in becoming more productive and proactive in the workplace.

Having experience on any leading ERP system is an extremely valuable skillset in the marketplace. Instead of seeing this as a threat to their job security, team members should see this as a great opportunity to enrich their skillsets on a modern system and as a chance to build "career capital" to become a more marketable professional (Vanderkam, 2012).

Lastly, there may be general stubbornness of an individual determined not to change, However, the decision to move to a new ERP system will have already been made. The situation would be no longer just business as usual. Stubbornness cannot stand in the way of forward progress, and complacency would not be acceptable.

There has to be a willingness to trust in the process, which includes putting forth a right effort and attitude. The time being invested in the new software system will ultimately assist everyone in being more successful in the near future, so this person needs to quickly decide whether to be a part of it or not. As one begins to achieve success through this project and experiences positive tangible results, this will hopefully lead to a feeling of pride and the satisfaction of achievement.

Special Incentives Create Positive Vibes

In addition to relying on personal accountability and positive reinforcement, the ERP advocate can also turn to other ways to motivate people, such as using special incentives. While not a common practice when it comes to ERP implementations, using incentives will assist in driving employee behaviors in the workplace, especially when it comes to special initiatives, such as enabling active participation in the transformation (Panorama Consulting Group, 2013).

In a current state in which teams have effectively performed their jobs by maintaining corporate cultural norms through legacy software systems, manual processes, and hand-me-down knowledge, transformation represents a seismic shift in business operations. You are now asking your team to perform daily activities in the current state and perform special tasks for the purpose of moving toward a more desirable and efficient future state. The best way to get there is by motivating people to perform these special tasks to help the company reach this objective.

As part of the ERP implementation, there may be several goals of the organization, such as keeping the project within a reasonably planned timeline, staying within the original budget for the project, or achieving the ultimate positive outcome of going live on the new system. These are straightforward organizational objectives that may be used as goals to incentivize team members and drive very specific behaviors into action.

As mentioned earlier, the level of participation for each team member will vary throughout the project, so incentives need to be aligned with the roles and the responsibilities of the project team. Bonuses, rewards, and even pats on the back will inspire team members to be more productive, which means there will be a greater likelihood for the project to be successful.

Just remember to keep the approach simple, straightforward, and impactful for team members by following the suggestions below:

- Align the goals of key team members with the successful outcome of the ERP project
- Recognize individuals doing an outstanding job all throughout the process
- Provide bonuses, rewards, or kind notes for accomplishing successful project milestones

In taking this approach, you are encouraging teamwork and recognizing individuals for their increase in productivity, which helps the organization achieve a strategic goal. In addition to providing incentives, bonuses, and rewards, there are ways to simply create an aura of excitement within the organization for ERP implementation as another way of getting the most from your team.

Build Camaraderie

In addition to providing incentives, you need to reenergize the team by creating a level of enthusiasm throughout the organization for this journey. Remember, you are no longer maintaining the corporate cultural norms. You are embarking on a future state of transformation, which requires the revitalization of mind and spirit.

Here you can influence the overall environment by fostering camaraderie among team members. As team members grow together through the ERP implementation, they will support one another as productive members on the team. When team members have a deep sense of affiliation with one another, they are driven to take positive actions that benefit the business or, in this case, the ERP project.

Once again, it requires the executive sponsor to socially influence the corporate atmosphere so that there is an environment for building camaraderie among team members. This may be achieved through increasing general communications, specifying goals, creating open lines of individual dialogue and feedback, and socializing as a team.

Here is a short list of suggestions for building camaraderie among team members during the ERP journey:

- Announce the ERP strategy at a corporate meeting and then provide regular updates
- Promote corporate team building activities around the implementation
- Celebrate both small wins and large milestones with everyone
- Schedule team social events with snacks, food, or drinks
- Listen to feedback

There is nothing better than creating a level of excitement with the team members so that they are goal-driven, collaborating, and productively working toward achieving a successful ERP outcome. In speaking of camaraderie, Christine Riordan, president of Adelphi University and an expert in leadership development, writes, "It's about creating a common sense of purpose and the mentality that we are in it together" (Riordan, 2013).

With this approach, team members will begin to trust in the process and increase their level of engagement throughout the course of the ERP project. With an environment that fosters camaraderie, a team will be able to promote organizational change and achieve transformation.

Have an Explorer's Mentality

The project team plays a significant role in the implementation by reporting to the executive sponsor or sponsors, being the primary point of contact with the consultants, and coordinating tasks with team members. With a substantial amount of work going into planning, scheduling, and execution of the ERP implementation, this role is incredibly challenging for anyone.

The best way to navigate the journey is by having an explorer's mentality. As with many explorers, elements such as focus, preparation, creativity, and learning will be needed throughout the course of the ERP journey. As Jeff Bezos, the former CEO of Amazon, once said in reference to his corporate culture, "We have an explorer mentality, so we like to go pioneering" (Choi, 2013).

As an explorer, a person intentionally travels unfamiliar areas to encounter and learn as much as possible. On the ERP journey, the project team will have to navigate unfamiliar situations, work with unique personalities with different perspectives, embrace and learn new technology, and transform manual processes into automation. All along the way, there will be issues, challenges, roadblocks, and obstacles both internally and externally.

Externally, team members will need to steer through a situation containing a lot of unknowns, work with a team of consultants with several skillsets, follow an unfamiliar implementation methodology, and have to get comfortable taking ownership of a new ERP software system.

Although there will be a project plan to create the framework for the implementation, special circumstances may arise at any time. When unearthing new and unknown system requirements, team members may find that the solutions may evolve, and the project can deepen. This can naturally lead to expansion of project scope or an impact on the timeline.

Internally, team members will need to work through corporate elements, such as items affecting budget, timeline, and strategic objectives. There may be personnel issues dealing with team members who are inexperienced, slow moving, or not detailed in performing tasks. There will also be significant need to provide ongoing communications, such as project updates, solicitation of feedback from end users, and management of any items of concern so that everyone is continuously on the same page.

In having an explorer's mentality on the ERP journey, the project team can have a big-picture perspective while working on detailed tasks. The team members can be smart and highly experienced but still learning as much as possible along the way. When the project team focuses on execution, collaboration with others, and learning as much as possible, the ERP journey moves forward.

Doug Burgum, in his former role as president of Fargo, North Dakota-based Great Plains Software and later president of Microsoft Business Solutions, would routinely intertwine exploration themes into his keynote addresses for annual customer events. Whether it was Stampede (in Fargo) or Microsoft Convergence, his keynotes highlighted notable explorers such as Lewis and Clark (west of the Mississippi River), Ernest Shackleton (in the Antarctic), and the Wright brothers (with flight) to demonstrate how life, discovery, and organization are all journeys. As Burgum, a pioneer in the ERP industry and current governor of North Dakota, warmly noted at Convergence in 2005, "Humankind has been pursuing journeys since the very, very beginning" (Burgum, 2005).

In having an explorer's mentality, every task and activity completed will be a momentum-generating win in moving the ERP journey forward. With this approach, executive sponsors, primary stakeholders, and team members will experience the success of turning strategic vision into a reality.

Summary

It is absolutely reasonable for a company to focus the majority of its ERP software evaluation on features and functionality. However, time needs to be spent preparing for the implementation because once the ink dries on the contracts, the sales process quickly transitions to the ERP implementation.

ERP blogs, websites, and whitepapers highlight the importance of project management, methodology, training, and testing. While this information is valuable and perhaps critical, you cannot lose sight of the importance of the human element.

In working through transformation, Tammie Pinkston has pointed out, "Ignoring the people element is a recipe for failure, ensuring employees will provide more resistance and take longer to adapt" (Pinkston, 2022). This is why it's important to embrace people in ways most of us can understand.

The executive sponsor has to be focused on providing leadership, but the sponsor also plays a significant role in what football coach Bill Walsh referred to as "creating the culture of the team" (Walsh, et al., 2010). There are several ways to get people excited, such as offering special incentives and building camaraderie across the entire organization.

All these tools and resources need to be leveraged, but what is also needed is an emphasis on an explorer's mentality. Here is where team members can take on several important traits, such as optimism, patience, and courage (Tillard, 2020).

Hold the vision. Trust the process.

—Unknown Author

21
THE ERP IMPLEMENTATION METHODOLOGY

Once you select a consultant to partner with on your ERP journey, there will be a brief transition from a sales process to the project itself by onboarding the team into implementation methodology. The ERP implementation methodology will guide in the planning, build-out, data migration, testing, training, and eventual cutover to the new ERP system.

To increase the probability of success in each project, the software development community mandates that the partner ecosystem follow a standard implementation methodology that is consistent and repeatable across customers and industries. While some partners follow a standard approach and methodology created or mandated by a particular developer, other partners have developed their own process standards.

Based on leading practices, evolution of the marketplace, and project management, ERP implementation methodologies usually follow a similar set of phases through the progression of the project—from start to finish (any partner not following an implementation methodology creates a huge red flag). The best implementation partners follow the methodology as if it were a pro football coach's Sunday playbook.

The most successful ERP implementation partners personalize the approach and methodology to the business requirements of the client and to the team members working on the project. In personalizing the methodology, the partner makes sure the process provides the necessary structure along with the flexibility to work within a corporate culture and the team's personalities.

Although there may be variations from one partner to another partner, the example below represents a standard ERP implementation methodology, which can take a project from start to finish:

Example of a Traditional ERP Implementation Methodology

Analysis

The analysis phase is the first step in the progression, and it establishes an overall framework for the rest of the project (JOVACO Solutions, 2016). The analysis phase assists in confirming the attributes of the deployment, which begins with the high-level conversations for confirming the software capabilities being deployed, confirming the roles and responsibilities of people involved in the project, and determining the desired go-live date on the calendar.

These conversations should include the project leaders (a lead consultant from partner assigned to lead the project and team members from the client assigned to lead the project), executive sponsor (client CEO, CFO, or financial controller), and subject matter experts (consultants assigned by the partner and team members assigned by the client) to discuss the strategic vision and establish alignment among all the primary stakeholders. With these early sessions, the lead consultant will be able confirm the primary objectives for the project and for everyone in the process.

With high-level objectives identified, the lead consultant will begin to walk through how the system will be configured in meticulous detail. These are the details that will be used to eventually set up and configure the new system. The consultants will touch on items, such as the chart of accounts, the data residing in the existing legacy systems and spreadsheets, the manual flow of processes, the critical business reports, and the mapping of system integrations.

In addition to fleshing out all the details, the analysis phase is used to introduce the importance of a communication plan. The communication plan will be a combination of written and verbal communications between the partner and the project stakeholders on a consistent basis to provide project updates. This creates a channel for communication for completed and upcoming activities. And it incorporates any unforeseen or special circumstances needing to be discussed in more detail.

Ultimately, the overall success of the project will tie back to the meetings and discussions taking place in the analysis phase. Here are the high-level goals of the phase:

- Identify and confirm the project team.
- Confirm the features and functionality being deployed.
- Agree on a project timeline.
- Establish a communication plan.

Design

Upon completing the analysis, the next phase is the design. The design phase is significant since the information gathered by the consultants will be transcribed into formal project deliverables for the client. These deliverables provide the blueprint for the entire project, encompassing the software features and functionality to be deployed, the project structure and framework, and the standards for success established by the executive sponsors.

The project deliverables will include (but may not be limited to) a project plan (often referred to as a business requirements document (BRD), communication plan, task list, roles and responsibilities, flow charts and diagrams, special reports, and mapping of system integrations (Boogaard, 2022). These documents will require time, planning, and execution to be created, distributed, and confirmed with the primary stakeholders.

The project plan lists specific functionality to be deployed in the ERP system, such as the general ledger, accounts payable, accounts receivable, fixed assets, invoicing, etc. For each one of these modules, the project plan contains the necessary configuration and corresponding tasks with assigned responsibilities (partner and client). All these tasks combined will be used to form a timeline of activities leading up to the planned go-live date on the calendar.

The communication plan offers a policy-based approach for conveying information to the primary stakeholders of the project (Waida, 2022). Verbal and written communications scheduled on a weekly or biweekly basis for the duration of the project will assist with the flow of information, such as change in management, the unexpected crisis, and gathering feedback from team members.

The data migration plan outlines the process of identifying, extracting, massaging, and transferring data so that it can be migrated to the new system (Petters, 2021). The plan will highlight the specific data from the legacy system needing to be uploaded into the new ERP system, and it will include a timeline for the client to extract it. Once the data is extracted, the client will need a reasonable amount of time to massage the information (by removing outdated information, such as old vendors, assets, and employees) before it is uploaded into the new system. As part of the plan, the consultant will provide a series of templates so that the data can be properly formatted for transfer and upload into the new ERP system. A list of examples includes the chart of accounts, general ledger history, customers, vendors, inventory items, fixed assets, and employees (in circumstances of a payroll deployment).[4]

The system integration plan will highlight each of the subsystems part of the software landscape that need to incorporate data into the new ERP system, such as CRM, expense management, and payroll. The system integration plan will identify each of these subsystems, the data that needs to be integrated, the mapping to the location in the ERP system, the technical method (API, SOAP (Simple Objects Access Protocol), manual import), and how the data will be authenticated (Fischer, 2017).

In addition to each of these deliverables, any specialized reports needing to be accessed as part of the initial going live process need to be identified. These typically include financial statements, such as income statement, balance sheet, and cash flow. However, there may be special reports for your business—such as sales reports, dashboards, and key performance indicators—that need to be finely tuned for executive management. While the most difficult reports will likely be developed by the consultant, the reporting plan will include the training of team members on how to take advantage of reporting, query, and dashboard tools available in the system. This will assist in the user adoption, team ownership, and gaining of insight into the business in real-time.

---

4 On a side note, while some businesses may wish to have the transactional history come across to the new system, this can be cost prohibitive. The subledger transactional data constitutes a one-to-many relationship, which means there are several touch points throughout the system. For instance, on a sales transaction, there are multiple touchpoints, including the customer, the invoice, the item, and the payment. Since the data of each historical transaction is intermingled throughout the system, the process of extracting this information is time-consuming and expensive. While it's possible to do, it does require a developer to write scripts and perform a lot of testing to move this data from the legacy system to the new ERP. Although many accountants want to keep this information, it is not a suggested approach.

Process diagrams often assist in illustrating the transition of a manual business process toward a new, automated process. The development of this documentation requires time to build and develop but will assist in creating the overall structure in the ERP implementation.

Building off the analysis phase, the design phase will provide a necessary blueprint for building the new system implementation and providing a game plan on how the partner and the client will work together throughout the process. Here is a list of the deliverables from this phase:

- Project plan with responsibilities, task list, and timeline
- Communication plan
- Data migration plan
- System integration plan
- Report plan

Development

While the first phases of the implementation are based on planning and preparation, the development phase is about action and execution. It is the longest portion of the project. The development phase requires the greatest amount of time and effort because of the progression in configuration, establishment of security settings, performance of data imports, creation of reports, and system integration setup and testing.

Beginning with the software being installed on-premises or provisioned via the cloud, the security will be applied to the system based on the roles and privileges of team members within the organization. There are multiple layers of security in the ERP system, starting from single-sign-on (SSO) authentication into the system and extending to the application layer, including access to screens and specific fields. Security provides control and minimizes exposure to vulnerabilities, assisting with separation of duties, industry compliance, and fraud prevention.

In addition to security, system configuration is one of the most important aspects of the development phase. Each of the modules will be setup and configured based on the business requirements discussed in the earlier phases and will determine how the system will be used. With system configuration, the consultant will apply the software setting to items, such as the chart of account structure, currencies, payment terms, methods of depreciation, and inventory valuation methods. The configuration of the system is intended to align with the current processes, cover unique business situations, and assist in creating automation.

Once the system has been configured, data migration can begin. The clean, summarized legacy data will be uploaded multiple times throughout the course of the implementation so that the client may review the data and ensure that it lines up properly in the new system. There may naturally be several tweaks along the way, so having the data prepared for import in advance works the best. With this approach, there is no need to run two systems in parallel, which saves precious time.

With data in the system, the process of report creation and modification can begin. In most instances, there will be a need for financial reports (income statement and balance sheet), operational reports, purchase orders, invoices, checks (if still manually cutting checks to pay vendors), and colorful dashboards (a visual display of key performance indicators (KPIs). In addition to creating reports, the level of accessibility, the method of delivery, and the timing of report distribution have to be established as well.

Just as detailed as the report writing, the process of system integration will require absolute precision. The application developers assigned to the project by the partner will incorporate the data sources, the destination, and the creation of the integration process between subsystems. The integration development process will be based on a trigger for data movement, the method of authentication, and the actual data import (going one way or two ways). The integration process will need to be built and tested several times during this phase in order to achieve automation between multiple systems in the software landscape.

The development phase turns all the plans into action. The execution of this phase is based on an iterative process (a cyclical progression of refining and tweaking) dedicated to establishing specific capabilities in the ERP system. The phase includes:

- Applying security to the application
- Setup and configuration of modules
- Data migration
- Report creation
- Building system integrations

Deployment

Deployment is the final phase of the project, and it has all the finishing touches of the implementation process that need to be performed. Similar to an airplane on a path for final descent, each of the remaining items in the deployment phase represents a final checkpoint for going live (in production) on the new ERP system. Here is where you need to buckle your seat belts and land the airplane.

User Acceptance Testing

The process of user acceptance testing (UAT) is the last step of the configured ERP software testing process and is required for the client. It is the client's responsibility to the primary stakeholders, subject matter experts, and the eventual system users to dedicate significant time testing the system and making sure the ERP software meets the defined requirements based on real-world-user case scenarios (the consultants are not going to be the primary users of the system) (Prophet Business Group, 2014).

While UAT is tedious, time-consuming, and often frustrating, the rigorous process is absolutely necessary. The client walking through use-case scenarios is the only way to confirm that the setup and configuration will work for the business in real-world situations. It's an *all-hands-on-deck* process because if there are any remaining tweaks or adjustments to the configuration that need to be performed, this is the time to get it done.

As a leader or project manager on the client side, it's important to emphasize the importance for team members to perform UAT and hold people accountable for getting it done. A well-tested system has the greatest probability for running smoothly in production. Once the client performs UAT and confirms all the inputs and outputs are correct, the software system is ready to go into production (go live).

Training

The best way to get the most out of the ERP system is through formal training on the new software. With formal training, users will be able to perform tasks correctly, increase the level of productivity within the organization, and eliminate errors, excuses, inefficiencies, and potential risks.

The training sessions will be based on the modules and reporting tools deployed as part of the ERP implementation and will require the new system users' full and active participation. The training sessions may include certain topics—such as general ledger, financial reporting, invoicing, and inventory management—so users in their various roles, the teams, or the departments receive the necessary training in the areas of their responsibility.

In addition to the training on the software modules, a couple of team members need to be trained in the system administration role within the organization. The system administrator will setup future users, apply security roles, assist with passwords, and be able to provide daily maintenance of the system.

Since the formal training is taking place as part of the deployment phase, each of the training sessions will include the recently uploaded company data along with the new settings and configuration. Having the training on your own data creates familiar, real-world situations and will assist the new users in comprehending the content being presented.

These sessions may be performed on-site, at a training center, or over the web through cloud-based tools and technology exemplified by Zoom, Webex, Teams, etc. With global workforces, remote workers, and multiple time zones, the location of the training center or trainee really does not matter. Over the last several years, online training has become a fixture for corporations educating employees, so this information may be presented in the same way.

However, what will matter is that a learning environment is established so that training sessions have full participation without needless interruption or potential distractions. There should be no checking of email, text messaging, or surfing the internet while participating in these training sessions.

There needs to be an *all-in effort and positive attitude* about the formal training so that team members have the opportunity to increase their knowledge and skills on the new software package. That also means avoiding any temptation to skip training sessions or perhaps skimp on the training budget. The formal training will provide team alignment and productivity in moving to the new system. And with everyone on the same page, there is a greater chance to achieve immediate success.

Final Data Conversion

Throughout the development phase of the project, legacy data will have been uploaded into the system, perhaps many times. With each repetition of data being loaded into the system, there has to be testing and tweaking to the software to ensure the configuration aligns with business needs.

Before going live on the new system, there will be one final data upload to incorporate the most current data possible into the system, including the chart of accounts, general ledger history, customers, vendors, inventory items, and employees. In addition, the open accounts receivable and open accounts payable balances will be brought into the system.

With this final data upload, all new transactions will be performed in the new system with the legacy software serving as a reference system. Over time, the legacy software will no longer be needed. It will fade away and become irrelevant to the software landscape.

Go-Live Cutover

After several months of planning, building, and testing, all the hard work culminates with the project going live. Going live is the climax of the project and the moment of truth in using the new system in a production environment that leaves the legacy system behind. The new ERP system will be the system of record for performing transactions, generating reports, and making business decisions.

In reaching this point, the team needs to be prepared to ensure that the go-live cutover goes smoothly. Before *flipping-the-switch*, it will be important to run through a final checklist to confirm everything is ready, such as the security having been properly setup, the software having been configured and tested, the most recent data having been migrated, the training having been completed, and a support plan having been ready to be put in place.

On the day of the go-live cutover, the consultant will play an active role answering questions, assisting with difficult transactions, and making sure everything is functioning well. The cutover process may continue throughout the entire week to ensure the team is comfortable transitioning to the new system.

Begin Support Plan

The last step of the deployment phase is to put a support plan in place for the team utilizing the new ERP system. In transitioning to a new system, a support plan provides the software users with a personalized method for receiving technical assistance to resolve issues, alleviate difficulties, and answer questions.

The majority of ERP implementation consulting firms offer support plans based on the desired level of accessibility for technical assistance, ranging from *call us when you need us* all the way to *unlimited support* incidents. A support plan provides access to technical support from consultants through phone calls, email, and an online web portal during business hours. The larger consulting firms may have a call center that may be contacted 24/7, 365 days/year to create a support incident for issue resolution. Support tickets track the interaction between the client and the support team from initial issue through resolution (Seymour, 2022).

Whether basic or enhanced—silver, gold, or platinum—there needs to be a support plan in place so that team members have a resource to resolve issues pertaining to the software, security, and reporting needs. You should work with the consulting partner to evaluate each of the available options and what services are included, and then select a support plan that best fits your organization.

The deployment phase is the final phase of the implementation and puts the ERP system into production. Once each of the tasks below is completed, the ERP system is ready for users in a real environment.

- User acceptance testing and validation
- End-user training

- Final data conversion
- Go-live cutover
- Begin support plan

Operation

Operation is the concluding phase of the project, which marks the utilization of the new ERP system. Similar to learning how to ride a bicycle for the first time, this is the final push to find your balance and to begin pedaling on your own.

Once the new system is live and stable, the consultant will schedule a meeting to formally close the project. The project closing meeting assists in the discussion of all aspects of the project, including the capabilities that have been deployed, the consulting time billed compared to the project budget, and any potential functionality to be deployed in the future.

As part of the conversation, there will undoubtedly be functionality—such as workflows, reports, dashboards, or even system integrations—that did not make it into the project plan for ERP deployment. With the platform in place, these enhancements may be added at any time in the future. The project closing provides an opportunity to discuss a framework and timeline for any additional functionality to be deployed in the future.

Also, as part of the meeting, the consultant will present a final project sign-off document. The document will be a letter indicating the project has been completed and will require the written authorization by the project executive sponsor. If for any reason there are any open items, issues, or outstanding deliverables with the consultant, the document should not be signed. You should sign the document only when the project is complete (even if it is after the project close meeting) because once the project is closed, it is closed permanently.

Lastly, the client will begin to use the support plan as the primary method for technical assistance, issue resolution, and asking questions. The team of consultants who worked on the project will be headed to another client for another project, so they will no longer be as readily available. Here the client team has to transition from calling the primary implementation consultant for help to reaching out to the support group for any necessary assistance.

With users logging into the system each day to perform their tasks and responsibilities, they become acclimated to the new environment. What was once foreign and perhaps intimidating is now familiar and a part of the business processes and corporate culture. Ultimately, the new ERP system will help team members be more productive and achieve their goals, and it will help the business become more successful. Hooray for user adoption!

The operation phase is the concluding phase of the project and measures the success of the implementation. Once each of the tasks below is complete, the ERP project comes to an end.

- Hold project closeout meeting, exchange feedback, and address project acceptance sign-off document
- Plan future projects or system enhancements (as needed)
- Transition to ongoing support model

Summary

The ERP implementation methodology is a proven and repeatable framework based on thousands of successful implementations and leading practices. Furthermore, the implementation methodology works across different industries, technical environments, and customer sizes.

The documentation, content, and tools help to personalize the deployment based on the business requirements. The tools and content serve as a guide for the planning, configuration, data migration, integration mapping, testing, training, and eventual cutover into production.

For anyone new to exploring ERP software and embarking on the journey, the implementation methodology increases the probability for success and turning a strategic vision into reality.

The secret of getting ahead is getting started.

—*Mark Twain*

22
ERP IMPLEMENTATION
APPROACHES

The previous chapter highlighted the traditional ERP implementation methodology, which is comprised of multiple phases and based on leading practices. The ERP implementation methodology is designed to be practical, repeatable, and workable within several client environments.

However, there are a couple of variations to this approach, and they may be used to achieve the same goal. These approaches are used to align with client corporate culture and the personality of executive leadership or perhaps to reflect potential budgetary constraints.

These variations represent both ends of the spectrum: the ability to slow the project down through a design first engagement or the capacity to speed up the timeline with a rapid implementation. Both approaches provide businesses with options for deploying a new ERP system that accommodates a budget, a timeline, and a desire for control.

The good news is that each option is based on the same methodology, tools, and processes, so there is consistency and continuity with the approach and the ultimate strategy to go live on a new

ERP system. However, no two businesses approach an ERP project the same way. There are priorities, agendas, concerns, and budgets. Therefore, it is good to know these options exist.

- Design first—cautious, methodical, and deliberate
- Rapid implementation—basic and accelerated
- ERP methodology—waterfall versus agile

Design First ERP Approach—Cautious, Methodical, and Deliberate

Design first is a unique approach centered on performing the initial planning stages of the implementation (analysis and design phases) as a single project in advance of the full implementation. With this approach, ERP customers may begin the implementation by taking a small, cautious step to gain confidence before having to commit to the entire project and before purchasing software licenses.

The design first approach assists in formalizing the discovery conversations beyond the normal sales process and placing them in a more substantive context so that the most critical details are fleshed out. In situations where there are highly complex business requirements, several unknown variables needing to be discussed in greater detail, or trepidation in committing to the full implementation, this approach can be an essential steppingstone.

At the end of the design first project, there will be a natural decision point: move forward with the next phases of the full implementation or walk away from the project entirely. With a defined purpose and specified parameters, decision makers have more control and a greater level of comfort.

As with the beginning phases of all ERP implementations, the consultant works directly with the primary stakeholders and with the client's subject matter experts to confirm the business system requirements, process data flows, legacy data to be migrated, and necessary system configuration. If there are any special requirements that have not been discussed during the sales discovery process, they will be naturally unearthed in conversations during this engagement.

These conversations will also be used to identify that the task's team members are comfortable performing as part of the project and to verify with confidence the specific software needing to be deployed as part of the implementation. All of the information gathered will be compiled into the project deliverables, such as a project plan, communication plan, a task list of responsibilities with a timeline, and final software configuration and pricing.

Furthermore, the consultant and client will establish a cadence so that there is structure, progress, and flow between teams. When this happens, everyone is aligned toward the common goal, business objective, and strategic vision. This will assist in generating a level of comfort in advance of the full implementation.

The design first process is advantageous for businesses wishing to move to a new ERP system because it creates confidence in the solution, generates momentum for the project, and minimizes exposure.

Project #1: Design First (Analysis and Design)

Special Note—Please be aware that not everyone in the ERP community is excited about performing a design first project for a prospective ERP client. Developers selling both software and services directly to customers incent their teams to sell as much software licensing as possible, and they may be unwilling to entertain this approach. In addition, smaller resellers dependent upon immediate software margins for liquidity and survival may also be reluctant to promote this approach. Once again, take the time to evaluate implementation partners and consultants in advance. And discuss whether the design first approach may be an available option and whether it is right for your business.

Once the design first project is complete and there is a decision to move forward with the remainder of the ERP implementation, it will be time to formalize the second project. The second project covers the remaining phases of the ERP deployment: development, deployment, and operation.

At this point, the partner or consultant will create a second statement of work to formalize the engagement and provide an updated quotation for procuring the software licensing. All of the project deliverables created as part of the design first engagement will be utilized for the full ERP deployment.

Project #2: ERP Deployment (Development, Deployment, and Operation)

Separating the full implementation into two separate projects can be tremendously beneficial. By beginning the project and investing time, hard work, energy, and resources into the process, the client gains assistance in building confidence in the solution and approach.

While some hesitate in a one-stage process by excessively focusing on the unknowns and thus making "no decision," others, using the design first approach, generate confidence, which leads to positive results and momentum. Therefore, design first is the ultimate cautious approach to the ERP implementation.

Rapid ERP Implementation—Basic and Accelerated

The rapid ERP implementation is designed to be a short, fast-paced, and repeatable deployment strategy for small businesses. It leverages many attributes from the full ERP implementation methodology, but it does so in an accelerated fashion focused primarily upon the final phases of the deployment.

The way a rapid ERP implementation strategy is developed is by establishing specific project parameters for the deployment. Those parameters might include a limited number of users, very little data to be migrated (in some cases no data), core modules to be configured, the leveraging of out-of-the-box reports, and the offering of a predetermined set of training sessions. These parameters are measurable conditions that can be used to establish an accelerated timeline, fixed budget for the project, and rapid time-to-value.

Ideally suited for small businesses moving away from basic entry-level accounting software, a rapid ERP implementation leverages only basic back-office capabilities, such as the general ledger, accounts receivable, accounts payable, bank reconciliation, and, in some instances, fixed assets. That's it. There is no room in a rapid deployment for advanced ERP capabilities such as supply chain management, manufacturing, payroll, human resources, or project accounting.

Furthermore, a rapid ERP implementation leverages *plain vanilla*, out-of-the-box functionality to create a basic platform. So there will be limited personalization with no customizations, system integrations, or workflows to automate business processes. To avoid confusion, the partner will typically provide a list containing the capabilities that are considered *in or out of scope* for the project. Unfortunately, there can be no deviation from this offering because it can compromise the project parameters, so this is likely to be a *take-it or leave-it* proposition, which merits consideration.

The benefit of this type of an approach is the ability to put a basic ERP platform in place in a relatively short period of time at a fraction of the cost of a full implementation. Depending on your business situation, this type of move may please your banker, accountant, or investors. Whatever the situation, a small business can move from an entry-level system to a modern system in a short time for less money.

Although the rapid ERP approach is not for everyone, it can be extremely beneficial in the right circumstances. If you are part of a small company with a limited budget wishing to move off an entry-level system and the company has very basic system requirements, then this may be a significant opportunity.

However, there can be drawbacks to this type of approach, especially if there is a desire to have more than a basic system with limited data, few reports, and no personalization. With *no bells or whistles*, it's truly a *get-what-you-pay-for model*, which is great for some people but not for everyone.

Good candidates for the rapid ERP approach would be some start-ups, family-owned businesses, or traditional small businesses that have experienced recent growth. Ultimately, it is important to know this type of approach is available so that you can take advantage of it if you need it.

Statement of Work—Rapid ERP Implementation (Deployment and Operation)

ERP Implementation Methodology—Waterfall Versus Agile

In presenting information on the implementation approaches, it would be a mistake not to recognize the growing appreciation in the middle market for an ERP deployment based on an "agile" methodology. Agile methodology is more familiar in development circles as a way to create software through collaboration with several fast iterative development cycles (sprints) in an effort to achieve quick value (Altvater, 2017).

In moving beyond ground-up software development projects, the agile methodology has made its way into the realm of packaged business applications, including enterprise resource planning. It began with partners implementing enterprise-sized systems for the largest American companies in an effort to reduce the implementation time, and now it has made its way to the middle market (Roberts, 2016).

The rationale for the agile process is based on deploying a specific piece of functionality, such as invoicing or accounts payable checks, one at a time rather than deploying all the functionality at once. Proponents of this approach argue this is a more flexible and quicker way for customers to go live on a new system compared with the traditional waterfall method.

The ERP implementation approaches listed in this book are based on a waterfall methodology. The best way to describe the waterfall methodology is through the previous illustrations. The phases follow a linear process, beginning with analysis and design and followed by development, deployment, and operation.

There are certainly elements of agile methodology interwoven into the waterfall approach, but perhaps not enough for agile protagonists. The advantages of the agile methodology maybe appealing, but it's not for everyone. Accounting and finance teams have to carefully manage their daily responsibilities as well as take ownership of tasks during an ERP implementation. Furthermore, these teams understand and are comfortable working on the familiar approach of strategy, execution, and results.

ERP applications designed for the middle market are considered *commercial, off-the-shelf, packaged software* offering *out-of-the-box* functionality. These systems are designed to be setup and configured rather than being developed for each new customer through several sprints.

While this discussion may be regarded as old school versus new school, in some ERP philosophical circles, the traditional way of deploying ERP to the middle market has been proven and is not going away any time soon. If you wish to pursue an agile approach, there are partners in the marketplace ready to assist.

Summary

The majority of the ERP software implementations will continue to be based on the traditional approach and methodology. However, in special circumstances, there are options for business to essentially move more deliberately or even perhaps accelerate the implementation.

It is important to know that these options do exist. Partners, consultants, developers, and anyone providing professional services may prefer the traditional full ERP implementation approach because it's better for planning consulting resources and staying busy.

Partners willing to accommodate each one of these ERP implementation approaches clearly differentiate themselves from others since they offer clients flexibility through normal and special circumstances. In addition, it is a great indication of the consultant's willingness to partner with all types of clients.

But it ain't about how hard you hit. It's about how hard you can get hit and keep moving forward; how much you can take and keep moving forward. That's how winning is done!

—*Rocky Balboa*

23
CHALLENGES ON THE ERP JOURNEY

The path to success on the ERP journey is not a straight line. With solid implementation methodologies, leading practices, and valuable professional experience, there are plenty of opportunities for poor decisions, making mistakes, wasting precious time, or simply experiencing unforeseen circumstances. Inexplicably, challenges are going to come up along the ERP journey.

The good news is that many of these challenges happen all the time in the middle market, so they can be identified, addressed, and handled. The bad news is that, left unaddressed, these challenges can lead to negative consequences affecting the budget, timeline, user adoption, or even the success of the project.

These challenges may arise from anyone at any point in time. They can be in the form of management decisions, changes in personnel, personal agendas, someone with an axe to grind, or pure laziness.

Whatever the situation may be, this project will bring out both the best and worst of intentions from people, some of which you may never expect.

Nevertheless, it makes sense to gain familiarity with the most common challenges experienced on the ERP journey so that they can be identified and overcome as much as possible.

Redesigning the Chart of Accounts

One of the benefits of moving to a new ERP system is redesigning the chart of accounts to match the current state of the business. As a company grows and operations become more sophisticated, there is often a need for better reporting on process segments and departmental responsibilities.

If there is a desire to change the chart of accounts, take the time necessary in advance for having internal meetings and discussions to determine the new structure. The foundation of an ERP system is the chart of accounts, so any redesign needs to be done before starting the project (Shurland, et al., 2021).

Once the new structure has been developed, the consultant will be able to use a chart of accounts mapping template to transfer the old account structure from the legacy system to the new account structure in the new ERP system. Once the new chart of accounts is setup in the ERP system, the general ledger history can be imported for reporting purposes.

If the process of redesigning the new chart of accounts takes longer than expected, this can impact the beginning of the project, overall timeline, and perhaps even the budget. There is no single event that slows down the ERP project more than not having the new chart of accounts structure prepared before the project kickoff.

Lack of Responsibility

One of the biggest reasons an ERP project fails to achieve expectations is lack of responsibility. Having responsibility means the willingness to take on extra obligations and duties, having accountability for actions, and following through on the commitment of achieving a high standard.

The lack of responsibility can take place at any level of the organization. It does not matter if you are the president, CEO, CFO, financial controller, IT director, accounts payable clerk, or project manager. If there is not a willingness to take responsibility for the project, or your particular piece of the project, there is no way the new ERP system will work the way it was initially intended (Miller, 2021).

Through the acceptance of responsibility, there becomes an emotional connection between team members (including executive management) with the final result of the project, causing team members to take pride in the success or be very disappointed in the failure. When team members accept responsibility, they have a higher level of engagement and participation in the project (Edinger, 2012).

With this emotional connection, team members will take the time to gain familiarity with the system, proactively participate in the design, training, and testing, and ask questions. The willingness to perform tasks and learn a new system leads to confidence, professional growth, and a successful ERP implementation.

If the ERP implementation is unsuccessful, then there will ultimately be consequences, ranging from light to severe. It is easy to place the blame on other people, such as the consultants. However, when the home team is clearly unprepared and not following through on assigned tasks, it is hard to blame others, make excuses, or bemoan the situation.

When owners or CFOs of businesses refuse to take responsibility for their systems, they point their fingers at the consultants, complain about spending money, and blame the software systems. This type of leadership by example only permeates through an entire organization (Phillips, 2013).

The consequences of this situation may include having to continue living with the manual tasks and processes, team members fumbling around in the new system, and continuous error messages. There is nothing worse than trying to work around a software system that is not fully aligned with your business.

Have the right effort, attitude, and organizational willingness to accept responsibility. Ultimately, this is your company, your project, and your system. When the consultants walk out the door, they want to leave the system in your good hands. Accepting responsibility for the project makes a huge difference.

Unrealistic Go-Live Date

In formulating a time line for an ERP implementation, it is imperative to plan a realistic go-live date for the new system. The go-live date is important. It is agreed upon by the client and the consultant as to when the new system will be ready to be used in production.

All planning of implementation tasks will be based on a time line leading to the go-live date. However, from time to time, there may be unforeseen circumstances during the project.

As you all know, life sometimes happens. Tasks may take longer than anticipated, team members may have other commitments, unpredictable events may take place, or an unexpected change in personnel may occur. Whatever the situation, when life happens, there is a need to be flexible. Correspondingly, sometimes there is a need to push the go-live date further back on the calendar to extend the timeline.

With more time, team members and consultants can adjust to the situation so that essential tasks can be completed and the project finished properly. Yet occasionally there are executives and managers who are obsessed with the go-live date, and they may be unwilling to budge from it. In these circumstances, the lack of flexibility suddenly creates an unrealistic go-live date and a burden for everyone.

The ERP implementation is based on a delicate balance of tasks, time commitment, and project time line. When the go-live date become unrealistic, there is a *cause-and-effect* impact to the project.

In this scenario, executives and managers may be tempted to cut important steps from the implementation to save time. For example, they might want to cut user acceptance testing or even user training. These decisions compromise the integrity of the project and create several problems down the road (Mink, 2019).

In most instances, dealing with less time means doubling down on the effort to complete tasks. Team members have to increase their commitment by taking on more tasks than originally anticipated while the consultant has to add more billable resources to the project.

The addition of consulting resources to the project places stress on the budget, thus leading toward a more expensive implementation. The prospect of team members taking on an increase in workload can become more professionally stressful and time-consuming, and it can negatively affect work/life balance.

Companies go live on new business systems all year long, so the easiest approach is to accept the circumstances and be willing to slightly push the go-live date back on the calendar. If that is not possible, there are creative ways to approach the impending go-live date without increasing the size of the project.

One option is to plan a *rolling go-live* so that functionality goes into production in smaller increments over an extended period of time. With a rolling go-live, the base financial platform goes into production first (at the time of the original go-live date). It is then followed by more advanced ERP functionality a short time later. For instance, financial management might go live on January 1, followed by supply chain management going live on February 1, and manufacturing going live on March 1. The rolling go-live strategy assists in keeping the original go-live date, but it then effectively uses the calendar to spread out the remaining tasks so that neither the project budget nor the team's morale is negatively impacted.

In addition to a rolling go-live strategy, an ERP system can go live into production without all the historical financial data (general ledger) having already been migrated. As a way of saving time, the historical financial data may be *back-filled* into an ERP after going live.

In this situation, a company can maintain the go-live date with a system containing master records (customers, vendors, and inventory items) and opening balances (accounts payable, accounts receivable, sales orders, and purchase orders). The historical financial data may be imported after going live so that comparative financial statements can be generated in the new system.

When life happens, instead of obsessing over the go-live date, have a willingness to be flexible. There are several adjustments that can be made during the project to assist with the time line, such as pushing out the go-live date, having rolling go-live dates, or a back-filling historical financial data. Having flexibility down the home stretch of the implementation will assist in achieving better results.

Running Parallel

The strategy of running parallel is based on an approach of slowly transitioning to the new ERP system from the old legacy system by running both systems simultaneously. Once the new system proves to be working correctly, then the team will transition away from the old legacy system to adopt the new system.

In order for the strategy of running parallel to work, users need to enter data into two systems each day. The process of running parallel equates to doubling the daily workload. The doubling of a daily workload is not only time-consuming, but it is also detrimental to morale and is, quite frankly, a waste of time (Chow, 2019).

Needless to say, running parallel is outdated and not recommended. The ERP software systems in the marketplace today either have the ability to create a test company or provision a sandbox. These are valuable tools used by consultants to assist customers in avoiding having to run systems in parallel.

In performing a data conversion, the consultant will use a test company or sandbox as a destination for importing data from the legacy system. Having data in the new system and the legacy system provides the ability to compare the results. The data migration process will be performed a few times (as necessary) throughout the implementation so that data is tested and validated until there is comfort with the new system. Before going live, there will be one final import to bring the most current data into the new software.

The ability to import data multiple times is by far easier, more efficient, and less time-consuming than running parallel. If you are ever in a meeting in which running parallel is suggested by ownership, management, or one of your peers, quickly ask one of your consultants to weigh in on the topic so that potentially better alternative approaches may be discussed in more detail.

Executive Sponsorship Changes Midproject

In business, players change all the time and from all levels of the organization. However, it is challenging when there are executive-level sponsor changes transpiring during the ERP implementation.

With the project already in progress, it does not matter which executive position has new leadership in the organizational hierarchy. If there is a new president, CEO, CFO, or CIO coming aboard, this person will want to understand in detail the plan of action and strategy for the ERP implementation.

Depending on the new executive's role in the organization, it is reasonable to assume this executive may want to know the touch points for a particular department, team, and budget. However, if the new executive is CFO or CIO, this person is likely inheriting the project sponsorship and can impact its direction positively or negatively.

When a new executive joins the ERP implementation midproject, one of two results is going to happen. The good leader will listen to the team and the consultants, appreciate the circumstances, and play a key role in the success of the project. The not-so-good leader will want to take control and change how things are being done. The former is good while the latter really wants everyone to know that *there's a new sheriff in town.*

Regardless of the personality of the new executive, when a situation such as this arises, take time to explain how the strategy was developed, share all the corresponding documentation, and show the progress completed. This is a person you are going to want to have on the team as the new sponsor to help get the project across the finish line, so it's important that the person understands as much as possible and as soon as possible (Couch, 2017).

If the explanation of strategy and documentation is thorough, odds are that the new executive will believe the project is going in the right direction. However, be aware that the new executive will provide input on the project and may offer suggestions based on first-hand professional experience. It will be absolutely key for this person to *get fingerprints on the project* for it to be successful.

Alternatively, if the new CFO or CIO does not believe the project is going well, that executive will take immediate action. That could consist of suggesting alternative software applications, bringing in consultants worked with at another company, or choosing to *pull the plug* on the project altogether. All are bad options.

Remember, if there is a change in an executive sponsor midproject, simply *tap the brakes* and do whatever it takes to get the new sponsor *on the team* as fast as possible. There is a strong chance you may have to make some adjustments in the project approach to gain the new executive's full buy-in, but if that's what it takes, it's probably the best route to take. Be ready to pivot as needed, but strive to keep the overall implementation moving forward to gain positive yardage.

Software Is Not Perfect

With any new ERP software system, there are features and function-ality, system capabilities, and enhancements developed to meet the needs of most business requirements. With the time it takes to imple-ment the ERP system, it's important to know software is not per-fect. As Brian Rue, the CEO and co-founder of Rollbar points out, "Software is an ongoing process that can always get better because perfection isn't attainable" (Rue, 2021).

Software is constantly being enhanced and updated for the pur-pose of better usability, more extensibility, and new features. In cases where there may be gaps, this is an opportunity to become creative using workarounds, such as reports or perhaps even a spreadsheet.

A new ERP system may provide a company with 95 percent of everything needed to fulfill its business requirements and critical business processes. To close any remaining gaps, there is the option of custom development, special modifications, and specific reports.

Whatever the circumstance, the software is never going to be per-fect. There will be workarounds, manual imports, the need for extra reports, and so on. This is normal, so there is no need to worry about every single little detail. The goal is to address as many business requirements as possible and move forward.

The former COO of Facebook, Sheryl Sandberg, considered this one of her favorite sayings: "Done is better than perfect" (Sandberg & Scovell, 2013). Have confidence in knowing the new system is going to work extremely well and move your company onto the new ERP system.

User Adoption

The users of any new software learn the system capabilities through active participation during the project and through completing formal training before going live. These users will eventually spend the majority of their workday using the new system, performing tasks and processing transactions, so emphasizing user adoption from the beginning to the end of the project is imperative (Kaushik, 2022).

The executive sponsor, project manager, and consultants need to be unified in establishing a clear expectation: team members need to proactively participate by fulfilling their assigned roles (big or small) on the project. For example, proactive participation in user acceptance testing and the training sessions provide valuable real-world simulations to gain insight, familiarity, and knowledge about how to successfully perform daily tasks and assume daily responsibilities.

It does not take a degree in rocket science to know the difference between working hard or hardly working. Proactive participants exhibiting a strong effort and a positive attitude have a desire to learn and want to develop new skills. These team members will work hard at using the new system, being open to making mistakes, learning from them, and working on the necessary adjustments. As Johann Wolfgang von Goethe wrote, "Everything is hard before it is easy" (Allauthor, 2022).

If team members are not participating in the user acceptance testing, playing a part in the training workshops, or trusting the overall process, user adoption happens at an unacceptably slow pace and can be detrimental to the success of the project. Even worse, a lack of effort and poor attitude can be contagious, which leads team members down a path of openly questioning the usefulness of a new system.

It will be up to the executive sponsor to move quickly to understand why there is resistance to user adoption and whether it ties back to a specific individual or perhaps a technical limitation. Although the issue can be technical in nature, the lack of user adoption is most often attributed to the refusal of an individual (or team of individuals) to learn or use a new system and weak leadership to enforce the use.

The clear expectation of user adoption established by executive sponsors, project managers, and consultants needs to remain a constant throughout the course of the project. Once the system is in production, the users can be self-sufficient, having learned the system navigation and how to perform daily tasks, create shortcuts, and personalize screens to achieve an overall positive user experience.

Sabotage

Going beyond traditional user adoption issues, one of the toughest challenges is discovering that a member of your team is sabotaging the project (Panorama Consulting Group, 2012). To be more specific, a team member can sabotage the ERP system implementation through complacency, resistance to change, personal interests, or refusing to embrace the future stated vision behind a new ERP system.

Initially, the saboteur may be difficult to recognize. It may be a person you have worked with for several years and often have relied upon in the workplace. It can be a person with a significant amount of responsibility within the organization. To exacerbate the situation, this person may be not only a coworker but also a close personal friend.

No matter who's the saboteur, when the project kicks off, everything will appear normal. However, this person will likely become vocal in meetings, voicing thoughts, concerns, and apprehensions. These viewpoints become a means of taking the much larger ERP conversation offtrack, slowing down progress, and delaying the project.

As time goes on, the saboteur will become more irritated and openly speak negatively about the project and the consultants. The saboteur will *hijack conversations*, place blame on others, and point a finger at the consultants, accusing them of *not understanding the business*. This person will stand around the water cooler openly criticizing the project by predicting its eventual failure. Nothing is safe from the saboteur; this person is willing to throw anyone or anything under the bus as a means of acting out some particular frustration.

Assuming the trail of verbal negativity is not obvious, the saboteur's actions will ultimately prove to be a personal undoing. The saboteur will undoubtedly handle assigned tasks, duties, or responsibilities with a lack of urgency or the necessary follow-through, which will eventually affect the project. Instances of falling short on assignments and expectations are all *red flags* of a person working to negatively affect the outcome of the project.

If not addressed as early as possible, the actions of the saboteur may turn chronic, poisoning the corporate culture and becoming detrimental to the overall mission of the project. In these cases, this person may have to be removed from the project, assigned somewhere else within the organization, or worst of all, terminated.

The executive sponsor, project manager, and consultants have to observe the attitudes, behaviors, and activities of team members throughout the course of the project. While the saboteur may turn out to be the person you least expect to be that way, the goal is to recognize and address the situation quickly. In doing so, the amount of harm the project experiences can be limited as much as possible.

Summary

When it comes to the ERP journey, there are always going to be challenges. When an unforeseen situation or circumstance arises (and it will), it may take time, patience, and hard work, but have confidence in knowing everything can be figured out.

Remember, the goal is to tackle these situations, address concerns, and ensure there is alignment among team members while keeping the project moving forward. Ultimately, if the project stays within budget and time line and people are using it, executive management and the project sponsors will be happy.

OPTIMIZATION AND BENEFITS OF THE ERP JOURNEY

We must never become too busy sawing to take time to sharpen the saw.

—Dr. Stephen R. Covey

24
BEYOND IMPLEMENTATION—
MAINTENANCE AND
OPTIMIZATION

Congratulations. You made it. Once you have led your team to a successful ERP implementation, you will be able to switch gears from project mode to a more comfortable, ongoing operations approach.

However, this does not mean the work ends. It's really only the beginning. Just as everything in life requires a form of maintenance, such as your house, car, mind, and body, so does your ERP software system (Durmonski, 2022).

Devoting energy and care toward maintaining the ERP system is essential to ensure ongoing operational efficiency. The reason is simple: Everything is in a state of constant change (DiGerolamo, 2021). Basic examples of change include advancements in tools and technology, new software features and functionality, turnover in team members, and the daily execution of the business growth strategy.

In addition to being in a state of constant change, the market place demands innovation and modernization more than ever before. When it comes to products and services, customer expectations are continuing to rise while competitors are out there lurking in the shadows with a goal of disrupting the industry (Murphy, 2021).

Without ongoing maintenance, ultimately gaps will surface between how the ERP system is functioning and the actual needs of the business. Left unchecked, these gaps can become a massive new spreadsheet, the latest disparate system requiring duplicate entry, or another time-consuming manual process.

Beyond ongoing care and maintenance, there will eventually be a need for system optimization. Opportunities for optimization arise during evolutionary stages of the business, such as onboarding a new acquisition, adopting new accounting standards, preparing for an initial public offering, or simply taking advantage of more advanced capabilities of the existing ERP system (Panorama Consulting Group, 2020).

A long-term system strategy is based on paying attention, performing ongoing maintenance, and being committed to optimization. With follow-through of this system strategy, the ERP system will continue to scale up to meet the growing business needs now and into the future.

Below are several suggestions well worth consideration.

Pay for a Support Plan

Once live on a new ERP system, there needs to be a transition from the project to an ongoing support plan for normal break-and-fix matters. The implementation consultant should offer support plan options to assist in resolving issues, troubleshooting, and answering miscellaneous questions.

In advance of going live, there needs to be a dialogue with the consultant to understand the support plan options, corresponding pricing, and the standards included in the service-level agreement. Once a support plan is agreed upon, this may have to become a new line item in the annual budget. It is realistic to budget between 10 percent and 25 percent of your initial implementation on an annual basis for a support plan (Amado & Paulo Belfo, 2021).

A support plan provides system users with a reliable resource to turn to when they need help. Undoubtedly, transactions will be processed incorrectly, someone will get locked out of the system, or a new user will need to be allowed access to the system. In addition, a support plan will help to keep small issues from becoming bigger ones and keep team members focused and working on productive activities (Flinchbaugh, 2021).

Train New Employees on the ERP System

When a new hire joins your organization, there should be an onboarding process to assist in socializing the team member to necessary knowledge, skills, tools, and processes in order to become effective in the organization. Assuming this person will be in finance, purchasing, sales, operations, or production, then the onboarding process needs to include formal training on the ERP system.

Too many businesses try to save money by relying on *hand-me-down knowledge* instead of paying for formal training. Without proper training on the software system, the new person is likely to fumble around, try to gain experience through trial and error, and simply be less productive.

In order to succeed, new hires need to understand how to perform their jobs. There are several ways to provide suitable training to new team members. Consultants provide training online or in person (and may be available as part of the support plan). Many ERP developers offer online training tools. Also, meaningful training might be developed in-house.

There are dozens of tools available online for creating instructional videos based on screen recording, such as iSpring Suite, Brainshark, and LinkedIn Learning (Nguyen, 2019). These tools assist in creating a modern learning environment for new team members who need to be trained on ERP functionality and company best practices. These tools make a big difference to team members, especially those from younger generations.

When team members do not understand how to use the ERP system, a gap is created between the software system and the needs of the business. The best way to eliminate this potential gap is by incorporating an ERP software training strategy for new hires and existing team members so that they are productive as soon as possible for as long as possible.

Participate in Local User Groups

Software user group participation has surged over the last several years across the United States. If there is a desire to learn more about an ERP software system, find a local user group and plan to participate. As Anthony Rotoli, CEO of Terra Dotta, writes, "User groups exist to facilitate knowledge-sharing and communication among individuals who use the same technology" (Rotoli, 2021).

User groups usually meet on a monthly basis, providing a forum for users to gain insight, network with local professionals, and see features and functionality first-hand through presentations and demonstrations. These forums offer *tips and tricks* on how to use the software better, to provide insight into the system roadmap, and to gain exposure to third-party software enhancements, which may be useful to your company.

With the information gathered and learned during these meetings, there is an opportunity to bring *gold nuggets* of newfound knowledge back to the workplace and realize immediate benefits. In addition, this is a great way to maintain control of the ERP system and support the ongoing needs of the business.

Send Staff to Annual National Conferences

Nearly all the mainstream horizontal ERP software developers and vertical developers host an annual customer conference. These conferences are planned in exacting detail, offering attendees product news and information, system advancements, and numerous activities in an extremely social environment.

These national conferences consist of keynote speakers, expert-driven presentations with demonstrations, and insight into the strategic product roadmap for future enhancements and development. Also, there may be a substantial product exposition representing the software ecosystem, with developers exhibiting the enhancements and extensions they have created for an ERP system.

Participants at an annual conference will have plenty of opportunities to learn more about the software, meet subject-matter experts in person, and network with peers in similar roles (Delaney, 2017). The experience can be very inspiring and also beneficial for learning new technologies, best practices, and helpful tips.

Yes, sending team members to Las Vegas, Orlando, or New Orleans for a national conference can be expensive. However, choosing to send staff to a national conference is not only an investment in each team member's professional growth but also an investment in the skills, tools, and ideas they will be bringing back to the workplace.

Meet with Consultant/Support Team on a Regular Basis

Often overlooked, meeting with your consultant or support team on a regular basis is tremendously beneficial in maintaining productivity, ensuring collaboration, and solving potential issues. Having an open dialogue with the consulting partner assists in understanding the system's performance, improving how your team uses the system, identifying gaps in functionality, or taking advantage of opportunities for optimization. Besides, getting an outsider's opinion may uncover findings, suggestions, or recommendations (even if this information confirms what you may already know) that can be very useful.

ERP Optimization and Continuous Improvement

Optimization is the process of enhancing the ERP system's capabilities beyond its original specifications and expectations so that it meets the growing needs of the business. It is best to pursue ERP optimization if either the current system is not operating to its full potential or there is a natural evolution of the business.

In a post implementation scenario, one hopes a reasonable amount of energy is already being dedicated to ongoing maintenance and upkeep of the system so that it's operating at or near its full potential. Therefore, the greater need for ERP optimization occurs during evolutionary periods of the business when the environment becomes more complex.

The internal environment becomes more complex when there is organic growth of the business model, such as starting a new line of products or services. Similarly, bringing outsourced services back in-house, including supply chain management and manufacturing, adds significant complexity to the business.

In addition to organic growth, mergers and acquisitions can add complexity, and they happen frequently in the middle market (Scavo, 2022). A new acquisition often demands the integration of personnel, the migration of data from another legacy system, and the deployment of additional features and functionality.

With real-world scenarios occurring all the time, the only way to bring the ERP system forward is through optimization and "continuous improvement" (Covey, 1989). In these situations, ERP optimization may be in training, data migration, setup and configuration of new software modules, creation of new reports, or integration with new, disparate systems.

Beyond the changing internal environment, there are several external conditions that may push a company toward ERP optimization. For instance, authorities, such as the Financial Standards Accounting Board (FASB) and the International Accounting Standards Board (IASB) release new accounting and financial reporting standards each year. These new standards can directly impact how businesses report on assets, liabilities, debts, inventory, revenue, equity, and taxes.

Working collectively in recent years, FASB and IASB have created new standards, such as ASC 606 for revenue recognition and ASC 842 to record all leases on the balance sheet (INAA Group, 2022). In both instances, these standards have directly impacted middle market businesses (public and private) across several industries.

Accounting professionals need to be familiar with these standards, their effective dates, and the plans to implement them accordingly. In order to meet these standards, ERP optimization is absolutely necessary. In this scenario, ERP optimization includes the deployment of revenue recognition and lease accounting modules (these may also be third-party enhancements) so that businesses may adopt these new standards.

Outside of these internal and external environmental conditions, the biggest reason for ERP optimization is the preparation for an initial public offering (IPO) to become a publicly traded and owned company. All companies desiring to go public are required to go through a Sarbanes-Oxley readiness assessment to show that the company is compliant (Christensen, 2019).

In terms of ERP optimization, there will need to be significant controls in place, including information security, segregation of duties, and financial reporting standards. Business processes need to be well-defined within the ERP system so that any regulatory professional can certify their completeness (Petters, 2020). The entire process requires a significant investment in resources, including a consultant to assist with ERP optimization and, of course, a risk advisory consultant to perform the readiness assessment.

The best place to start is by engaging a consultant to perform a system review or gap analysis to assist in creating a roadmap for optimization. These formal engagements are designed to identify the current state of the system, the desired future state of the system (goals, targets, compliance, etc.), and recommendations and necessary tasks relating to how to get there.

Although this type of project may be performed with resources in-house, engaging a consultant from the outside brings significantly more experience, expertise, and skills in formulating the roadmap to optimization. These projects are smaller in scope, staffed with experienced subject-matter experts, and they are absolutely necessary when it comes to the ERP system meeting the needs of an evolving business.

The process of ERP optimization may be achieved by creating complex reports, building system integrations, automating processes with workflows, or deploying new functionality. Organizations running on-premises systems can optimize the system by performing upgrades, applying service packs, or loading any new releases. In addition, enhancing user training, updating security, and modifying the chart of accounts are all examples of ERP optimization.

There are several environmental influences that compel the need for ERP optimization. If the ERP system is not brought forward or enhanced, then it will eventually become stagnant. Instead of allowing stagnation with the ERP system, you should plan to continually optimize the system. The benefits of ERP optimization include getting optimal performance, improving efficiency, and achieving the desired results.

Summary

While a new ERP system is a significant investment of time and resources, the maintenance and optimization are equally important. There are always going to be new advances in technology and an ever-changing business environment. Therefore, you have to look beyond the original implementation and plan to adjust to changing circumstances. These changing circumstances include investing in team members, engaging with consultants, and committing to ERP optimization.

The only impossible journey is the one you never begin.
                                                    —*Anthony Robbins*

25
THE BENEFITS OF THE SUCCESSFUL ERP JOURNEY

There is a natural relationship between the ERP journey and the growth strategy for middle market companies. While this statement may seem indistinct, the interconnectivity between these initiatives can become a key differentiator for many businesses.

In the middle market, organizations expand their business through the calculated execution of a growth strategy. A growth strategy can be based on starting a new line of business, expanding into new markets, boosting throughput, acquiring another business, or obtaining new assets to increase the size of a business (Maxwell, 2010).

Whichever method is the chosen path for creating growth, there has to be a plan of action for it to become reality. As with any good plan, there need to be achievable goals, significant research, the right tools and resources in place, and strong execution.

Whether working in a garage or at a desk, having the right tools and resources is imperative to the successful completion of any task or activity. In this case, having the right tools and resources means having the necessary funding, knowledgeable consultants, and a functional ERP software system (Brody, 2021).

A functional ERP system handles financial transactions by performing functions such as processing sales and purchase orders, tracking inventory, depreciating assets, monitoring cash flow, and reporting to investors. The system manages advanced transactions, such as supply chain, manufacturing, project accounting, or revenue recognition.

A company embracing the capabilities of a new system will be able to accelerate momentum and have a much better chance of successfully turning goals into reality. These capabilities help fuel the drive toward great pursuits, such as onboarding new acquisitions, maintaining regulatory compliance, taking an emerging business global, or preparing for an initial public offering.

In understanding the benefits of the ERP journey, several immediate advantages become evident for executive management and team members. Those advantages include the disappearance of a reliance on massive spreadsheets, a need for duplicate data entry among disparate systems, and having to live with inadequate reports. These are just a few examples that can bring dramatic change to any organization.

Today, consultants and marketing gurus often label this process "digital transformation." Maybe this classification is correct since there is significant technical and cultural transformation taking place. These improvements allow executive management and team members to save valuable time, which in turn leads to more efficiency and productivity in the workplace (Krishanu, 2021).

However, the centerpiece of any successful ERP journey is a company transcending boundaries and getting to the next level. The company will experience improvements, gains, and increased revenue. It is here that you can highlight many significant benefits of a successful ERP journey.

Automating Manual Processes

In business there are standard processes and operating procedures, such as the creation of sales orders and purchase orders and the fulfillment of inventory. All too often these processes are based on manual tasks and time-intensive activities.

Here you see paper documents, massive spreadsheets, numerous emails, and internal meetings used in an effort to constantly track information. The practice of passing information back and forth throughout an organization only increases the risk of making mistakes and raises the exposure to making poor decisions (Tilleli, 2022).

With a new ERP system, several manual processes become technology-enabled, leading to greater simplicity and automation. Familiar business processes, such as order to cash, procure to pay, requisition to check, and bank reconciliation can now seamlessly flow through the system.

Furthermore, complex manual processes can be powered with workflow automation. With workflow, predefined business rules can be applied to basic activities, data, and files so that specific processes, such as invoice approvals, expense approvals, or new accounts setup can be automated and executed (Pratt & Gillis, 2022).

Automating manual processes saves time and creates the opportunity for businesses to be more productive as more time is spent on purpose-filled tasks and activities to generate more revenue. In addition, automation allows for more consistency across corporate processes, which reduces risks, errors, and bad decisions (Long, 2018).

Make Decisions Based on Data

Across all industries, there are experienced professionals making decisions each day based on intuition and spreadsheets. Without having functioning technical systems or reporting tools, these decision makers rely heavily on intuition or leading by gut feeling.

While *trusting your gut* works well for some and does reflect significant experience, this singular approach becomes less reliable as the complexity of the business increases (Bonabeau, 2003). When it comes to complicated processes and situations, decisions have to be made based on evidence and analytics.

With a new ERP system, each transaction is recorded, so data resides in a database, reports, and dashboards. Critical information regarding sales, inventory, and financial performance becomes translated into factual metrics that can be used for making decisions. There are several metrics every company should be able to access. They include the following:

- Strategy—measure overall performance and accountability
- Business objectives—sales targets, service response time, customer satisfaction
- Operational metrics—department contributions, overhead, capacity, people, etc.
- Financial metrics—financial statements, budget versus actuals, forecasts, etc.

With an ERP system in place, professionals can perform analysis of dynamic data captured through a single source of truth. With real-time information and insight, professionals can confidently make important and time-sensitive decisions based on genuine data.

Bring Customers into Focus

Regardless of industry, all companies have to deliver quality products and services to customers on a consistent basis to generate revenue. The most successful companies are able to establish relationships, create loyalty, and grow a strong base of revenue-generating customers.

Since there will always be competition from rivals, new products and services coming to market, alternative price options, and industry disruption in a competitive marketplace, there is no room for taking for granted that a customer will return in the future (Newman, 2014).

It is also no longer acceptable to just know who your customers are. The days of ranking the "top ten" customers and subjectively labeling them as an A, B, or C are over. Today you have to understand the characteristics of each customer in order to provide each customer with the best possible experience (Jones, 2022).

With the new ERP system, you can bring customers into focus. Valuable customer information no longer has to be pieced together from multiple applications, spreadsheets, or other data silos. Team members can collaborate across departments on one platform creating a single source of truth for each customer.

Within a system-driven environment, data can be used to enhance the customer experience. Customer segmentation by industry, size, revenue, geography, and purchase history includes data points that can be tracked, analyzed, and used to determine the value of a customer (Nguyen, 2021). Trends, patterns, and seasonality can be identified and used to better know your customer.

In understanding this critical information, a more proactive approach may be used in putting customers first and building a lasting emotional connection. Proactively assisting customers in their own success creates more opportunities, such as cross-selling, upselling, and generating future referral business (Smith, 2022).

The new ERP system can unlock the data to bring customers into focus. Accessible information coming from a single source of truth can now be used to understand customers, enhance their experience, and cultivate valuable long-term relationships to increase revenue growth.

A Platform for Growth

As a company executes its plan or mission, it can be confident in knowing the new ERP system serves as a platform for growth in several ways. Most notably, the ERP system will contribute technologically, strategically, and economically as the business transforms from basic to complex.

From a technical perspective, the ERP system leverages the latest in technology and may be scaled to include additional functionality at any point in time. There can be confidence in knowing the platform can take on a heavier workload, a higher volume of transactions, and a significant amount of data storage for the foreseeable future.

With the added capacity, there is an opportunity to become more strategic when it comes to execution of the growth strategy. The ERP system will not only assist the business in being able to grow with its customers, but it will also put the business in a better position to acquire other companies.

Becoming active in mergers and acquisitions can provide significant growth and diversification to an organization. With an ERP system, the process of onboarding new teams, departments, and customer data can now simply be a part of the acquisition playbook.

Furthermore, the ERP system will have the capability to continue to be enhanced, so the functionality can reflect the natural broadening of the business. For instance, there may be a need to establish a multichannel approach to sales, marketing, and serving valued customers.

Whether it is moving into e-commerce or establishing a partner channel, the options available for expansion become limitless. The ability to seamlessly deploy online shopping carts and web portals will provide customers with multiple touch points and insight into real-time sales and inventory.

In growing the bottom line, the ERP system will also assist economically by providing accurate financials for investors, bankers, and potential buyers. Banks review income statements and balance sheets when extending credit, and potential investors conduct buy-side due diligence before ever writing a check.

The ERP can also play a huge role in a business exit strategy. If entrepreneurs wish to sell ownership stakes to another company or investors, they will have to provide insight into income statements, balance sheets, cash management, and evolutionary milestones. Having the single source of truth in an ERP system may even assist in eventually achieving a large payday.

Beyond a business exit strategy, there may be a desire for taking the company public. There are more ways to go public than ever before because of special purpose acquisition companies (SPACs). Regardless of the vehicle, having an ERP system with audited financial statements and role-based security is a necessity in such circumstances.

The ERP system is truly a platform for growth for any company trying to orchestrate success through a rapidly changing environment. The system assists technologically, strategically, and economically. There is no other software package, appliance, or tool that can provide a greater impact than the ERP system.

Corporate Governance and Compliance

Gillan and Starks (1998) succinctly define corporate governance as "the system of laws, rules, and factors that control operations at a company" (Gillan & Starks, 2003). The ERP system plays a considerable role in corporate governance and compliance for businesses in all industries. It is the main system for incorporating rules, controls, processes, and approvals that manage a company's daily activities.

Having internal controls in place ensures the integrity of financial information and is the essence for corporate governance and compliance (Sineriz, 2019). These controls assist with establishing a separation of duties, they reduce the opportunity for fraud, and they create the necessary audit trails for regulations, industry compliance, and annual audits (Turner & Owhoso, 2009).

At the end of the day, the ERP system provides a technology-enabled mechanism for limiting exposure by promoting accountability and preventing fraudulent activities. Furthermore, it ensures that adequate safeguards are in place for meeting financial reporting and fiduciary responsibilities.

Professional Experience

Playing an active role in a successful ERP project is a big deal. It is worthy of placement on a professional résumé and of being highlighted on your LinkedIn profile with emphasis on first-hand experience. Working on a successful ERP implementation demonstrates the ability to work hard, be organized, collaborate with teammates on special initiatives, and assist a company in reaching new heights.

Remember, ERP implementation experience and direct software experience are highly marketable skills, and they can lead to professional growth opportunities (Algerson, 2022). These opportunities can include jobs in accounting, project management, application development, consulting, and executive management (Do You Even ERP, 2021). These opportunities may assist in moving up the organizational chart at your company or perhaps being recruited by another company in the future.

It's good to be known for getting complex projects completed. These are highly marketable skills that are transferrable to nearly any workplace situation. As author and philosopher Ayn Rand once wrote, "The ladder of success is best climbed by stepping on the rungs of opportunity" (Rand, 2022).

Improve Work-Life Balance

A modern ERP system has a positive impact on the professional working environment. For instance, the month-end close process will become shorter, the process of generating and distributing financial reporting will become easier, and team members will be able to perform their jobs from the office or work from home.

When manual, time-consuming tasks and activities are automated, having to work nights and weekends becomes less likely, which reduces stress and the chance of burning out (Sanfilippo, 2021). Furthermore, the automation is likely to allow team members the opportunity to spend more of their personal time with family, friends, interesting hobbies, or other meaningful activities that enhance their lives (Snyder, 2022).

When people are able to prioritize both professional and personal activities, they are able to improve their work-life balance. Both companies and team members experience the benefits of work-life balance through increased productivity, higher morale, lower turnover, and better overall experience.

CONCLUSION

Business professionals spend too much time in the software evaluation process while not budgeting enough time for the implementation. The path to acquiring software can be straightforward and should not be made more complex than it really needs to be.

The amount of time spent on meetings, conference calls, software presentations, and question-and-answer sessions can easily take several months and may become a burden for team members. Much of the time spent reviewing several systems can be more effectively used on preparing for an ERP implementation.

In addition, decision makers sometimes get frugal by trying to cut ERP implementation costs, most notably through negotiating billable rates, limiting project management, or cutting away necessary functionality or reporting tools from the scope of the project. All of this is done to lower the overall price point of this special project.

A word from the wise: **When it comes to a new ERP system, you get what you pay for**. Scrimping on the little things leads to issues down the road. The term *garbage in, garbage out* not only relates to data, but it also refers to consulting skills, system design, processes alignment, configuration, and reporting.

While *putting one over* on a vendor may feel satisfying, this should be viewed as a maneuver that may potentially compromise the success of the initiative. Instead of trying to chisel away at the software configuration and implementation to lower costs, be willing to pay the full price to get the best—but ask for valuable incentives.

When paying full price for the implementation, the client should feel empowered to ask the partner (or software developer) for valuable incentives, such as free training, a credit for being a reference, special discounts on early payments, or perhaps free passes to an annual software conference. These incentives can truly impact the success of the implementation and enhance the long-term relationship with the partner.

In the long run, which is more valuable—cutting $5,000 from the implementation budget by downplaying the need for training or having the partner invest $5,000 into additional free training for your team? Deep down, you know the correct answer to this question.

Wise Words from One of the Best

With anything in life, it is always better to do things right the first time. Although it may take time, discipline, financial investment, and alignment of team members, the end result will speak for itself.

As Jim Auer often said to new prospective clients throughout his celebrated ERP sales career, "Years from now you won't remember the day you started the project or the day you went live, but what you will remember is whether it was done right." When it's done right, the ultimate benefit of this journey is having the ERP system become one of your company's best assets.

REFERENCES

Agrawal, A. & Selimkhanov, I., 2020. *Operational Improvement: A Private Equity Roadmap to ERP.* [Online]
Available at: https://trajectoryinc.com/blog/operational-improvement-a-pe-roadmap-to-erp/
[Accessed 10 May 2022].

Alexandra, 2021. *Land and Expand, the Business Model Worth Billions.* [Online]
Available at: https://mentomics.com/land-and-expand-then-explode/
[Accessed 23 June 2022].

Algerson, 2022. *Calling All Accounting Professionals With ERP Experience!* [Online]
Available at: https://blog.execu-search.com/accounting-finance/calling-all-accounting-professionals-with-erp-experience/
[Accessed 28 May 2022].

Ali, M., 2017. *GoodReads.com.* [Online]
Available at: https://www.goodreads.com/quotes/200873-don-t-count-the-days-make-the-days-count
[Accessed 27 April 2022].

Allauthor, 2022. *"Everything Is Hard Before It Is Easy".* [Online]
Available at: https://allauthor.com/quotes/171129/
[Accessed 13 November 2022].

Altuit Inc., 2022. *The Altuit Process: 5Ds Define, Discover, Design, Develop, Deploy.* [Online]
Available at: https://www.altuit.com/projects/the-altuit-process-5ds
[Accessed 17 October 2022].

Altvater, A., 2017. *What is Agile Methodology? How It Works, Best Practices, Tools.* [Online]
Available at: https://stackify.com/agile-methodology/
[Accessed 20 May 2022].

Amado, A. & Paulo Belfo, F., 2021. Maintenance and Support Model within the ERP Systems Lifecycle: Action Research in an Implementer Company. *Procedia Computer Science*, p. 582.

Anderson, P. M., 2019. *What Are The Secrets Of Private Equity?* [Online]
Available at: https://www.perryanderson.global/blog/2019/3/13/pe
[Accessed 24 June 2022].

Apollo, B., 2019. *RFPs: how to avoid being column fodder.* [Online]
Available at: https://www.inflexion-point.com/blog/rfps-how-to-avoid-being-column-fodder
[Accessed 1 May 2022].

Arians, B. & Anderson, L., 2017. *The Quarterback Whisperer: How to Build an Elite NFL Quarterback.* 1st ed. New York: Hachette Book Group, Inc.

Azeem, R., 2019. *"The Secret of Getting Ahead Is Getting Started"* - Mark Twain. [Online]
Available at: https://medium.com/@ramshaazeem/the-secret-of-getting-ahead-is-getting-started-mark-twain-b57334695009
[Accessed 2 May 2022].

Baldwin, J. G., 2021. *How to Start Your Own Private Equity Fund.* [Online]
Available at: https://www.investopedia.com/articles/markets/100515/how-start-your-own-private-equity-fund.asp
[Accessed 8 May 2022].

Barber, F. & Goold, M., 2007. *The Strategic Secret of Private Equity.* [Online]
Available at: https://hbr.org/2007/09/the-strategic-secret-of-private-equity
[Accessed 21 June 2022].

Baseball-Reference.com, 2022. *No-decision.* [Online]

Available at: https://www.baseball-reference.com/bullpen/No-decision
[Accessed 1 May 2022].

Bly, L., 2020. *What Is Best-of-Breed Technology?* [Online]
Available at: https://www.okta.com/blog/2020/09/best-of-breed-technology/#:~:text=%E2%80%9CBest%2Dof%2Dbreed%20technology, tools%20that%20serve%20specific%20purposes.
[Accessed 26 April 2022].

Bolton, D., 2019. *Why Product Recalls Are Often A Compliance Issue.*
[Online]
Available at: https://blog.etq.com/product-recalls-regulatory-compliance-qms-software
[Accessed 14 June 2022].

Bonabeau, E., 2003. *Don't Trust Your Gut.* [Online]
Available at: https://hbr.org/2003/05/dont-trust-your-gut
[Accessed 27 May 2022].

Boogaard, K., 2022. *How To Write a Business Requirements Document (Template Included).* [Online]
Available at: https://www.wrike.com/blog/how-write-business-requirements-document/#What-is-a-business-requirements-document-BRD
[Accessed 20 May 2022].

Booth, K., 2021. *ERP IMPLEMENTATION: PLANNING, ANALYZING AND DESIGNING.* [Online]
Available at: https://www.epcgroup.net/erp-implementation-planning-analyzing-and-designing/
[Accessed 17 October 2022].

Bridgwater, A., 2018. *What are software accelerators?* [Online]
Available at: https://www.computerweekly.com/blog/CW-Developer-Network/What-are-software-accelerators
[Accessed 30 April 2022].

Brody, J., 2021. *Growth Strategies 2019: Choosing the Right Path for Your Business.* [Online]
Available at: https://ladder.io/blog/growth-strategies
[Accessed 27 May 2022].

Bryan, W. J., 1999. *PassItOn.com.* [Online]
Available at: https://www.passiton.com/inspirational-quotes/7201-destiny-is-no-matter-of-chance-it-is-a-matter
[Accessed 27 April 2022].

Burgum, D., 2005. *Doug Burgum: Convergence 2005.* [Online]
Available at: https://news.microsoft.com/2005/03/07/doug-burgum-convergence-2005/
[Accessed 2 May 2022].

Byrd, J., 2022. *Importance and Benefits of Electronic Medical Billing.* [Online]
Available at: https://www.relatient.com/electronic-medical-billing/
[Accessed 13 June 2022].

Byrne, D., 2022. *QuoteFancy.com.* [Online]
Available at: https://quotefancy.com/david-byrne-quotes
[Accessed February 2022].

Cameron, P., 2022. *Automation Advantages: 5 Benefits of Automation.* [Online]
Available at: https://www.helpsystems.com/resources/guides/automation-advantages-5-benefits-automation
[Accessed 7 June 2022].

Cantelme, D., 2016. *Business Parks: Cost-Effective Communities.* [Online]
Available at: https://businessfacilities.com/2016/08/business-parks-cost-effective-communities/
[Accessed 18 May 2022].

Capitalism.com, 2019. *16 Inspirational Warren Buffet Quotes on Life, Business, and Choices.* [Online]
Available at: https://www.capitalism.com/warren-buffett-quotes/
[Accessed 7 January 2020].

Carucci, R., 2016. *Midsize Companies Shouldn't Confuse Growth with Scaling.* [Online]
Available at: https://hbr.org/2016/07/midsize-companies-shouldnt-confuse-growth-with-scaling

[Accessed 11 May 2022].

Celestix, 2014. *Planning your Remote Access Strategy.* [Online]
Available at: https://celestix.com/2014/05/planning-remote-access-strategy/
[Accessed 6 May 2022].

Chai, W., Brush, K. & Bigelow, S. J., 2022. *What is PaaS? Platform as a service definition and guide.* [Online]
Available at: https://www.techtarget.com/searchcloudcomputing/definition/Platform-as-a-Service-PaaS
[Accessed 6 May 2022].

Chandler, R., 1953. *The Long Goodbye.* 1st Edition ed. London: Hamish Hamilton.

Chen, J., 2021. *Analysis Paralysis.* [Online]
Available at: https://www.investopedia.com/terms/a/analysisparalysis.asp#:~:text=Analysis%20paralysis%20is%20an%20inability,an%20inability%20to%20pick%20one.
[Accessed 1 May 2022].

Chen, J., 2022. *Private Equity.* [Online]
Available at: https://www.investopedia.com/terms/p/privateequity.asp
[Accessed 2022 9 May].

Choi, J., 2013. *The Risky Mentality that Made Jeff Bezos So Successful.* [Online]
Available at: http://blog.idonethis.com/the-risky-mentality-that-made-jeff-bezos-so-successful/
[Accessed 1 May 2022].

Choudhury, P. (., 2020. *Our Work-from-Anywhere Future.* [Online]
Available at: https://hbr.org/2020/11/our-work-from-anywhere-future
[Accessed 8 May 2022].

Chow, A., 2019. *Ways You Are Sabotaging Your ERP Implementation. Going Parallel.* [Online]
Available at: https://www.apcommerce.com/articles/ways-you-are-sabotaging-your-erp-implementation-going-parallel/

[Accessed 24 May 2022].

Christensen, C., 2019. *Sox Readiness.* [Online]
Available at: https://www.ipohub.org/sox-readiness/
[Accessed 4 May 2022].

Cisco, 2018. *2018 Cisco Cybersecurity Report: Special Edition SMB.*
[Online]
Available at: https://www.cisco.com/c/dam/global/hr_hr/solutions/
small-business/pdf/small-mighty-threat.pdf
[Accessed 24 April 2022].

Cloudflare Inc, 2021. *What is the cloud? | Cloud definition.* [Online]
Available at: https://www.cloudflare.com/learning/cloud/what-is-the-
cloud/
[Accessed 7 October 2022].

Cloudwell, C., 2022. *Technology is helping SMBs to become a global
force - More and more small-to-medium-size businesses (SMBs) are
using technology to punch above their weight against much larger
competitors.* [Online]
Available at: https://www.wsj.com/ad/article/execdigest-technology
[Accessed 10 May 2022].

CNBC Staff, 2021. *CNBC Disruptor | 50.* [Online]
Available at: https://www.cnbc.com/2021/05/25/these-are-the-
2021-cnbc-disruptor-50-companies.html#:~:text=The%20
2021%20CNBC%20Disruptors%20are, generation%20of%20
billion%2Ddollar%20businesses.
[Accessed 17 June 2021].

Cohn, M., 2022. *SPACs and IPOs pose challenges for SOX
compliance.* [Online]
Available at: https://www.accountingtoday.com/news/spacs-and-ipos-
pose-challenges-for-sox-compliance#:~:text=Section%20404%20
of%20the%20Sarbanes, along%20with%20an%20auditor's%20
attestation.
[Accessed 13 June 2022].

Constable, S., 2021. *How the Enron Scandal Changed American Business Forever.* [Online]
Available at: https://time.com/6125253/enron-scandal-changed-american-business-forever/
[Accessed 24 April 2022].

Couch, C., 2017. *When a Sponsor Departs An Executive Shuffle Can Put a Project at a Disadvantage; Strong Project Managers Know How To Cope.* [Online]
Available at: https://www.pmi.org/learning/library/when-sponsor-departs-strong-project-managers-cope-10761
[Accessed 24 May 2022].

Covey, S. R., 1989. *The 7 Habits of Highly Effective People: Powerful Lessons in Personal Change.* New York City: Simon & Schuster.

D., L., L., S., T., J. & SageStar, 2017. *Tell me everything about Private Equity in the ERP (enterprise resource planning) space. Specifically, what trends are present, which firms are most active, and the type of organization they seek.* [Online]
Available at: https://askwonder.com/research/tell-everything-private-equity-erp-enterprise-resource-planning-space-69mglmy44
[Accessed 24 June 2022].

Davies, R. & Huey, D., 2017. *Why CFOs need a bigger role in business transformations.* [Online]
Available at: https://www.mckinsey.com/~/media/McKinsey/Business%20Functions/Strategy%20and%20Corporate%20Finance/Our%20Insights/Strategy%20and%20corporate%20finance%20special%20collection/Final%20PDFs/McKinsey-Special-Collections_RoleoftheCFO.ashx
[Accessed 24 April 2022].

Davis, I., 2014. *Reflections on corporate longevity.* [Online]
Available at: https://www.mckinsey.com/business-functions/strategy-and-corporate-finance/our-insights/reflections-on-corporate-longevity
[Accessed 29 April 2022].

Delaney, D., 2017. *4 reasons companies should send their staff to conferences.* [Online]
Available at: https://www.tennessean.com/story/money/2017/06/26/4-reasons-companies-should-send-their-staff-conferences/424773001/
[Accessed 26 May 2022].

Deloitte, 2018. *Connecting Small Businesses in the US 2018.* [Online]
Available at: https://www2.deloitte.com/us/en/pages/technology-media-and-telecommunications/articles/connected-small-businesses.html
[Accessed 10 May 2022].

Deloitte, 2021. *Fast Break | A way to design and manage TSAs to achieve a fast and clean separation.* [Online]
Available at: https://www2.deloitte.com/content/dam/Deloitte/us/Documents/mergers-acqisitions/us-ma-consulting-fastbreak-080908.pdf
[Accessed 20 June 2022].

DiGerolamo, D. A., 2021. *A Constant State of Change - Marcus Aurelius, Heraclitus, and the change that binds us.* [Online]
Available at: https://medium.com/the-stoic-within/a-constant-state-of-change-d95394222d8
[Accessed 3 May 2022].

Do You Even ERP, 2021. *What Does ERP Experience Required Mean? (Job Description).* [Online]
Available at: https://doyouevenerp.com/erp-experience/
[Accessed 28 May 2022].

Dominguez, D., 2013. *The Perfect is the Enemy of the Good.* [Online]
Available at: https://www.optimissa.com/lo-perfecto-es-enemigo-de-lo-bueno/
[Accessed 1 May 2022].

DumbLittleMan, 2011. *7 Must Read Life Lessons from Benjamin Franklin.* [Online]

Available at: https://www.businessinsider.com/7-must-read-life-lessons-from-benjamin-franklin-2011-7

[Accessed 24 April 2022].

Dungy, T., 2022. *Turning a Losing Culture Into a Winning One.* [Online]

Available at: https://www.allprodad.com/turning-a-losing-culture-into-a-winning-one/

[Accessed 21 June 2022].

Durmonski, I., 2022. *Everything in The World Requires Maintenance.* [Online]

Available at: https://durmonski.com/self-improvement/everything-requires-maintenance/

[Accessed 3 May 2022].

Dweck, C., 2020. *TED Talks - The power of believing that you can improve.* [Online]

Available at: https://www.youtube.com/watch?v=_X0mgOOSpLU

[Accessed 5 May 2022].

Edinger, S., 2012. *Three Ways Leaders Make Emotional Connections.* [Online]

Available at: https://hbr.org/2012/10/three-ways-leaders-make-an-emo

[Accessed 23 May 2022].

Elkington, R., 2021. *We need to talk about science outreach.* [Online]

Available at: https://biotrib.eu/we-need-to-talk-about-science-outreach/#:~:text=Carl%20Sagan%20said%3A%20%E2%80%9CWe%20live, thought%20was%20never%20so%20contemporaneous.

[Accessed 24 April 2022].

Emerson, R. W., 1993. *Self-Reliance and Other Essays.* Dover Thrift Edition ed. Mineola: Dover Publications Inc.

Ergun, C., 2019. *Finance Stack - Integration Technology Solutions for CFOs.* Denver, The CFO Leadership Council.

Ernst & Young LLP, 2008. *The changing role of the financial controllers.* [Online]

Available at: https://thesunflowergroup.co.uk/wp-content/
    uploads/2017/07/EY_Financial_controller_changing_role.pdf
[Accessed 17 January 2019].
Farris, C., 2020. *History of Digital Transformation.* [Online]
Available at: https://capacity.com/digital-transformation/history-of-
    digital-transformation/#:~:text=Yet%2C%20it%20was%20in%20
    2013, a%20response%20to%20changing%20times.
[Accessed 28 June 2022].
Fernando, J., 2021. *What Is an Initial Public Offering (IPO)?* [Online]
Available at: https://www.investopedia.com/terms/i/ipo.
    asp#:~:text=The%20period%20can%20range%20anywhere,
    underwriters%20can%20last%20much%20longer.
[Accessed 13 June 2022].
Financial Accounting Foundation, 2014. About the Codification.
    FASB Accounting Standards Codification®, Volume v 4.10, p. 5.
Fischer, J., 2017. *5 Questions to Think About When Planning System
    Integration.* [Online]
Available at: https://www.ariasolutions.com/5-questions-think-
    planning-system-integration/#:~:text=System%20integration%20
    planning%20is%20the, resource%20planning%20(ERP)%20
    systems.
[Accessed 20 May 2022].
Fisher, P. A., 1996. *Common Stocks and Uncommon Profits and Other
    Writings.* Hoboken: John Wiley & Sons Inc.
Flinchbaugh, J., 2021. *The power of solving small problems.* [Online]
Available at: https://www.fastcompany.com/90702029/the-power-of-
    solving-small-problems
[Accessed 25 May 2022].
Forleo, M., 2020. *Everything Is Figureoutable.* New York: Portfolio /
    Penguin.
Fortune Business Insights, 2022. *With 9.1% CAGR, ERP Software
    Market Worth USD 90.63 Billion by 2029.* [Online]
Available at: https://www.globenewswire.com/news-
    release/2022/08/29/2505744/0/en/With-9-1-CAGR-ERP-

Software-Market-Worth-USD-90-63-Billion-by-2029.
html#:~:text=29%2C%202022%20(GLOBE%20
NEWSWIRE),9.1%25%20during%20the%20forecast%20period.
[Accessed 9 October 2022].

Fowler, M., 2019. *MartinFowler.com.* [Online]
Available at: https://martinfowler.com/bliki/TechnicalDebt.
html#:~:text=Technical%20Debt%20is%20a%20metaphor,
interest%20paid%20on%20the%20debt.
[Accessed 15 November 2017].

Franklin, B., 2022. *BrainyQuote.* [Online]
Available at: https://www.brainyquote.com/quotes/benjamin_
franklin_141119
[Accessed 25 April 2022].

FranklinCovey, 2022. *Habit 7: Sharpen the Saw®.* [Online]
Available at: https://www.franklincovey-benelux.com/en/tips-tools/
habit-7-sharpen-the-saw/
[Accessed 4 May 2022].

Freedman, R., 2020. *5 CFO trends to watch in 2020.* [Online]
Available at: https://www.cfodive.com/news/5-cfo-
trends-2020/570234/
[Accessed 6 June 2022].

Freeman, J., 2019. *What is an API? Application programming
interfaces explained.* [Online]
Available at: https://www.infoworld.com/article/3269878/what-is-an-
api-application-programming-interfaces-explained.html
[Accessed 8 May 2022].

Friedman, T. & Smith, M., 2011. *Measuring the Business Value of
Data Quality,* Stamford: Gartner, Inc.

Gartner Inc., 2022. *Positioning technology players within a specific
market.* [Online]
Available at: https://www.gartner.com/en/research/methodologies/
magic-quadrants-research
[Accessed 28 April 2022].

Gartner, 2022. 7 Options To Modernize Legacy Systems. [Online]

Available at: https://www.gartner.com/smarterwithgartner/7-options-
to-modernize-legacy-systems
[Accessed 16 June 2022].

Gartner, 2022. *Gartner Glossary - Information Technology Glossary:
Chief Information Officer (CIO).* [Online]
Available at: https://www.gartner.com/en/information-technology/
glossary/cio-chief-information-officer#:~:text=The%20chief%20
information%20officer%20(CIO, the%20goals%20of%20the%20
business.
[Accessed 24 April 2022].

Gartner, 2022. *Gartner Glossary - Information Technology: Small
And Midsize Business (SMB).* [Online]
Available at: https://www.gartner.com/en/information-technology/
glossary/smbs-small-and-midsize-businesses#:~:text=A%20
small%20and%20midsize%20business, staff)%20are%20often%20
highly%20constrained.
[Accessed 24 April 2022].

Gates, B., 1999. *Business @ the Speed of Thought: Using a Digital
Nervous System.* 1st ed. New York: Warner Books Inc.

Gillan, S. L. & Starks, L. T., 2003. Corporate Governance, Corporate
Ownership, and the Role of Institutional Investors: A Global
Perspective. *Journal of Applied Finance - Fall/Winter 2003,* p. 20.

Goldstein, S., 2021. *ASC 842 Is Set To Disrupt Multiple Industries –
Is Yours One Of Them?* [Online]
Available at: https://trullion.com/blog/asc-842-is-set-to-disrupt-
multiple-industries-is-yours-one-of-them/#:~:text=It's%20
no%20surprise%20therefore%20that, and%20other%20
customer%2Dfacing%20businesses.
[Accessed 16 June 2022].

Gottfried, M. & Cooper, L., 2018. Billionaire's Secret Buyout
Formula: 110 Instructions and an Intelligence Test. *Wall Street
Journal,* 9 July.

Grammarist, 2022. Where there's a will there's a way. [Online]

Available at: https://grammarist.com/proverb/where-theres-a-will-
theres-a-way/
[Accessed 1 May 2022].

Greer, L., 2020. *Four Keys to a Healthy Workplace Hierarchy.*
[Online]
Available at: https://greatergood.berkeley.edu/article/item/four_keys_
to_a_healthy_workplace_hierarchy
[Accessed 7 June 2022].

Guha, R., 2014. *Executives with Cross Industry experience are more
effective in the majority of roles.* [Online]
Available at: https://www.linkedin.com/pulse/20140707151144-
4325489-executives-with-cross-industry-experience-are-more-
effective-in-the-majority-of-roles/
[Accessed 11 July 2022].

Harvard Business Review, 2016. *How Private Equity Firms Hire
CEOs.* [Online]
Available at: https://hbr.org/2016/06/how-private-equity-firms-hire-
ceos
[Accessed 10 May 2022].

Hasbro Studios LLC, 1985. *Running Away Leads Nowhere featuring
Shipwreck - 1980's G.I. Joe Knowing Is Half The Battle PSA,
YouTube, Uploaded by Mr. 80s Movies.* [Online]
Available at: https://www.youtube.com/watch?v=WPE9fciA9d4
[Accessed 24 April 2022].

Hayden, B., 2014. *Warren Buffett Knows It. Reinvesting in Your
Business Can Lead to Huge Growth.* [Online]
Available at: https://www.entrepreneur.com/article/241196
[Accessed 1 June 2022].

Hayes, A., 2021. *Middle Market Firm.* [Online]
Available at: https://www.investopedia.com/terms/m/middle-market.
asp
[Accessed October 2021].

Hayes, A., 2022. *White-Collar Crime.* [Online]

Available at: https://www.investopedia.com/terms/w/white-collar-crime.asp#:~:text=Examples%20of%20white%2Dcollar%20crimes, NASD)%2C%20and%20state%20authorities.
[Accessed 13 June 2022].

Hendrix, M., 2020. *Empowering Change: 3 Steps to Strengthen the 'Human Element' of Digital Transformation.* [Online]
Available at: https://www.infosysconsultinginsights.com/2020/08/19/empowering-change-3-steps-to-strengthen-the-human-element-of-digital-transformation/
[Accessed 2 May 2022].

Hikaru, U., 2022. *BrainyQuote.* [Online]
Available at: https://www.brainyquote.com/quotes/utada_hikaru_238923#:~:text=Utada%20Hikaru%20Quotes&text=I%20squeeze%20oranges%20every%20morning%20to%20make%20juice.
[Accessed 25 April 2022].

Hisrich, R. D. & Soltanifar, M., 2020. *Unleashing the Creativity of Entrepreneurs with Digital Technologies.* [Online]
Available at: https://link.springer.com/chapter/10.1007/978-3-030-53914-6_2
[Accessed 28 June 2022].

Holter, S. A., 2016. *What Layer of Functionality Do I Need in My ERP System?* [Online]
Available at: https://www.meadenmoore.com/blog/consulting/what-layer-of-functionality-do-i-need-in-my-erp-system
[Accessed 14 February 2018].

Holter, S. A., 2020. *The Cloud comes to Manufacturing and Distribution ERP Software.* [Online]
Available at: https://www.meadenmoore.com/blog/atc/the-cloud-comes-to-manufacturing-and-distribution-erp-software
[Accessed 8 May 2022].

IBM Cloud Education, 2021. *Intelligent Automation.* [Online]
Available at: https://www.ibm.com/cloud/learn/intelligent-automation
[Accessed 7 June 2022].

IMDb, 1996. *Independence Day (1996).* [Online]
Available at: https://www.imdb.com/title/tt0116629/characters/
nm0001065
[Accessed 24 April 2022].
INAA Group, 2022. *What's the Relationship Between IASB and
FASB?* [Online]
Available at: https://www.inaa.org/whats-the-relationship-between-
iasb-and-fasb/#:~:text=However%2C%20since%20many%20
companies%20operate,(ASAF)%20and%20other%20means.
[Accessed 26 May 2022].
Ingalls, S., 2021. *What Is a Client-Server Model? A Guide to Client-
Server Architecture.* [Online]
Available at: https://www.serverwatch.com/guides/client-server-
model/
[Accessed 8 May 2022].
Intrasinghathong, K., 2019. *QueBIT Blog: Five Steps to make your
planning models ready for ASC 606!* [Online]
Available at: https://blog.quebit.com/blog/quebit-blog-five-steps-to-
make-your-forecast-model-ready-for-asc-606
[Accessed 14 June 2022].
Jenkins, L., 2020. *ERP Integration: Strategy, Challenges, Benefits,
and Key Types.* [Online]
Available at: https://www.selecthub.com/enterprise-resource-planning/
best-erp-software-integrations/
[Accessed 20 February 2020].
Johnson, E., 2018. *Director of Information Technology* [Interview]
2018.
Jones, P., 2022. *The Importance Of Knowing Your Customer.* [Online]
Available at: https://www.convergehub.com/blog/six-principles-
knowing-your-customers-better
[Accessed 27 May 2022].
Jongen, R., 2019. *WTF Is The Principle of Affordable Loss?* [Online]
Available at: https://www.revelx.co/blog/principle-affordable-loss/
[Accessed 10 May 2022].

JOVACO Solutions, 2016. *The Analysis Phase of a Project: An Important Piece of Any Microsoft Dynamics 365 Implementation.* [Online]
Available at: https://www.erpsoftwareblog.com/2016/02/analysis-phase-project-important-piece-microsoft-dynamics-gp-implementation/
[Accessed 20 May 2022].

Kanaracus, C., 2009. *SAP project costs cited in jeweler's bankruptcy filing.* [Online]
Available at: https://www.computerworld.com/article/2530405/sap-project-costs-cited-in-jeweler-s-bankruptcy-filing.html
[Accessed 27 April 2022].

Kaplan, S., 2017. *The Business Consulting Industry Is Booming, and It's About to Be Disrupted: Every industry will be disrupted. Management consulting is next.* [Online]
Available at: https://www.inc.com/soren-kaplan/the-business-consulting-industry-is-booming-and-it.html
[Accessed 30 April 2022].

Kaushik, K., 2022. *ERP Adoption - 5 Lethal Mistakes to Avoid in the Post-Pandemic World.* [Online]
Available at: https://www.apty.io/blog/erp-adoption
[Accessed 3 May 2022].

KBV Research, 2019. *ERP Software Market Size.* [Online]
Available at: https://www.kbvresearch.com/erp-software-market/
[Accessed 27 April 2022].

Kenney, M., 2013. *Apples to apples: Comparing ERP costs accurately.* [Online]
Available at: https://www.erpsoftwareblog.com/2013/07/new-white-paper-apples-to-apples-comparing-erp-costs-accurately/
[Accessed 24 November 2022].

Kenton, W., 2022. *SWOT Analysis: How To With Table and Example.* [Online]
Available at: https://www.investopedia.com/terms/s/swot.asp

[Accessed 7 October 2022].

Khanduri, A., 2022. *People, Process, Technology: The PPT Framework, Explained.* [Online]
Available at: https://www.plutora.com/blog/people-process-technology-ppt-framework-explained
[Accessed 17 March 2022].

Kimberling, E., 2018. *Why Private Equity Firms Demand Successful ERP Implementations.* [Online]
Available at: https://blogs.solidworks.com/delmiaworks/private-equity-erp-implementations/
[Accessed 9 May 2022].

Knab, M., 2019. *Chart of Accounts: The Backbone of your business.* [Online]
Available at: https://medium.com/veriledger/setting-up-a-chart-of-accounts-f5b2d21abf34
[Accessed 6 June 2022].

Know Your Phrase, 2022. *You Can't Have Your Cake And Eat It Too.* [Online]
Available at: https://knowyourphrase.com/you-cant-have-your-cake-and-eat-it-too
[Accessed 28 April 2022].

Kokemuller, N., 2022. *Who Is Responsible for Developing Policies & Procedures?* [Online]
Available at: https://smallbusiness.chron.com/responsible-developing-policies-procedures-67162.html
[Accessed 7 June 2022].

Krikhaar, J., Loucks, J. & Sguazzin, M., 2018. *Mergers and Acquisitions in Tech, Media, and Telecom | Charting a well-defined integration strategy.* [Online]
Available at: https://www2.deloitte.com/content/dam/Deloitte/us/Documents/technology-media-telecommunications/us-mergers-acquisitions-tech-media-telecom.pdf
[Accessed 29 April 2022].

Krishanu, 2021. *4 Ways Enterprises Can Use Digital Transformation to Enhance Productivity.* [Online]
Available at: https://www.replicon.com/blog/ways-enterprises-can-use-digital-transformation-to-enhance-productivity/
[Accessed 4 May 2022].

Kruse, K., 2013. *What Is Leadership?* [Online]
Available at: https://www.forbes.com/sites/kevinkruse/2013/04/09/what-is-leadership/?sh=56ed14665b90
[Accessed 1 May 2022].

Lampton, J., 2019. *CREDIBILITY IS PARAMOUNT.* [Online]
Available at: https://sfmagazine.com/post-entry/may-2019-credibility-is-paramount/
[Accessed 3 June 2022].

Langer, N. & Heaton, S. B., 2022. *To Make Deals in the Middle Market, Private Equity Needs Cultural Literacy.* [Online]
Available at: https://hbr.org/2022/03/to-make-deals-in-the-middle-market-private-equity-needs-cultural-literacy
[Accessed 10 May 2022].

Lawver, M., 2022. *Understanding Terms: Main Street vs. Middle Market.* [Online]
Available at: https://goquantive.com/blog/understanding-terms-main-street-vs-middle-market/
[Accessed 11 May 2022].

LEADTO, INC., 2020. *LEAD-TO-X.* [Online]
Available at: https://www.lead-to.com/lead-to-x-experience
[Accessed 25 April 2022].

Ledgard, J., 2022. *The 'Go Big or Go Home' Startup Mantra is Flawed.* [Online]
Available at: https://kickofflabs.com/blog/the-go-big-or-go-home-startup-mantra-is-flawed/
[Accessed 10 May 2022].

Leese, C., 2020. *LEASE ACCOUNTING: AN OVERVIEW OF ASC 842.* [Online]

Available at: https://www.gaapdynamics.com/insights/
blog/2020/05/26/lease-accounting-an-overview-of-asc-842/
[Accessed 16 June 2022].

Liberto, D., 2022. *Chart of Accounts (COA) Definition: Examples and How It Works*. [Online]
Available at: https://www.investopedia.com/terms/c/chart-accounts.
asp
[Accessed 5 October 2022].

Littlefield, M., 2015. *Understanding Out-of-the-Box vs. Configured vs. Customized Software*. [Online]
Available at: https://blog.lnsresearch.com/blog/bid/204226/
Understanding-Out-of-the-Box-vs-Configured-vs-Customized-
Software
[Accessed 20 December 2017].

Lombardi, V., 2022. *Famous Quotes by Vince Lombardi*. [Online]
Available at: http://www.vincelombardi.com/quotes.html
[Accessed 1 May 2022].

Long, L., 2018. *How The Right Automation Road Map Helps Overcome Human Error*. [Online]
Available at: https://www.forbes.com/sites/
forbestechcouncil/2018/11/09/how-the-right-automation-road-map-
helps-overcome-human-error/?sh=78b7615d647f
[Accessed 27 May 2022].

Luu, A. & Thomson, J., 2019. *Solving the carve-out conundrum.*
[Online]
Available at: https://www.mckinsey.com/business-functions/
strategy-and-corporate-finance/our-insights/solving-the-carve-out-
conundrum
[Accessed 20 June 2022].

MacArthur, H., Burack, R., De Vusser, C. & Yang, K., 2022. *The Private Equity Market in 2021: The Allure of Growth*. [Online]
Available at: https://www.bain.com/insights/private-equity-market-in-
2021-global-private-equity-report-2022/

[Accessed 6 November 2022].

MacMillan, I., 2015. *Do you understand your company's knowledge assets?* [Online]
Available at: https://www.weforum.org/agenda/2015/04/do-you-understand-your-companys-knowledge-assets/
[Accessed 30 April 2022].

Management.Net, V. B., 2022. *Acceptance and Diffusion of Innovations.* [Online]
Available at: https://www.valuebasedmanagement.net/methods_rogers_innovation_adoption_curve.html#:~:text=The%20innovation%20adoption%20curve%20of, or%20Diffusion%20of%20Innovations%20Theory.
[Accessed 24 April 2022].

Maney, D., 2011. *Why the Middle Market Matters – Now More Than Ever.* [Online]
Available at: https://www.cnbc.com/id/44639661
[Accessed 17 December 2017].

Maslen, C., 2021. *5 Things You Need To Nail When Selling to the Mid-Market.* [Online]
Available at: https://www.gilroyassociates.com/thought-leadership/5-things-you-need-to-nail-when-selling-to-the-mid-market
[Accessed 11 May 2022].

Maslen, C., 2022. *Mid-Market Sales Strategies (Hint: They're Not Like Enterprise).* [Online]
Available at: https://www.gilroyassociates.com/thought-leadership/understanding-the-mid-market-how-to-approach-this-valuable-segment
[Accessed 11 May 2022].

Maxwell, S., 2010. *Business Growth Strategies- What are Business Growth Strategies?* [Online]
Available at: https://openviewpartners.com/blog/business-growth-strategies-what-are-business-growth-strategies/
[Accessed 26 May 2022].

McKinsey & Company, 2019. *Private equity exit excellence: Getting the story right.* [Online]
Available at: https://www.mckinsey.com/industries/private-equity-and-principal-investors/our-insights/private-equity-exit-excellence-getting-the-story-right
[Accessed 8 May 2022].

Mead, S., 2022. *Communicating Your Vision to Build Strategic Teams.* [Online]
Available at: https://cmoe.com/blog/communicating-vision-to-your-team/
[Accessed 6 June 2022].

Melville, H., 2021. *Moby Dick.* New York City: Quartro Publishing Group USA Inc.

Merriam-Webster, 2022. *Critical Mass.* [Online]
Available at: https://www.merriam-webster.com/dictionary/critical%20mass
[Accessed 29 April 2022].

Merriam-Webster, 2022. *Evaluate.* [Online]
Available at: https://www.merriam-webster.com/dictionary/evaluate
[Accessed 28 April 2022].

Miller, R., 2021. *Microsoft's shift to the cloud is a lesson in corporate evolution.* [Online]
Available at: https://techcrunch.com/2021/11/12/microsofts-shift-to-the-cloud-is-a-lesson-in-corporate-evolution/
[Accessed 8 May 2022].

Miller, T., 2021. *Top 10 reasons for ERP failure (and how to avoid it).* [Online]
Available at: https://www.erpfocus.com/erp-failure-10-reasons-why-your-erp-project-could-crash-article-540.html
[Accessed 23 May 2022].

Million Business Software, 2016. *What is the Importance of Business Software for an Organization?* [Online]
Available at: https://www.million.my/what-is-the-importance-of-business-software-for-an-organization/

[Accessed 17 December 2017].

Mink, L., 2019. *Should an Arbitrary Date Drive the Go-Live Decision?* [Online]
Available at: https://blog.briteskies.com/blog/should-an-arbitrary-date-drive-the-go-live-decision
[Accessed 24 May 2022].

Monterey, T., 2021. *How Do Private Equity Firms Improve Operations?* [Online]
Available at: https://www.ictsd.org/how-do-private-equity-firms-improve-operations/
[Accessed 8 May 2022].

Moore, G. A., 1991, 1992, 2002, 2014. *Crossing the Chasm, Third Edition.* New York: HarperCollins Publishers.

Morrow-Kondos, D., 2020. *It Takes a Village – Or Does It?* [Online]
Available at: https://www.tulsakids.com/it-takes-a-village-or-does-it/#:~:text=According%20to%20Wikipedia%2C%20%E2%80%9CIt%20takes,American%20culture%20several%20decades%20back.
[Accessed 28 April 2022].

Murphy, A., 2021. *How customer expectations are rising – and what to do about it.* [Online]
Available at: https://www.intercom.com/blog/bridging-the-customer-expectation-gap/#:~:text=Our%20recent%20report%20showed%20that,support%20team%20to%20fall%20into.
[Accessed 25 May 2022].

MyAccountingCourse.com, 2022. *What is Corporate Strategy?* [Online]
Available at: https://www.myaccountingcourse.com/accounting-dictionary/corporate-strategy
[Accessed 7 June 2022].

Newman, E., 2014. *Do not take your Customers for Granted.* [Online]
Available at: https://corp.yonyx.com/customer-service/customers-for-granted/
[Accessed 27 May 2022].

Nguyen, H., 2019. *How to Make Instructional Videos with Screen Recording.* [Online]
Available at: https://atomisystems.com/screencasting/how-to-make-instructional-videos-with-screen-recording/
[Accessed 26 May 2022].

Nguyen, T.-A., 2021. *Customer Segmentation: A Step-by-Step Guide for Growth.* [Online]
Available at: https://openviewpartners.com/blog/customer-segmentation/
[Accessed 5 May 2022].

Onion, B., 2015. *What is Middleware and Why Should You Care?* [Online]
Available at: https://blog.briteskies.com/blog/what-is-middleware-and-why-should-you-care#:~:text=Both%20the%20ERP%20and%20eCommerce, operations%20of%20the%20other%20system.
[Accessed 8 May 2022].

Panorama Consulting Group, 2012. *Internal Sabotage: A Critical Risk Factor of ERP Failure.* [Online]
Available at: https://www.panorama-consulting.com/internal-sabotage-a-critical-risk-factor-of-erp-failure/
[Accessed 3 May 2022].

Panorama Consulting Group, 2013. *Effectively Engaging Employees Throughout an ERP Implementation.* [Online]
Available at: https://www.panorama-consulting.com/effectively-engaging-employees-throughout-an-erp-implementation/
[Accessed 2 May 2022].

Panorama Consulting Group, 2020. *Using ERP Optimization to Get More Out of Your Current System.* [Online]
Available at: https://www.panorama-consulting.com/erp-optimization/
[Accessed 3 May 2022].

Parcells, B. & Demasio, N., 2014. *Parcells: A Football Life.* First Edition ed. New York: Three Rivers Press.

Parcells, S., 2015. *INTERCOMPANY TRANSACTIONS CAN SNOWBALL.* [Online]
Available at: https://sfmagazine.com/post-entry/april-2015-intercompany-transactions-can-snowball/
[Accessed 13 June 2022].

Park Place Technologies, 2022. *Hardware Lifecycle Management – Maximizing Value at Every Stage.* [Online]
Available at: https://www.parkplacetechnologies.com/blog/hardware-lifecycle-management-maximizing-value-at-every-stage/
[Accessed 11 October 2022].

Patel, K., 2022. *Private Equity Due Diligence: How to Conduct It Properly.* [Online]
Available at: https://dealroom.net/blog/private-equity-due-diligence
[Accessed 9 May 2022].

Pathlock, 2022. *What are SOX Internal Controls?* [Online]
Available at: https://pathlock.com/learn/internal-controls-for-sox-compliance-a-practical-guide/
[Accessed 13 June 2022].

Pattinson, T., 2020. *Relational vs. non-relational databases.* [Online]
Available at: https://www.pluralsight.com/blog/software-development/relational-vs-non-relational-databases#:~:text=A%20relational%20database%20works%20by, data%20contained%20within%20a%20table.
[Accessed 7 June 2022].

Perkins, B., 2020. *What is ERP? Key features of top enterprise resource planning systems.* [Online]
Available at: https://www.cio.com/article/272362/what-is-erp-key-features-of-top-enterprise-resource-planning-systems.html#:~:text=Enterprise%20resource%20planning%20(ERP)%20software,2020%2011%3A30%20am%20PDT
[Accessed 4 December 2020].

Petters, J., 2020. *What is SOX Compliance? Everything You Need to Know in 2019.* [Online]

Available at: https://www.varonis.com/blog/sox-compliance
[Accessed 26 May 2022].

Petters, J., 2021. *Data Migration Guide: Strategy Success & Best Practices.* [Online]
Available at: https://www.varonis.com/blog/data-migration
[Accessed 20 May 2022].

Phillips, S., 2013. *ERP Disasters: Are Clients Incompetent (or are Consultants Mostly to Blame)?* [Online]
Available at: https://www.toolbox.com/tech/erp/blogs/erp-disasters-are-clients-incompetent-or-are-consultants-mostly-to-blame-101513/
[Accessed 23 May 2022].

Philosiblog, 2014. *Luck is what happens when preparation meets opportunity.* [Online]
Available at: https://philosiblog.com/2014/02/22/luck-is-what-happens-when-preparation-meets-opportunity/
[Accessed 24 April 2022].

Pieroux, A., 2017. *Your ERP Needs a Makeover.* [Online]
Available at: https://blogs.oracle.com/cx/post/your-erp-needs-a-makeover
[Accessed 17 February 2019].

Pinkston, T., 2022. *It's the People, People – Don't Overlook the Human Element of Digital Transformation.* [Online]
Available at: https://isg-one.com/articles/it-s-the-people-people-don-t-overlook-the-human-element-of-digital-transformation
[Accessed 2 May 2022].

Pirsig, R. M., 1981. *Zen and the Art of Motorcycle Maintenance: An Inquiry Into Values.* New Age Edition ed. New York City: Bantam New Age Books.

Pluralsight LLC, 2022. *Erasing tech debt: A leader's guide to getting in the black.* [Online]
Available at: https://www.pluralsight.com/blog/software-development/erasing-tech-debt

[Accessed 21 June 2022].

PoemAnalysis.com, 2022. *Good things come to those who wait.* [Online]
Available at: https://poemanalysis.com/proverb/good-things-come-
to-those-who-wait/#:~:text=%E2%80%9CGood%20things%20
come%20to%20those, circumstances%20and%20fail%20in%20
others.
[Accessed 1 May 2022].

Potts, B., 2018. *What is Best of Breed ERP?* [Online]
Available at: https://www.thirdstage-consulting.com/what-is-best-of-
breed-erp/
[Accessed 8 May 2022].

Pratt, M. K. & Gillis, A. S., 2022. *workflow automation.* [Online]
Available at: https://www.techtarget.com/searchcontentmanagement/
definition/workflow-automation
[Accessed 2022 27 May].

Prophet Business Group, 2014. *User Acceptance Testing: The Secret
to a Successful ERP Implementation.* [Online]
Available at: https://www.erpsoftwareblog.com/2014/06/
user-acceptance-testing-the-secret-to-a-successful-erp-
implementation/#:~:text=User%20acceptance%20testing%20is%20
the%20process%20of%20getting%20business%20users, to%20
lack%20of%20user%20adoption.
[Accessed 20 May 2022].

PwC, 2022. *Technology: Deals 2022 midyear outlook.* [Online]
Available at: https://www.pwc.com/us/en/industries/tmt/library/
technology-deals-insights.html
[Accessed 28 April 2022].

Rand, A., 2022. *Quotes and Aphorisms.* [Online]
Available at: https://quote-citation.com/en/aphorism/3753
[Accessed 5 May 2022].

Red Hat, 2018. *What is middleware?* [Online]
Available at: https://www.redhat.com/en/topics/middleware/what-is-
middleware
[Accessed 17 June 2019].

Ridler, M., 2019. *Procrastination or Prudence?* [Online]
Available at: https://medium.com/@realmikeridler/procrastination-or-prudence-842cd4913fa3
[Accessed 1 May 2022].

Riordan, C. M., 2013. *We All Need Friends at Work.* [Online]
Available at: https://hbr.org/2013/07/we-all-need-friends-at-work
[Accessed 1 May 2022].

Robbins, A., 2022. *Goodreads.com.* [Online]
Available at: https://www.goodreads.com/quotes/877199-the-only-impossible-journey-is-the-one-you-never-begin
[Accessed 4 May 2022].

Roberts, J., 2016. *Getting started with Agile for SAP – 8 steps to success.* [Online]
Available at: https://blogs.sap.com/2016/03/29/getting-started-with-agile-for-sap-8-steps-to-success/
[Accessed 20 May 2022].

Rocky Balboa. 2006. [Film] Directed by Sylvester Stallone. United States of America: Metro-Goldwyn-Mayer.

Rogers, E. M., 1962. *Diffusion of Innovations.* 1st ed. New York: The Free Press, A Division of Simon & Schuster, Inc.

Rosencrans, L., 2020. *How to choose the right ERP for digital transformation.* [Online]
Available at: https://www.techtarget.com/searcherp/feature/Five-keys-to-using-ERP-to-drive-digital-transformation
[Accessed 28 June 2022].

Rossier-Renaud, A. & Meier, O., 2022. *Managing Different Generations in the Mobile Workforce.* [Online]
Available at: https://mobilityexchange.mercer.com/insights/article/managing-different-generations-in-the-mobile-workforce
[Accessed 8 May 2022].

Rotoli, A., 2021. *Why Customer User Groups Are Integral To The Success Of Today's Technology Organizations.* [Online]
Available at: https://www.forbes.com/sites/forbesbusinesscouncil/2021/10/07/why-customer-user-

groups-are-integral-to-the-success-of-todays-technology-organizations/?sh=de7bce91f17b
[Accessed 26 May 2022].

Rue, B., 2021. *Why Error-Free Software Isn't The Goal.* [Online]
Available at: https://www.forbes.com/sites/
forbestechcouncil/2021/05/21/why-error-free-software-isnt-the-goal/?sh=9f1922a6da52
[Accessed 3 May 2022].

Saar, Y., 2022. *Solopreneurs are Changing the Face of the Economy.*
[Online]
Available at: https://www.entrepreneur.com/article/420714
[Accessed 10 May 2022].

Sandberg, S. & Scovell, N., 2013. *Lean In: Women, Work, and the Will to Lead.* 1st ed. New York City: Alfred A. Knopf.

Sanfilippo, M., 2021. *How to Improve Your Work-Life Balance Today.*
[Online]
Available at: https://www.businessnewsdaily.com/5244-improve-work-life-balance-today.html
[Accessed 9 June 2022].

Scavo, F., 2022. *How to Optimize Your ERP System.* [Online]
Available at: https://www.computereconomics.com/article.
cfm?id=1784
[Accessed 26 May 2022].

Schultz, C.-H., 2021. *On-Premises Comeback: Cloud Is Just One Side of the Story.* [Online]
Available at: https://thenewstack.io/on-premises-comeback-cloud-is-just-one-side-of-the-story/
[Accessed 8 May 2022].

Seedgrowth.Wordpress.com, 2015. *"Hold the vision, trust the process.".* [Online]
Available at: https://seedgrowth.wordpress.com/2015/09/26/hold-the-visiontrust-the-process/
[Accessed 2 May 2022].

Seuss, D., 1990. *Oh, the Places You'll Go!* New York: Random House Children's Books.

Seymour, J., 2022. *What is a Support Ticket (& Why We Don't Use That Term).* [Online]
Available at: https://www.helpscout.com/blog/support-ticket-system/#:~:text=%E2%80%9CSupport%20ticket%E2%80%9D%20is%20a%20term, resolved%2C%20the%20ticket%20is%20closed.
[Accessed 21 October 2022].

Shives, K., 2022. *From Zero to SOX Implementation: Sarbanes-Oxley Compliance.* [Online]
Available at: https://ssfllp.com/zero-sox-sarbanes-oxley-compliance/
[Accessed 13 June 2022].

Shurland, T. et al., 2021. *Optimizing your chart of accounts and why it matters.* [Online]
Available at: https://www2.deloitte.com/us/en/pages/operations/articles/chart-of-accounts-design.html
[Accessed 23 May 2022].

Sineriz, M. H., 2019. *Importance of Internal Controls in Corporate Governance.* [Online]
Available at: https://bizfluent.com/facts-6817611-importance-internal-controls-corporate-governance.html
[Accessed 28 May 2022].

Singaram, M. & Jain, P., 2018. *What is the Difference between Proof of Concept and Prototype?* [Online]
Available at: https://www.entrepreneur.com/article/307454
[Accessed 1 May 2022].

Sinha, S., 2020. *Lead to cash: Transform the buyer journey.* [Online]
Available at: https://www.the-future-of-commerce.com/2018/05/18/intelligent-sales-lead-to-cash/
[Accessed 3 March 2021].

Skelton, A., 2018. *The Microsoft Dynamics Sure Step Methodology.* [Online]

Available at: https://www.mercuriusit.com/the-microsoft-dynamics-sure-step-methodology/

[Accessed 30 April 2022].

Smith, M., 2022. *Customer Success: What It Means, Why It Matters, and More.* [Online]

Available at: https://www.helpscout.com/helpu/customer-success/

[Accessed 28 May 2022].

Snyder, J., 2022. *6 Easy Ways to Improve Your Work-Life Balance.* [Online]

Available at: https://thepalmergroup.com/blog/6-easy-ways-to-improve-your-work-life-balance/

[Accessed 9 June 2022].

Solis, B., 2022. *Digital Darwinism: How Disruptive Technology Is Changing Business for Good.* [Online]

Available at: https://www.wired.com/insights/2014/04/digital-darwinism-disruptive-technology-changing-business-good/

[Accessed 24 April 2022].

Star Wars: Episode VI—Return of the Jedi. 1983. [Film] Directed by Richard Marquand. United States of America: Lucasfilm, Ltd.

Survivor, 1982. *Eye of the Tiger.* [Sound Recording] (Scotti Brothers Records).

Thakur, M., 2022. *Accounting Controls.* [Online]

Available at: https://www.wallstreetmojo.com/accounting-controls/

[Accessed 13 June 2022].

The National Center for The Middle Market, 2022. *The National Center for the Middle Market - Promoting Growth of the U.S. Middle Market.* [Online]

Available at: https://www.middlemarketcenter.org/Media/Documents/MiddleMarketIndicators/NCMM_InfoSheet_FINAL_WEB.pdf

[Accessed 24 April 2022].

Tiles, K., 2013. *How Do Trees and Forests Grow?* [Online]

Available at: https://woodlandinfo.org/how-do-trees-and-forests-grow/

[Accessed 15 November 2022].

Tillard, P., 2020. *The Qualities of an Explorer - Then and Now.* [Online]
Available at: https://shackleton.com/blogs/articles/explorer-qualities#:~:text=Sir%20Ernest%20Shackleton%20believed%20that,%2C%20patience%2C%20idealism%20and%20courage.
[Accessed 1 May 2022].

Tilleli, F., 2022. *How Manual Processes Are Hurting Your Business.* [Online]
Available at: https://www.connectpointz.com/blog/how-manual-processes-hurt-your-business
[Accessed 27 May 2022].

Treece, D., 2021. *What Are Accounting Reports?* [Online]
Available at: https://www.businessnewsdaily.com/16092-what-are-accounting-reports.html
[Accessed 3 June 2022].

Turner, L. D. & Owhoso, V., 2009. Use ERP Internal Control Exception Reports to Monitor and Improve Controls. *Management Accounting Quarterly,* 10(3), pp. 41-50.

Tzu, L., 2022. *www.zenmoments.org.* [Online]
Available at: https://zenmoments.org/have-patience-lao-tzu/
[Accessed 1 February 2022].

U.S. Small Business Administration—Office of Advocacy, 2019. *United States Small Business Profiles for 2019.* [Online]
Available at: https://www.sba.gov/sites/default/files/advocacy/2018-Small-Business-Profiles-US.pdf
[Accessed 9 May 2022].

Umar, T., 2020. *What is Leavitt's Diamond Model?* [Online]
Available at: https://changemanagementinsight.com/what-is-leavitts-diamond-model/
[Accessed 7 March 2022].

Valentine, A. C., 2021. *BABY BOOMERS, GENERATION 'X' AND GENERATION 'Y' IN THE WORKPLACE: A MELTING POT OF EXPERTISE.* [Online]

Available at: https://www.resource1.com/baby-boomers-generation-x-and-generation-y-in-the-workplace-a-melting-pot-of-expertise/
[Accessed 24 April 2022].

Vanderkam, L., 2012. *What the Most Successful People Do Before Breakfast: And Two Other Short Guides to Achieving More at Work and at Home.* New York: Penguin Group (USA).

VelocityGlobal, 2022. *How to Manage a Smooth HR Transition in International Mergers and Acquisitions.* [Online]
Available at: https://velocityglobal.com/blog/how-to-manage-a-smooth-hr-transition-in-international-mergers-and-acquisitions/
[Accessed 21 June 2022].

Voltaire, 1996. *YourDictionary.com.* [Online]
Available at: https://quotes.yourdictionary.com/author/quote/541957
[Accessed 27 April 2022].

Waelter, A., Kaplan, B., Gibson, A. B. & Krumwiede, K., 2018. *Stepping Outside the Box: Elevating the Role of the Controller.* [Online]
Available at: https://www.imanet.org/-/media/7ad27dc4d26c44adbc92c452b7444726.ashx
[Accessed 3 June 2022].

Waida, M., 2022. *What Is a Project Communication Plan?* [Online]
Available at: https://www.wrike.com/blog/what-is-a-project-communication-plan/
[Accessed 20 May 2022].

Walsh, B., Jamison, S. & Walsh, C., 2010. *The Score Takes Care of Itself: My Philosophy of Leadership.* 1st ed. New York: Penguin Group.

Weldon, D., 2015. *Why 'rip and replace' IT projects are worth the effort.* [Online]
Available at: https://www.cio.com/article/242703/why-rip-and-replace-it-projects-are-worth-the-effort.html
[Accessed 8 May 2022].

Westerman, G., Bonnet, D. & McAfee, A., 2014. *The Nine Elements of Digital Transformation.* [Online]
Available at: https://sloanreview.mit.edu/article/the-nine-elements-of-digital-transformation/
[Accessed 5 July 2022].

Whatman, P., 2022. *What is a financial controller? The role & keys to effectiveness.* [Online]
Available at: https://blog.spendesk.com/en/what-is-a-financial-controller
[Accessed 3 June 2022].

Wiktionary, 2022. *there is a new sheriff in town.* [Online]
Available at: https://en.wiktionary.org/wiki/there_is_a_new_sheriff_in_town
[Accessed 21 June 2022].

Willink, J. & Babin, L., 2015. *Extreme Ownership: How U.S. Navy SEALs Lead and Win.* 1st ed. New York: St. Martin's Press.

Windows Server Brain, 2022. *Terminal Services History.* [Online]
Available at: https://www.serverbrain.org/terminal-2000/terminal-services-history.html
[Accessed 6 May 2022].

Wong, D., 2022. *Step by Step: What you Should Know About the Order-to-Cash Process.* [Online]
Available at: https://www.salesforce.com/products/cpq/resources/what-to-know-about-order-to-cash-process/
[Accessed 2022 25 April].

Wooden, J. & Jamison, S., 2005. *Wooden on Leadership: How to Create a Winning Organization.* New York: McGraw-Hill.

workato, 2022. *Work Automation Index 2022: APJ.* [Online]
Available at: https://public-workato-files.s3.us-east-2.amazonaws.com/Uploads/work-automation-index.pdf
[Accessed 24 October 2022].

YouTube, 2019. *How To Recognize Winning Stocks (Scuttlebutt Method) - Warren Buffett.* [Online]
Available at: https://www.youtube.com/watch?v=Ftiboqt1pt8
[Accessed 28 April 2022].

TAKE ME TO YOUR CONTROLLER

Printed in Great Britain
by Amazon

32380296R00201